EARLY AMERICAN FICTION

a reference guide

A
Reference
Guide
to
Literature

Everett Emerson
Editor

EARLY
AMERICAN FICTION

a reference guide

PATRICIA L. PARKER

G.K.HALL &CO.

70 LINCOLN STREET, BOSTON, MASS.

Copyright © 1984 by Patricia L. Parker.
All rights reserved.

Library of Congress Cataloging in Publication Data

Parker, Patricia L.
  Early American fiction.

  Includes bibliographical references and index.
  1. American fiction—18th century—History and criti-
cism—Bibliography. I. Title.
Z1231.F4P25 1984   016.813′2   84-3734
[PS375]
ISBN 0-8161-7999-9

This publication is printed on permanent/durable acid-free paper
MANUFACTURED IN THE UNITED STATES OF AMERICA

Contents

Contents

The Author

Patricia L. Parker has taught in the English Department at Salem State College in Salem, Massachusetts since 1968. She received her B.A. in 1963 from Western Maryland College, her M.A. in 1964 from the University of Chicago, and her Ph.D. in American Civilization in 1981 from New York University. In 1980 she published Charles Brockden Brown: A Reference Guide. In 1982-83 she taught as a Fulbright professor at Kyung Hee University in Seoul, South Korea, and then lived for six months in Japan where her husband was also a Fulbright professor. She is currently working on a literary biography of Susanna Haswell Rowson.

Preface

   This book is an annotated bibliography of books and articles
about American fiction before 1800, arranged chronologically within
subject headings. The fiction writers are for the most part those
found in Henri Petter's Early American Novel (1971), the definitive
study of early fiction. The one author whom Petter includes but this
book excludes is Joseph Dennie, whose Lay Preacher seems to be generally regarded as a series of essays rather than a work of fiction.
The Gleaner essays of Judith Sargent Murray might appear similar to
Dennie's work, but enough critics have called The Gleaner fiction to
merit its inclusion here. This study includes only authors generally
agreed upon as American, thus omitting Charlotte Ramsay Lennox but
including Helena Wells. In the case of an author who wrote both
fiction and nonfiction, such as Philip Freneau and Jeremy Belknap,
this guide annotates only criticism of the fiction. Therefore the
reader will find articles and books about Belknap's The Foresters but
not about his History of New Hampshire. Charles Brockden Brown, the
most frequently studied author of this early period, is covered in my
Charles Brockden Brown: A Reference Guide (Boston: G.K. Hall & Co.,
1981).

   The most questionable case of whether a work should be classified
as fiction is perhaps Samuel Peters's The History of Connecticut.
Although many critics have dubbed this work "fiction," they seem to
have done so in an effort to disparage it as history. Peters's
intent seems not to have been to create a work of fiction but to
wreak vengeance upon his countrymen who had treated him so roughly
during the Revolution. But then "intent" would not suffice as either
a necessary or a sufficient condition for determining whether a work
is fiction. Many early writers denied any intent to create imaginative literature for fear of moral censure, and the question of what
actually constitutes early American fiction has never been clearly
defined.

   The written commentaries on these fiction writers include full-
length studies, journal and periodical articles, newspaper articles,
English and American reviews, general studies of American literature,

and doctoral dissertations. When I have read dissertations in full, they appear under the year in which they were accepted; otherwise they appear under the year in which they were abstracted in <u>Disserta-</u> <u>tion</u> <u>Abstracts</u> <u>International</u>, and the annotation is taken from the published abstract. Most entries contain literary criticism, but biographies and bibliographies are included. I have aimed at completeness through 1980, but a few important items from 1981 and 1982 appear if they were obtainable. Any work I have not seen is marked with an asterisk. When I was unable to find a book or article because the source in which I found the item cited it incorrectly, I annotated the item "unlocated."

This guide is divided into separate sections for each individual author, as well as a section on general and thematic studies and one on anonymous works. The first section, "General and Thematic Studies," annotates general discussions of the development of American fiction and discussions of particular themes in more than one work. In a few cases, a work might be cited under this general section and in sections on several authors. The reader should consult the index for a complete list of citations for a book that discusses early fiction in general and various authors specifically, and for topics such as "Father Bombo's Pilgrimage," which refers to citations under both Philip Freneau and Hugh Henry Brackenridge. Cross-references within the text refer only to items within that section on a particular author.

The annotations either convey the point of view of the author or describe the work editorially. In the few instances in which the entire annotation appears in quotation marks, the annotation was written by the author of the work cited.

Names of authors generally appear in the entry as they appear in the publication, which may result in some variation.

Introduction

American fiction suffered a slow and difficult start. Many who
chose to write faced a conservative New England, where fiction did
not readily appeal. They, and those outside New England, often felt
rejected by printers who preferred to publish British works for which
they had to pay no authors' fees. Many simply chose not to write.
Following the Revolution the challenges of a developing government
and the immediacy of new commercial enterprises appealed to both the
young and the mature who might in another time and place have turned
to literature. For several decades the country made no place for the
professional man or woman of letters. Charles Brockden Brown, the
best known writer of the early period, endeavored in vain to earn a
living as a novelist and finally turned to translation and the writing of geography. Susanna Rowson came close to succeeding as a
professional writer, but she supplemented her income with her acting
and turned ultimately to the more respectable profession of educator.

Novelists both in and outside New England faced a critical public. Although Americans had steadily increased their purchases of
works by Goldsmith, Richardson, Fielding, and other English authors,
they received with caution the fiction offered by their fellow Americans. Newspapers and magazines frequently criticized fiction as
immoral and dangerous. The primary novel-reading audience, in this
country as in England, was thought to be young ladies, especially
vulnerable to the suggestions of exaggerated romanticism or tales of
incest, attempted rape, murder, and suicide which constituted much
early American fiction, especially in the magazines. Even novelists
themselves often inveighed against the fiction of seduction and
sentimentality, sometimes within the very pages of their own novels
of sentimentality and seduction.

In defense against moral censure, some novelists sought pro-
tection under cover of didacticism. In The Bloomsgrove Family, for
example, the Reverend Enos Hitchcock simply used the narrative form
as a vehicle for conveying his principles of education. Others
sought to defend themselves by writing under the guise of truth,
and more than one novelist simply turned a true story into a lurid

tale of seduction and abandonment or incest. The Coquette by Hannah
Webster Foster is based on the actual seduction of Elizabeth Whitman,
who died in Danvers, Massachusetts; The Power of Sympathy by William
Hill Brown publicized the embarrassing account of a love affair between prominent Bostonian Perez Morton and his wife's sister. Such
books served only to reinforce the moralists' judgment against
fiction.

But public condemnation could not curtail the extraordinary
inventiveness of early fiction writers. Their works do not fall
neatly into categories, for they demonstrated great variety: political allegory, Indian captivity narrative, a Portuguese political and
adventure narrative, Gothic stories, the biography of a woman soldier,
the tale of an Algerian captivity, and, of course, a trail of seduc-
tions, abandonments, suicides, and deaths of fair unfortunates. The
writers themselves included ministers, lawyers, and school mistresses.

Few writers thought of themselves as novelists or followed a
clear theory of the novel, and few felt sufficiently independent to
create distinctly American characters or use American settings. The
popular Charlotte Temple contained both British and American scenes,
but Charlotte's New York scarcely differed from Chichester. Gilbert
Imlay's The Emigrants and Hugh Henry Brackenridge's Modern Chivalry
portrayed the only pictures of the American frontier.

A good proportion of women joined the few who braved public
condemnation of novel writing, following the English tradition begun
by Aphra Behn (1640-89) and developed by Maria Edgeworth, Hannah
More, Fanny Burney and others. These women for the most part imitated the themes and subject matter of Samual Richardson, who had
brought to the English novel the world of the middle class and its
attendant values and virtues. English women's novels between 1770
and 1800 dealt with the home, with male characters existing chiefly
in their domestic aspects, as fathers, sons, or lovers. American
women writers of this period imitated their English sisters and for
the most part continued the sentimental tradition, although some
early American women writers, such as Foster and Rowson, in fact
undermined the conventions of the passive or docile female by creat-
ing heroines who refused to marry a respectable but boring minister
or who enjoyed sea adventures and could handle an attempted seduction
with a show of common sense. But such heroines became fewer in the
decades after the turn of the century, as women novelists increased
in number and in their acceptance of convention.

The study of early American fiction is relatively recent. For
many years both the public and literary critics ignored fiction
before Hawthorne, and literary historians viewed early literary forms
as unworthy of scholarly regard. Only Charles Brockden Brown merited
serious consideration, and most works by other writers remained out
of print. Only Lillie Deming Loshe (The Early American Novel, 1907)

and Arthur Hobson Quinn (<u>American Fiction. An Historical</u> and <u>Critical Survey</u>, 1936) could discuss early fiction authoritatively, because they alone had actually read the novels. But recent interest in the period of the new American Republic has focused increased attention on the novel as an indicator of national style and taste and on customs and manners. Interest in the nineteenth-century novel has led to a search for its origins in the eighteenth century, and concern with the eighteenth-century essay has led inevitably to examination of the fine line between essay and fiction. Thus interest in the novel before 1800 has steadily increased.

One question that has interested critics is the issue of which novel can actually be called "the first." Charlotte Ramsay Lennox has been called the first American novelist, but she published all her works in London. Michel Renee Hilliard d'Auberteuil has been credited with the earliest novel written and published in America, but his work was written in French. The relatively recent discovery of William Williams's <u>Mr. Penrose, Seaman</u> adds another contender for first place, and if short fiction is considered, Francis Hopkinson's "A Pretty Story" has been given the title. Generally, however, critical consensus is that William Hill Brown's <u>The Power of Sympathy</u> is the "first American novel."

Much remains to be understood about early American fiction. A canon of short fiction is extremely difficult to establish, since many early magazine stories were signed with pseudonyms and often came from English and European periodicals. Writers such as Samuel Relf and Mrs. Patterson remain virtually unknown. Many fictional works remain unexamined for their contribution to our understanding of America before 1800 and to our understanding of the development of American fiction. In 1976 Harrison Meserole made a plea for clearer understanding of early American fiction. That invitation remains open today.

Fiction Writers and Their Works

This list includes only works of fiction before 1800 by writers other than Charles Brockden Brown. It includes no anonymously written works. Anonymously published works show the author's name in brackets.

[Belknap, Jeremy.] The Foresters, an American Tale: Being a Sequel to the History of John Bull the Clothier. In a Series of Letters to a Friend. Boston, 1792. 2 vols.

Bleecker, Ann Eliza. The Posthumous Works of Ann Eliza Bleecker, in Prose and Verse. New York, 1793. (This contains "The History of Maria Kittle" and "The Story of Henry and Anne.")

Brackenridge, Hugh Henry. Modern Chivalry. Containing the Adventures of Captain John Farrago, and Teague O'Regan, his Servant. Part I. Vol. 1, Philadelphia, 1792; vol. 2, Philadelphia, 1793; vol. 3, Pittsburgh, 1793; vol. 4, Philadelphia, 1797. Part II. Vols. 1-2, Carlisle, Pa., 1804-5; [no volume 3 published]; vol. 4, Philadelphia, 1815.

Bradford, Ebenezer. The Art of Courting, Displayed in Eight Different Scenes; the Principal of Which are Taken from Actual Life, and Published for the Amusement of the American Youth. Newburyport, 1795.

[Brown, William Hill.] "Harriot; or, The Domestic Reconciliation." Massachusetts Magazine 1 (1789):3-7.

_____. Ira and Isabella; or, The Natural Children. A Novel, Founded in Fiction. Boston, 1807.

_____. The Power of Sympathy; or, The Triumph of Nature, Founded in Truth. Boston, 1789. 2 vols.

Butler, James. Fortune's Football; or, The Adventures of Mercutio. Founded on Matters of Fact. Harrisburgh, Pa., 1797-98. 2 vols.

Davis, John. The Farmer of New-Jersey; or, A Picture of Domestic
    Life. A Tale. New York, 1800.

_____. The First Settlers of Virginia, an Historical Novel. 2d ed.
    New York, 1805.

_____. The Original Letters of Ferdinand and Elizabeth. New York,
    1798.

[Digges, Thomas Atwood.] The Adventures of Alonzo: Containing Some
    Striking Anecdotes of the Present Prime Minister of Portugal. By
    a Native of Maryland, Some Years Resident in Lisbon. London,
    1775. 2 vols.

[Foster, Hannah Webster.] The Boarding School; or, Lessons of a
    Preceptress to her Pupils. Boston, 1798.

_____. The Coquette; or, The History of Eliza Wharton. Boston,
    1797.

Freneau, Philip. "Father Bombo's Pilgrimage." Edited by Lewis
    Leary. PMHB 66 (1942):459-78.

Hitchcock, Enos. The Farmer's Friend, or the History of Mr. Charles
    Worthy. Boston, 1793.

_____. Memoirs of the Bloomsgrove Family. In a Series of Letters
    . . . Containing Sentiments on a Mode of Domestic Education,
    Suited to . . . Society, Government, and Manners, in the United
    States of America. Boston, 1790. 2 vols.

Hopkinson, Francis. A Pretty Story: Written in the Year of Our Lord
    2774, by Peter Grievous, Esq., A.B.C.D.E. Philadelphia, 1774.

Imlay, Gilbert. The Emigrants, &c., or The History of an Expatriated
    Family, Being a Delineation of English Manners, Drawn from Real
    Characters, Written in America. London, 1793. 3 vols.

Mann, Herman. The Female Review: or, Memoirs of an American Young
    Lady; Whose Life and Character are Peculiarly Distinguished--
    Being a Continental Soldier for Nearly Three Years, in the Late
    American War. . . . Dedham, Mass., 1797.

Markoe, Peter. The Algerine Spy in Pennsylvania; or, Letters Written
    by a Native of Algiers on the Affairs of the United States of
    America, From the Close of the Year 1783 to the Meeting of the
    Convention. Philadelphia, 1787.

Mitchell, Isaac. The Asylum; or, Alonzo and Melissa. Poughkeepsie,
    N.Y., 1811. 2 vols.

Morgan, Joseph. The History of the Kingdom of Basaruah, Containing a Relation of the Most Memorable Transactions, Revolutions and Heroick Exploits in that Kingdom, from the First Foundation Thereof to the Present Time. . . . New York, 1715.

Murray, Judith Sargent. The Gleaner. A Miscellaneous Production by Constantia. Boston, 1798. 3 vols.

Patterson, Mrs. The Unfortunate Lovers, and Cruel Parents: A Very Interesting Tale Founded on Fact. 17th ed. n.p., 1797.

Peters, Samuel. A General History of Connecticut, from its First Settlement under George Fenwick, Esq. to its Latest Period of Amity with Great Britain; Including a Description of the Country and Many Curious and Interesting Anecdotes. London, 1781.

Relf, Samuel. Infidelity, or the Victims of Sentiment; a Novel, in a Series of Letters. Philadelphia, 1797.

Rowson, Susanna. Charlotte. A Tale of Truth. Philadelphia, 1794. 2 vols.

_____. Charlotte's Daughter: or, The Three Orphans. A Sequel to Charlotte Temple. Boston, 1828.

_____. The Fille de Chambre. Philadelphia, 1794.

_____. The Inquisitor; or, Invisible Rambler. Philadelphia, 1793. 3 vols.

_____. Mentoria; or The Young Lady's Friend. Philadelphia, 1794. 2 vols.

_____. Reuben and Rachel; or, Tales of Old Times. Boston, 1798.

_____. Sarah, or The Exemplary Wife. Boston, 1813.

_____. Trials of the Human Heart. Philadelphia, 1795. 4 vols.

Sherburne, Henry. The Oriental Philanthropist, or True Republican. Portsmouth, N.H., 1800.

[Tyler, Royall.] The Algerine Captive, or, the Life and Adventures of Doctor Updike Underhill: Six Years a Prisoner Among the Algerines. Walpole, N.H., 1797. 2 vols.

_____. The Yankey in London. New York, 1809.

Wells, Helena. Constantia Neville; or, The West Indian. 2d ed. London, 1800. 3 vols.

_____. The Step-Mother; a Domestic Tale from Real Life. By Helena Wells, of Charles Town, South-Carolina. 2d ed. London, 1799. 2 vols.

Williams, William. Mr. Penrose: The Journal of Penrose, Seaman. By William Williams, 1727-91. With an introduction and notes by David Howard Dickason. Bloomington, 1969.

[Wood, Sarah.] Amelia; or, The Influence of Virtue. Portsmouth, N.H., 1802.

_____. Dorval, or the Speculator. Portsmouth, N.H., 1801.

_____. Ferdinand and Elmira: A Russian Story. Baltimore, 1804.

_____. Julia, and the Illuminated Baron. Portsmouth, N.H., 1800.

_____. Tales of the Night. Portland, N.H., 1827.

_____. "War, the Parent of Domestic Calamity: A Tale of the Revolution." In A Handful of Spice: Essays in Maine History and Literature. Edited by Richard S. Sprague. Orono, 1969.

Abbreviations

AEB   Analytical and Enumerative Bibliography

AL   American Literature: A Journal of Literature, History,
           Criticism, and Bibliography

AN&Q   American Notes & Queries

AQ   American Quarterly

BB   Bulletin of Bibliography

BC   The Book Collector

BSUF   Ball State University Forum

CRevAS   Canadian Review of American Studies

DAI   Dissertation Abstracts International

EAL   Early American Literature

EALN   Early American Literature Newsletter

ECS   Eighteenth-Century Studies (Davis, Calif.)

EJ   The English Journal

Hispania   Hispania: A Journal Devoted to the Interests of the
           Teaching of Spanish and Portuguese (Cincinnati)

HLQ   Huntington Library Quarterly: A Journal for the
           History and Interpretation of English and American
           Civilization

JEGP   Journal of English and Germanic Philology

MLN   Modern Language Notes

NCHR	North Carolina Historical Review
N&Q	Notes and Queries
NEQ	The New England Quarterly: A Historical Review of New England Life and Letters
PAR	Performing Arts Resources
PBSA	Papers of the Bibliographic Society of America
PMHB	Pennsylvania Magazine of History and Biography
PMHS	Proceedings of the Massachusetts Historical Society
PMLA	Publications of the Modern Language Association
SAF	Studies in American Fiction
SLitI	Studies in the Literary Imagination (Atlanta, Ga.)
SLJ	Southern Literary Journal
SP	Studies in Philology
SSF	Studies in Short Fiction (Newberry, S.C.)
SWR	Southwest Review
TSLL	Texas Studies in Literature and Language: A Journal of the Humanities
VMHB	Virginia Magazine of History and Biography
WGCR	West Georgia College Review
WMQ	William and Mary Quarterly
WS	Women's Studies: An Interdisciplinary Journal

Bibliography

I. General and Thematic Studies and Literary Influences

1876.1   LATHROP, G.P. "Early American Novelists." Atlantic
          Monthly 37 (April):404-5.
               Briefly discusses literature before Charles Brockden
Brown. Sees Tyler's Algerine Captive as the only effort to provide
an American fiction prior to Brown.

1901.1   BRONSON, WALTER COCHRANE. A Short History of American
          Literature. Boston: D.C. Heath, pp. 91-101.
               To trace the transition from true narrative to fiction,
gives brief biographical account and critical evaluation of some
early prose fiction writers.

1902.1   WEGELIN, OSCAR. Early American Fiction 1774-1830: A
          Compilation of the Titles of Works of Fiction, by Writers
          Born or Residing in North America, North of the Mexican
          Border and Printed Previous to 1831. Stanford: The
          compiler.
               Bibliography of primary sources. Reprinted: 1963.2.

1903.1   TRENT, WILLIAM PETERFIELD. A History of American Literature
          (1607-1865). New York: D. Appleton & Co., pp. 187-212.
               Describes the cultural dependency of the new nation until
literature began to share the evolution of political, industrial, and
social development. Ascribes literary primacy to Philadelphia.
Traces the development of poetry and drama. In fiction, finds "practically no works of fiction to chronicle for America, except the small
beginnings made by literary ladies." Notes Rowson, Brackenridge and
Tyler before Charles Brockden Brown, "the first professional man of
letters."

1907.1   DAVIS, RICHARD BEALE. "Arthur Blackmore: The Virginia
          Colony and the Early English Novel." VMHB 75 (January):
          22-34. Reprint. In Literature and Society in Early
          Virginia, 1608-1840. Baton Rouge: Louisiana State Uni-
          versity Press, 1973, pp. 77-96.
               If it could be shown that either of Arthur Blackmore's
novels published in London in 1720 and 1723 was composed in Virginia,
it would be the first American novel. Blackmore spent ten years in
Virginia and might have composed his novels there.
               Describes Blackmore's life, the novels, and their polit-
ical background.

1907.2   LOSHE, LILLIE DEMING. The Early American Novel. New
          York: Columbia University Press, 131 pp.
               A "comprehensive account of the earliest attempts at novel
writing." Includes descriptions of the stories because the works are
so little known and are often inaccessible. The chapters are: "The
Didactic and the Sentimental," "The Gothic and the Revolutionary,"

"Early Historical Novels and Indian Tales," and "Cooper and His Contemporaries." Includes a bibliography of novels to 1830 and a bibliography of secondary sources. Reprinted: 1958.1.

1909.1   STANTON, THEODORE, in collaboration with members of the faculty of Cornell University. A Manual of American Literature. New York and London: G.P. Putnam's Sons, Knickerbocker Press, pp. 107–111.
       Attributes the dearth of good writers after the revolution to the proscription of Loyalists, the exaggerated value set on political theories, and the concentration on individual states rather than the union.

1912.1   VAN DOREN, CARL. "The Beginnings of Fiction." In The American Novel. New York: Macmillan Co., pp. 1–15.
       Briefly surveys the first English fiction read in the colonies. Notes the early American apathy to fiction. Cites The Power of Sympathy by Morton as the first novel, and briefly cites and summarizes other novels. Revised: 1940.4.

1917.1   LONG, WILLIAM J. Outlines of English and American Literature. New York: Ginn & Co., pp. 365–67.
       The popularity of Charlotte Temple indicates widespread interest in fiction, but early American romances have interest only for historical students. Brown, however, is worth remembering.

1917.2   VAN DOREN, CARL. "Fiction 1: Brown, Cooper." In The Cambridge History of American Literature. Edited by William Peterfield Trent et al. Vol. 1, Colonial and Revolutionary Literature. Early National Literature. New York: G.P. Putnam's Sons, pp. 284–87.
       Traces the development of novel reading and novelists' reliance on nature and Richardson. Briefly discusses Morton, Foster, Brown, Brackenridge, and Tyler as predecessors to Charles Brockden Brown.

1918.1   BRADSHER, EARL. L. "Some Aspects of the Early American Novel." Texas Review. 3 (April):241–58.
       Describes the spiritual and political transitions of the period when the novel first came into being. Notes that Goethe's Werther seemed the archfiend to many, and describes popular opposition to fiction. Quotes from the preface to The Asylum for expression of critical theory, and notes the reluctance to distinguish between the novel and the historical narrative. Cites examples of the "hysterical striving for effect" and the struggle for variety.

1925.1   COAD, ORAL SUMNER. "The Gothic Element in American Literature Before 1835." JEGP 24:72–93.
       In England and America, Gothic stories were "a natural reaction against the rationality, restraint and unimaginativeness of

neo-classic literature." The Gothic idea appeared in poetry and drama, but only in fiction did it achieve its best.
        Traces Gothicism in various fictional works to 1835.

1926.1   WILLIAMS, STANLEY THOMAS. "The Era of Washington and
        Jefferson." In The American Spirit in Letters. Pageant
        of America Series, edited by Ralph Henry Gabriel. New
        Haven: Yale University Press, pp. 76-93.
        Literature continued to be imitative after the Revolution, but newspapers and magazines flourished. The growth of an independent literature in the essays and fiction of this era were omens of things to come.

1927.1   McDOWELL, TREMAINE. "Sensibility in the Eighteenth-
        Century American Novel." SP 24 (July):383-402.
        Defines sensibility and its use in thirty-six American novels. Notes the chief physical manifestations, the problems of applying sensibility to social ends, and the deliberate excitement of sensibility as an end in itself. Acknowledges, with qualifications, European and English influences and discusses the effects of sensibility.

1929.1   BROWN, HERBERT ROSS. "Elements of Sensibility in the
        Massachusetts Magazine." AL 1:286-96.
        The Massachusetts Magazine was written largely by and for women. Seduction was a constant theme of its stories, but the most striking evidence of public taste afforded by this magazine "is the vogue of sentimentality in general, and sensibility, in particular." Extravagant affectation and the diction of sensibility were criticized, but the critics were in the minority.

1932.1   . "Richardson and Sterne in the Massachusetts Maga-
        zine." NEQ 5 (January):65-82.
        Examines the influence of Sterne and Richardson on fiction in the Massachusetts Magazine, 1789-96. Describes characteristics of and cites examples of fiction of the period. Finds that contemporary fiction imitated Richardson and Sterne and parodied Sterne.

1932.2   KNIGHT, GRANT COCHRAN. American literature and Culture.
        New York: Ray Lond & Richard R. Smith, pp. 96-103.
        Before the fiction of Washington Irving, Charlotte Temple exemplified the kind of stories people preferred, but Modern Chivalry shows they also enjoyed satire. Charles Brockden Brown was the "Father of the American novel."

1933.1   SINGER, GODFREY FRANK. "Epistolary Fiction in America." In
        The Epistolary Novel: Its Origin, Development, Decline, and
        Residuary Influence. Philadelphia: University of Pennsyl-
        vania Press, 21 pp.

A chronological survey of American epistolary novels,
summarizing plots and describing characteristics. Reprinted:
1963.1.

1935.1   PATTEE, FRED LEWIS. "The Fight for the Novel." In The
          First Century of American Literature 1770-1870. New York:
          D. Appleton-Century Co., pp. 81-94.
          "The novel is as old as the Republic--not a trace of it
before 1789." Various prejudices operated against the growth of
literature, but various novelists managed to distinguish themselves.
By 1820 arguments against the novel became thunderous.

1936.1   BOYNTON, PERCY H. Literature and American Life. Boston:
          Ginn & Co., pp. 188-98.
          Fiction developed after 1789 and was met with injunctions
against novel reading. Fiction to 1830 consisted chiefly of historical and domestic subjects, but none of the novels were distinctively
American in method or manner. This early fiction foreshadows the
feminization of American culture, as novels portrayed the perils to
which ladies were susceptible.

1936.2   FLORY, CLAUDE REHERD. "Economic Criticism in American
          Fiction, 1792-1900." Ph.D. Dissertation, University of
          Pennsylvania, 261 pp.
          An examination of the novelist's criticism of the social
scene. Deals with "matter rather than method." Refers to two American novelists before 1800, Hugh Henry Brackenridge and Royall Tyler.
Chapter one, "Man's Inhumanity to Man," discusses race, class, and
general economic injustice. Chapter two, "Signposts to Utopia,"
describes reforms suggested by novelists. Chapter three describes
"Literary Characteristics of American Fiction Treating Economic
Themes."

1936.3   LEISY, ERNEST E. "The Novel in America: Notes for a
          Survey." SWR 22 (Autumn):88-99.
          Various obstacles faced the early American novelist, but
Brackenridge, Rowson, Foster, and Charles Brockden Brown overcame
them.

1936.4   QUINN, ARTHUR HOBSON. American Fiction: An Historical
          and Critical Survey. New York: Appleton-Century-Crofts,
          pp. 3-39.
          Discusses the tentative beginnings of American fiction in
the works of Franklin and Hopkinson. Summarizes The Power of Sympathy
as the first American novel. Describes the satirical novels of adventure by Brackenridge, Tyler, and Imlay, and the sentimental novels of
Rowson and others. Concludes with a lengthy discussion of Charles
Brockden Brown as the first professional man of letters.

1937.1   ORIANS, G. HARRISON. "Censure of Fiction in American
          Romances and Magazines, 1789-1810." PMLA 52:195-214.

Cites instances of printed disapprobation of novels between 1790 and 1815 in magazines and books. Quotes some novelists' reactions and their claims to truth and morality. Shows how liberal critics discriminated between good and bad novels on ethical grounds and how occasional defenses of novels appeared. Concludes: (1) there must have been a considerable audience who believed novels were subversive; (2) the atmosphere of the 1790s and after "was a little frigid for the ambitious novelist," though the reading public did enlarge; (3) "charges were leveled particularly against the mawkish, melodramatic character of the novel"; (4) what standing the novel did have was primarily among feminine readers; and (5) attacks on the novel in America became noticeable as soon as the novel seemed likely to gain ground.

1939.1   WRIGHT, LYLE H. <u>American Fiction, 1774-1850</u>: <u>A Contribution toward a Bibliography</u>. San Marino: Huntington Library, 246 pp.

The most nearly definitive bibliography to date. Lists editions of 2,772 novels, romances, tales, and short stories, as well as fictional biographies, travels and sketches, allegories, tract-like tales, and similar works, all entered under author's names. Locates copies in nineteen libraries and two private collections. See also 1980.5.

1939.2   _____. "A Statistical Survey of American Fiction." <u>Huntington Library Quarterly</u> 2 (March):309-318.

A survey of American fiction through 1850 based on tabulations from 1939.1. From 1770 to 1819, found only ninety titles of fiction, not sufficient to merit the flood of antifiction criticism. Concludes that most of the criticism must have been directed at the so-called novels and "true stories" in magazines of the period. Calls for further study in the history of American fiction. Includes a bibliography of best sellers before 1850.

1940.1   BLACK, FRANK GEES. <u>The Epistolary Novel in the Late Eighteenth Century</u>. University of Oregon Publications, no. 2. Eugene: University of Oregon Press, 184 pp.

Examines English and American novels between 1781-1800 to show "what the epistolary novel typically amounted to, what peculiar virtues it had, what devices it employed, what subjects it treated, what writers it occupied, why it was so considerably utilized, and why it so abruptly gave way to other methods." Includes a bibliography of 816 epistolary novels.

1940.2   BROWN, HERBERT ROSS. <u>The Sentimental Novel in America, 1789-1860</u>. Durham: Duke University Press, 780 pp.

Traces in popular fiction "some manifestations of the sentimental mind." Is primarily concerned with "social trends, forces, creeds, movements, and literary fashions." Chapters on early fiction include "The Triumph of the Novel," "Richardson and

Seduction," "The Elegant Epistolarians," "Sterne and Sensibility," and
"The Sentimental Formula." Reprinted: 1959.1.

1940.3   MAYNADIER, GUSTAVUS HOWARD. The First American Novelist?
         Cambridge, Mass.: Harvard University Press, 79 pp.
         Credits Charlotte Ramsay Lennox with being the first
American novelist. Notes the little biographical information avail-
able about her and summarizes the plot of The Life of Harriot Stuart.
Finds Lennox "timidly American," for she never gave full names to
American places. Summarizes Euphemia, which uses American scenes.
Notes Johnson's high regard for Lennox and cites the only extant
biography. Summarizes The Female Quixote.

1940.4   VAN DOREN, CARL. "The Beginnings of Fiction." In The
         American Novel 1789-1939. Rev. and enl. ed. New York:
         Macmillan Co., pp. 3-14.
         Describes the apathy toward fiction at the time of the
Revolution. Describes satires, sentimental novels, and the works of
Charles Brockden Brown. Revision of 1912.1.

1945.1   PAINE, GREGORY. "American Literature a Hundred and Fifty
         Years Ago." SP 42 (April):385-402.
         Briefly mentions and describes the main fictional and
nonfictional works of the late eighteenth century.

1948.1   KOLLER, KATHRINE. "The Puritan Preacher's Contribution to
         Fiction." HLQ 11 (August):321-40.
         Puritans contributed significantly to the development of
the novel. They used literary devices such as dialogue in their
religious instruction.

1950.1   HART, JAMES D. The Popular Book: A History of America's
         Literary Taste. New York: Oxford University Press,
         pp. 51-66.
         Describes American fiction during the second half of the
eighteenth century, its sources, characteristics, and audiences.
Shows how sentimental novels flourished under the influence of
Richardson and Sterne but how Goethe's Werther gave the novel of
sensibility a pathological taint.

*1952.1   PALMER, ORMOND E. "Some Attitudes Toward Fiction in
         America to 1870 and a Bit Beyond." Ph.D. Dissertation,
         University of California.

1952.2   WAGENKNECHT, EDWARD. Cavalcade of the American Novel:
         From the Birth of the Nation to the Middle of the Twentieth
         Century. New York: Holt, Rinehart & Winston, pp. 1-13.
         Discusses the contenders for the title "first American
novel" and holds for The Power of Sympathy. Notes the provocative
themes of incest, seduction, and suicide, and the popularity of
Gothicism. Notes various novelists' use of American history, and

finds <u>Modern Chivalry</u> the most important book before Charles Brockden Brown.

1957.1   MARTIN, TERENCE.   "Social Institutions in the Early American
         Novel."   <u>AQ</u> 9 (Spring):72-84.
             A study of the early American novel to 1820 for its
insights into the quality and texture of American life. Most novels
of the period are historical or sentimental. Writers of both visual-
ized the action of their novels within the framework of some social
form, and the institutions of the nation and the family are func-
tional in both historical and sentimental fiction. In historical
fiction, the institution of the nation is negative; in sentimental
novels the family is treated sympathetically according to a formula.
             Constructs a hypothetical novel to illustrate what novels
of the day were like.

1957.2   STIMSON, FREDERICK S.   "Spanish Inspiration in the First
         American Adventure Stories."   <u>Hispania</u> 40 (March):66-69.
             Early North American writers drew from Spain, Mexico, and
the West Indies for their settings, plots, and characters. Spanish
settings were sometimes authentic, sometimes insignificant. Plots
were often based on intrigue and skirmishes in Spanish American
struggles for independence. Themes dealt with Spanish elements of
romance, mystery, intrigue, and cruelty. Spanish characters were
often viewed with admiration mixed with caution.

1958.1   LOSHE, LILLIE DEMING.   <u>The Early American Novel</u> 1789-
         1830. New York: Frederick Ungar Publishing Co., 131 pp.
             Reprint of 1907.2.

1959.1   BROWN, HERBERT ROSS.   <u>The Sentimental Novel in America,</u>
         1789-1860. New York: Pageant Books, 780 pp.
             Reprint of 1940.2.

1959.2   CHARVAT, WILLIAM.   <u>Literary Publishing in America,</u> 1790-
         1850. Philadelphia: University of Pennsylvania Press,
         94 pp.
             Limited to "writers to whom both art and income were
matters of concern." Includes one chapter on publishing centers and
the factors that helped or hindered them, one chapter on author-
publisher relations after 1819, and one chapter on "literary genres
and artifacts" which discusses the public image and self-image of
writers.

1961.1   MARTIN, TERENCE.   <u>The Instructed Vision: Scottish Common
         Sense Philosophy and the Origins of American Fiction.</u>
         Bloomington: Indiana University Press, 197 pp.
             Reviews Scottish Common Sense philosophy and its recep-
tion in the colonies and the early Republic, and then shows how the
metaphysical principles of Common Sense thought supported the American predisposition to regard imagination as suspect, how these

principles lay behind the American attitude toward fiction, and how that attitude prepared the way for the "romance."

1963.1   SINGER, GODFREY FRANK. "Epistolary Fiction in America." In The Epistolary Novel: Its Origin, Development, Decline, and Residuary Influence. New York: Russell & Russell.
       Reprint of 1933.1.

1963.2   WEGELIN, OSCAR. Early American Fiction 1774-1830: A Compilation of the Titles of Works of Fiction, by Writers Born or Residing in North America, North of the Mexican Border and Printed Previous to 1831. Gloucester: Peter Smith.
       Reprint of 1902.1.

1965.1   MOORE, JACK BAILEY. "Native Elements in American Magazine Short Fiction 1741-1800." DA 25, No. 9, p. 5261A.
       A detailed examination of original short fiction. Shows how it became domesticated by combining new materials with old forms. Describes the most frequently represented types of the American Indian, the black, the Yankee, the Southerner, and the middle-class American. Examines the sentimental convention, the combination of native elements with fantasy, the comedy, and the realism.

1965.2   PEARCE, ROY HARVEY. The Savages of America: A Study of the Indian and the Idea of Civilization. Rev. ed. Baltimore: Johns Hopkins Press, pp. 196-99.
       The images, themes and strategies involving the noble savage were used in drama and poetry but not in fiction. We do not know why. Before Cooper we find a scattering of savages, noble and ignoble, in magazine fiction. Bleecker and Charles Brockden Brown used the figure of the ignoble savage to achieve horror.

1965.3   SPILLER, ROBERT E. "New Wine in Old Bottles." In The Third Dimension: Studies in Literary History. New York: Macmillan Co., pp. 66-88.
       Tries to answer two questions: What was the nature of the literary movement in the last decade of the eighteenth century and in what ways was it distinctly American? Discusses the periodical essay, poetry, and the novel. Cites The Power of Sympathy as the first novel. Notes the sentimentality of Charlotte Temple, the burlesque of Modern Chivalry, and the pseudo-Gothic tale of Charles Brockden Brown. Attributes the rise and fall of this literary movement to the timing of the transfer of culture from western Europe.

1968.1   CHARVAT, WILLIAM. The Profession of Authorship in America, 1600-1800: The papers of William Charvat. Edited by Matthew Bruccoli. Columbus: Ohio State University Press, pp. 5-28.
       Discusses the beginnings of professionalism in Barlow, Thomas Paine, and Joseph Dennie. Describes the Philadelphia-New York

cultural center by examining the publications of Rowson and Charles
Brockden Brown.

1968.2   FREE, WILLIAM J.   "American Fiction in the <u>Columbian</u>
          <u>Magazine</u> 1786–1792:   An Annotated Checklist." <u>BB</u>
          25:150–51.
          An annotated list of twenty-eight American fiction works.
Determines native American fiction on the basis of: (1) the identity
of the author as American; (2) an American setting, theme or character; and (3) a pseudonymn or an American dateline.

1968.3   HOLT, CHARLES CLINTON.   "Short Fiction in American
          Periodicals, 1775–1825." <u>DA</u> 28:4131–32A.
          "Although the larger portion of short fiction in American
periodicals in the half-century following the Revolutionary War
showed a slavish adherence to the eighteenth-century British literary
tradition, a significant body of work depended upon native experience
and reflected attitudes peculiar to the new republic. American
editors, desirous of both personal profit and national prestige,
issued a challenge to local writers to contribute material which
would establish the new country as a source of significant literature. The response to this challenge, largely amateurish and anonymous, represented the genesis of a new genre. By the turn of the
century, the clamor for a national literature of note had produced a
number of 'tales,' 'histories,' 'sketches,' and 'stories' based on
some aspect of life in the new environment."

1970.1   KABLE, WILLIAM S.   Introduction to <u>Three Early American</u>
          <u>Novels</u>. Columbus: Charles E. Merrill, pp. 2–4.
          Briefly surveys eighteenth-century English novels.
Explains the American reluctance toward fiction. Cites <u>The Power of</u>
<u>Sympathy</u> as the first American novel.

1971.1   GRAY, JAMES L.   "The Development of the Early American Short
          Story to Washington Irving." <u>DAI</u> 32:1471A.
          Finds the background of the American short story in the
English periodical essay and English periodical short fiction. Examines the influence of the American periodic essayist on the development of short fiction. Concludes that American short magazine
fiction did not develop in a coherent pattern and that American
writers imitated English sentimental fiction. When the sentimental
form was modified, the change occurred accidentally, not consciously.

1971.2   PETTER, HENRI.   <u>The Early American Novel</u>. Columbus:
          Ohio State University Press, 500 pp.
          A descriptive and critical survey of the American novel
to 1820. Indicates the assumptions and concerns of the age "with
respect to the possibilities and limitations of fiction and the genre
of the novel, its moral soundness and its role within literary and
national traditions." Parts I and II "take stock of the views,
materials, and resources of the readers, novelists, and critics;

Parts III and IV focus on the novels that grew out of these views, materials, and resources." Includes synopses of all novels treated and a bibliography of primary and secondary sources.

1972.1   WINANS, ROBERT BOCKEE. "The Reading of English Novels in
          Eighteenth-Century America." Ph.D. Dissertation, New York
          University, 308 pp.
              Contrary to the traditional view, eighteenth-century
Americans read novels widely. In addition to Richardson, they read
Goldsmith, Sterne, Smollett, Fielding, and lesser-known novelists.
American taste was determined by English taste, and regional differ-
ences were minimal. Scholars have misinterpreted eighteenth-century
reading habits. See also 1975.4.

1973.1   GREEN, MARTIN. "The God that Neglected to Come: American
          Literature 1780-1820." In History of Literature in the
          English Language. Vol. 8, American Literature to 1900,
          edited by Marcus Cunliffe. London: Barrie & Jenkins,
          pp. 72-104.
              Asks why the god of literature refused to come to America
during this period. Cites eighteenth- and nineteenth-century critics
who have tried to answer the question. Divides writers according to
their cities and asks how the city helped or hindered him. Considers
writers from Hartford, Philadelphia, New York and Boston. Concludes
that "the trouble seems to have been that a provincial culture,
hitherto quite flourishing, was blighted by the strains of
revolution."

1974.1   PITCHER, EDWARD W. "Some Sources for the Fiction of the
          Massachusetts Magazine (1789-96)." PBSA 74
          (October-December):383-86.
              Most of the 325 short stories in the Massachusetts Maga-
zine were reprints from English magazines and miscellanies.
              Cites particular sources for a number of stories.

1974.2   STEIN, ROGER B. "Pulled Out of the Bay: American Fiction
          in the Eighteenth Century." SAF 2 (Spring):13-36.
              An attempt to define American sea fiction before Cooper.
Describes the difficulty of the search for sea-related fiction and
locates the problem in the specific choices which the American artist
of the eighteenth century made about subject matter and shaping form
in American fiction.
              Finds clarification in Franklin's Autobiography which views
the sea as disordered or vacant. Notes the sea voyages in various
authors who associate the sea with disorder. Finds these authors
achieve balance between the religious writings of the seventeenth
century and the romantic writings of the nineteenth.

1975.1   McALEXANDER, PATRICIA JEWELL. "The Creation of the American
          Eve: The Cultural Dialogue on the Nature and Role of
          Women in Late Eighteenth-Century America." EAL 9
          (Winter):252-66.

Examines the change in the image of women from the colonial period, when women were viewed as sexual, self-sufficient, and active, to the nineteenth century, when women were considered pure, pious, submissive, and domestic. Classifies positions in the cultural dialogue in political terms: conservative, liberal, and radical. Finds that the cult of passion was spread covertly in the sentimental novel which officially promoted conservative values.

1975.2   NYDAHL, JOEL MELLEN. "Utopia Americana: Early American Utopian Fiction 1790-1864." DAI 35:7263A.
Defines a utopia as a fictional representation of an ideal society. Examines utopian literature in general and American utopian literature in particular. Traces the history of pre-Civil War utopian fiction.

1975.3   STODDARD, RICHARD, and FRANCIS KNIBB KOZUCH. "The Theatre in American Fiction, 1774-1850: An Annotated List of References." PAR 1:173-212.
Examined 1,815 of the titles in Wright and annotated the 116 most useful to historians. Includes several works of early American fiction.

1975.4   WINANS, ROBERT B. "The Growth of a Novel-Reading Public in Late Eighteenth-Century America." EAL 9 (Winter): 267-75.
Scholars have traditionally misconceived late eighteenth-century reading taste because of the condemnation of novels and the tendency to use American printing output as an indication of that taste. In fact, the American reading public was largely a novel-reading public, as shown by the growth of booksellers, social libraries, and circulating libraries. "The evidence demonstrates . . . that in late eighteenth-century America, a constantly- and rapidly-expanding reading public was reading novels with increasingly greater frequency than it read other kinds of books." See also 1972.1.

1977.1   BÉRANGER, JEAN. "Histoire des genres et discours de l'histoire dans la littérature américaine a l'époque de la révolution." In La France et l'esprit de 76. Colloque du bicentenaire de l'indépendance des États-Unis. Établis et présentés par Daniel Royot. Clermont-Ferrand: Association pour les publications de la Faculté des lettres et sciences humaines, pp. 132-48.
"This article surveys the various literary genres used in America during the revolutionary period, with special emphasis on the historical discourse. The suggestion is that genres do not exist as perfectly separate literary systems. Compatability and/or confusion explain transfers. The appearance of the novel as a form is discussed. Generally the theory is that an essential factor for the development of an American literature is the immersion in the struggle for independence." In French. [Annotation by the editors.]

1977.2   BONNET, JEAN-MARIE. "Le point de vue théorique des
          romanciers dans les préfaces des premiers romans américains
          (1783-1820)." In La France et l'esprit de 76. Colloque du
          bicentenaire de l'independance des États-Unis. Établis et
          présentés par Daniel Royot. Clermont-Ferrand: Association
          pour les publications de la Faculté des lettres et sciences
          humaines, pp. 163-73.
          "This study attempts to show how American novelists re-
sponded to the harsh criticisms leveled against the novel in the
1800s. By a careful study of all extant prefaces it shows that most
novelists thought that their main function was to please the moralist,
not the literary critic. Before Cooper, novelists rarely thought of
the novel in terms of fiction and were content to guarantee that it
was 'based on truth.'" In French. [Annotation by the editors.]

1977.3   MESEROLE, HARRISON T. "Some Notes on Early American Fiction:
          Kelroy Was There." SAF 5 (Spring):1-12.
          Calls for a fuller exploration of literary and general
magazines before 1850 and for a fuller examination of literary
annuals and gift books of the nineteenth century. Sees the most
challenging task as the reassessment of the early American novel.
Notes the scarcity of texts for teaching early American fiction.
Calls for a modern edition of Rebecca Rush's Kelroy (1812).

1977.4   SPENGEMANN, WILLIAM C. The Adventurous Muse: The
          Poetics of American Fiction, 1789-1900. New Haven:
          Yale University Press, 284 pp.
          An examination of the interrelations between American
travel-writing, European literature, and romantic aesthetics.
Chapter one traces the evolution of the poetics of adventure from
Columbus's letters to Richard Henry Dana. Chapter two follows the
migration of the poetics of domesticity from eighteenth-century
England to America, where they came into conflict with novels like
Modern Chivalry. Chapter three examines two early expressions of the
adventurous muse in fiction, The Algerine Captive and Arthur Gordon
Pym.

1977.5   WARD, WILLIAM S. "American Authors and British Reviewers
          1798-1826: A Bibliography." AL 49 (March):1-21.
          Lists over 450 reviews and articles dealing with over
forty American authors. Includes Charles Brockden Brown, Susanna
Rowson, and Royall Tyler.

*1978.1   HARADA, KEUCHI. "America Shosetsu no Hattan" [Origin of
          American novels]. In America shosetsu no tenkai [Develop-
          ment of American novels]. Edited by Katsuji Takamura and
          Iwao Iwamoto. Tykyo: Shohakusha, pp. 3-16.
          Citation not verified.

1978.2   PITCHER, EDWARD W. "Signatures and Sources for Fiction in
          Webster's American Magazine (Dec. 1787-Nov. 1788)." EAL
          8 (Spring):102-6.

An annotated checklist of nineteen fictional works showing that seventeen definitely originated in British sources and two
probably did.

1978.3 _____. "Sources for Fiction in The Royal American Magazine. (Boston, 1774-5)." AN&Q 17:6-8.
Another step toward the goal of cataloging and identifi-
cation of fiction in early American magazines. An annotated checklist sequentially arranged by date of appearances. Lists sources.

1979.1 ISANI, MUKHTAR ALI. "Far From 'Gambia's Golden Shore':
The Black in Late Eighteenth-Century American Imaginative
Literature." WMQ 36:353-72.
A survey of views of blacks presented in tales, frag-
ments, visions, dialogs, and verse before the nineteenth century.

1979.2 PITCHER, EDWARD W. "Fiction in The Philadelphia Minerva
(1795-1798): A Contribution toward the Establishment of the
American Canon." RALS 9:3-23.
Catalogs all the distinct stories in the Minerva and
indicates sources and translations. Finds fifty-one of the 227
stories by American authors.

1979.3 _____. "The Un-American Fiction of The American Moral
& Sentimental Magazine, with a Comment on the 'Captivity
Narrative.'" EAL 14 (Winter):312-15.
Argues against the theory that American pseudonyms or
local datelines indicate the American authorship of a piece of fic-
tion. Shows the British sources for the ten short stories in Thomas
Kirk's American Moral & Sentimental Magazine. Notes that captivity
narratives by 1760 were parodied and comically written.

1979.4 WILSON, JANICE CRABTREE. "The General Magazine and Impar-
tial Review: A Southern Magazine in the Eighteenth
Century." SLJ 11 (Spring):66-77.
In an examination of this representative eighteenth-
century magazine, includes summaries of the fictional works published
in it.

1980.1 DAUBER, KENNETH. "American Culture as Genre." Criticism
22:101-15.
Compares the question "Which is the first American
novel?" to "Which is the first English novel?." Proposes that the
"great American novel is but the first American novel seen from
another perspective," because the great American novel would authorize a new, distinctly American writing. Finds in the rhetoric of
Charlotte Temple, The Scarlet Letter, and works by Melville the key
to understanding the culture of the period of each novel.

1980.2 DAVIDSON, CATHY N. "Mothers and Daughters in the Fiction of
the New Republic." In The Lost Tradition: Mothers and
Daughters in Literature. Edited by Cathy N. Davidson and
E.M. Broner. New York: Frederick Ungar, pp. 115-27.

"Places the sentimental novel within a specific social
context of 'feminist' debate and also discusses the sentimental
novel, with its emphasis on the proper path to procreation, as a
warning to a rootless young nation." [Annotation by Cathy N.
Davidson.]

1980.3   PITCHER, EDWARD W. "Anthologized Short Fiction in
          Eighteenth-Century America: The Example of The American
          Bee." EAL 15 (Winter):247-51.
               A checklist of fiction in the anthology, The American Bee
(1797). The twenty-six items derive primarily from American
magazines.

1980.4   _____. "Fiction in the Boston Magazine (1783-1786):
          A Checklist with Notes on Sources." WMQ 37:478-83.
               Traces all reprinted pieces to their first appearance in
British periodicals or miscellanies, collections, and translations.
Has tried to establish authorship. Includes sixty-six entries.

1980.5   _____. "Some Emendations for Lyle B. Wright's
          American Fiction 1774-1850. PBSA 74 (April):143-45.
               Adds authors to Wright's list (1939.1) and shows where
several stories first appeared.

1980.6   REYNOLDS, DAVID SPENCER. "Polishing God's Altar: The
          Emergence of Religious Fiction in America, 1785-1850."
          DAI 41:255A.
               A study of some 250 American writers to advance the
following thesis: "During a period of widespread liberalization and
secularization of Christianity, a growing number of Americans . . .
adopted fictional modes and devices with the aim of refreshing doctrine. Both fictionalists and mainstream clergymen moved progressively away from such Puritan literary ideals as logic and unsullied
spirituality toward the more earthly mixture of anecdotal persuasion,
romantic ideality and heroic action that characterized popular religion after the Civil War." Analyzes the Oriental tale, the non-
Oriental visionary mode, fiction by Calvinists, liberals, writers of
biblical paraphrase and by Roman Catholics, and a small body of
satirical or combative novels.

1982.1   DAVIDSON, CATHY N. "Flirting with Destiny: Ambivalence and
          Form in the Early American Sentimental Novel." SAF 10
          (Spring):17-39.
               A reinterpretation of the origins of American fiction
which establishes the critical climate in which the first American
novelists wrote. Assesses the accommodations American writers had to
make to the critics. Separates the conventional apologetics from the
more subtle attempts to circumvent the prescribed formulae for fiction in general and sentimental fiction in particular. Discusses the
debates on women's rights in sentimental novels from Tenney to Wells,
and examines in detail The Coquette.

II. Anonymous Works

1907.1   LOSHE, LILLIE DEMING. The Early American Novel. New York:
         Columbia University Press, pp. 17-18.
             Summarizes the plots of The Hapless Orphan and
Constantius and Pulchera. Reprinted: 1958.1.

1918.1   BRADSHER, EARL L. "Some Aspects of the Early American
         Novel." Texas Review 3 (April):252-54.
             Describes several anonymous novels as examples of
writers' fear of making their novels too interesting and their
straining to achieve variety.

1927.1   McDOWELL, TREMAINE. "Sensibility in the Eighteenth-
         Century American Novel." SP 24 (July):382-402.
             Cites examples of sensibility in Ferdinand and Elizabeth
and The Hapless Orphan.

1929.1   _____. "An American Robinson Crusoe." AL 1:307-9.
             The Female American, an anonymous work published in 1790,
demonstrates an instance of an imitation of Robinson Crusoe. The
book has little intrinsic worth but is unique in its introduction of
the South American Indian and its close imitation of an English
novelist.

1932.1   FULLERTON, BRADFORD M. Selective Bibliography of American
         Literature 1775-1900: A Brief Survey of the More Important
         American Authors and a Description of their Works. New York:
         William Farquhar Payson, pp. 1-2.
             Includes Amelia and The Hapless Orphan.

1932.2   BROWN, HERBERT ROSS. "Richardson and Sterne in the
         Massachusetts Magazine." NEQ 5 (January):65-82.
             Cites several examples of anonymous short fiction in the
Massachusetts Magazine and shows how the stories imitated Richardson
and Sterne.

1933.1   SINGER, GODFREY FRANK. The Epistolary Novel: Its
         Origin, Development, Decline, and Residuary Influence.
         Philadelphia: University of Pennsylvania Press, pp. 196-97.
             Brief mention of The Hapless Orphan.

1936.1   BOYNTON, PERCY. Literature and American Life. Boston:
         Ginn & Co., pp. 195-96.
             Constantius and Pulchera is perhaps the worst of the crop
of seduction novels. It reads like a parody of the genre.

1936.2   QUINN, ARTHUR HOBSON. American Fiction: An Historical
         and Critical Survey. New York: D. Appleton-Century Co.,
         pp. 5-6, 14, 22-23.

Amelia is neither a short story nor a novel, but it has
interest and historical significance. The Unfortunate Discovery
imitates English sentimental fiction and is flawed by minor characters' interjections of their autobiographies. Constantius and
Pulchera is absurd. The Hapless Orphan is a remarkable example of
the novel of disaster.

1939.1   WRIGHT, LYLE H. American Fiction, 1774-1850: A Contribu-
         tion toward a Bibliography. San Marino: Huntington
         Library, 246 pp.
              The most nearly definitive bibliography to date.
Includes anonymous works.

1948.1   COWIE, ALEXANDER. The Rise of the American Novel.
         New York: American Book Co., pp. 20-21, 29-30.
              The Hapless Orphan contains a worldly heroine with
a shocking philosophy, and the novel apparently has no moral.
Constantius and Pulchera "is one of the most extravagant American novels ever written," both in style and content.

1952.1   WAGENKNECHT, EDWARD. Cavalcade of the American Novel:
         From the Birth of the Nation to the Middle of the Twentieth
         Century. New York: Henry Holt & Co., p. 7.
              Brief mention of Amelia.

1958.1   LOSHE, LILLIE DEMING. The Early American Novel 1789-1830.
         New York: Frederick Ungar Publishing Co., 131 pp.
              Reprint of 1907.1.

1962.1   MOORE, JACK B. "A Traditional Motif in Early American
         Fiction. 'The Too Youthful Solitary.'" Midwest
         Folklore 12 (Winter):205-8.
              "The Boy Who Had Never Seen a Woman," a traditional
popular story in England and Europe, appeared in an American version
in The Timepiece and Literary companion in 1798. Philip Freneau may
have been the author.

1964.1   MOORE, JACK B. "'The Captain's Wife': A Narrative Short
         Story before Irving." SSF 1 (Winter):103-6.
              This story appeared in The Gentleman and Lady's Town and
Country Magazine, 1789. Though the author is unknown, he was probably American. The story "combines fancy, folklore, and the American
experience in an imaginative manner, producing an interesting and
aesthetically satisfying short story." See 1978.1.

1965.1   PEARCE, ROY HARVEY. The Savages of America: A Study of
         the Indian and the Idea of Civilization. Rev. ed.
         Baltimore: Johns Hopkins Press, pp. 169-99.
              Briefly mentions "Yonora: An American Indian Tale" which
appeared in the South Carolina Weekly Museum in 1798.

1966.1   MOORE, JACK B. "Black Humor in an Early American Short
          Story." <u>EALN</u> 1 (Summer):7-8.
              Summarizes the plot of "Child of Snow" which appeared in
the <u>Massachusetts Magazine</u>, 1797. Sees the story as written by an
American, and describes its humor as black. See 1966.2; 1978.3.

1966.2   JANTZ, HAROLD. "Note." <u>EALN</u> 1 (Winter):16.
              "Child of Snow" is not of American origin as Jack Moore
indicated (see 1966.1). It is an old European tale. See also
1978.3.

1966.3   MOORE, JACK B. "A Neglected Early American Short Story."
          <u>AN&Q</u> 4 (February):84-86.
              "Something Unaccountable," published in the <u>Massachusetts
Magazine</u>, 1789, used the American scene and displayed a good sense of
short story form.

1967.1   _____. "The First 'Narrative of the Unpardonable Sin.'"
          Conconcordia College <u>Discourse</u> 10 (Summer):274-83.
              "Narrative of the Unpardonable Sin" first appeared in the
<u>Theological Magazine</u>, 1796. Its theme relates to the American expe-
rience and to American literature of a later period.

1967.2   SANDERLIN, R. REED. "A Variant Version of 'The Child of
          Snow.'" <u>EALN</u> 2 (Fall):22-26.
              Prints a variant of "The Child of Snow" entitled "The Son
of Snow," which appeared in a Pennsylvania newspaper in 1793. Notes
the differences between the two versions and speculates on the relationship between them. See 1966.1-2.

1968.1   KETTLER, ROBERT RONALD. "The Eighteenth-Century American
          Novel: The Beginning of a Fictional Tradition." Ph.D.
          Dissertation, Purdue University, pp. 55-60, 61-69, 69-71,
          71-73, 138-44.
              Examines <u>Amelia</u> as an example of the use of fiction to
teach a moral lesson, and describes the characters as types and the
theme as an adaptation of Richardson. Discusses <u>Constantius and
Pulchera</u> as an example of the didactic tale which may have been
written as an allegory to illustrate the operations of politics.
Notes that <u>The Fortunate Discovery</u> contains the stereotyped character
and situation of most early American novels, and describes the plot
and characterization of <u>Fidelity Rewarded</u>. Sees <u>The Hapless Orphan</u>
as exemplifying the theme of terror in early American novels and
finds its American scene not beautiful but stressful.

1969.1   WRIGHT, LYLE H. <u>American Fiction, 1774-1850: A Contri-
          bution toward a Bibliography</u>. 2d rev. ed. San Marino:
          Huntington Library, passim.
              Lists editions and locations of ten anonymous works writ-
ten before 1800.

1970.1   KABLE, WILLIAM. Introduction to <u>Three Early American</u>
          <u>Novels</u>. Columbus: Charles E. Merrill, pp. 2-4.
              Briefly mentions "The Golden Age," a sixteen-page alle-
gory which appeared in 1785.

1974.1   STEIN, ROGER B. "Pulled Out of the Bay: American Fiction
          in the Eighteenth Century." <u>SAF</u> 2 (Spring):20-21, 31-32.
              <u>Constantius and Pulchera</u> treats the sea in perfunctory
and conventional language, yet the fundamental perspective on sea
experience is the same as in other early fiction: it defines social
and emotional disorder. The book lacks the total unity of <u>Charlotte</u>
<u>Temple</u>.

1974.2   TILLINGHAST, CHARLES ALLEN. "The Early American Novel: A
          Critical Revaluation." Ph.D. Dissertation, Syracuse
          University, pp. 78-80, 88-90, 90-91.
              Discusses the use of the theme of terror in <u>The Hapless</u>
<u>Orphan</u>. Interprets the relationship between Amelia and Doliscus in
<u>Amelia</u> as a parable of the relationship between England and America.
Finds that <u>Constantius and Pulchera</u> confirms the moral superiority of
Americans.

1975.1   McALEXANDER, PATRICIA JEWELL. "The Creation of the American
          Eve: The Cultural Dialogue on the Nature and Role of Women
          in Late Eighteenth-Century America." <u>EAL</u> 9 (Winter):261.
              Notes that <u>Ferdinand and Elizabeth</u> was one of the Amer-
ican imitators of Werther with his suicidal adulterous love.

1976.1   MOORE, JACK B. "Making Indians Early: The Worth of
          'Azakia.'" <u>SSF</u> 13 (Winter):51-60.
              Examines the plot, structure, narrative technique and
meaning of the short story "Azakia" which appeared in the <u>American</u>
<u>Museum</u>, the <u>Vermont Magazine</u>, and the <u>New York Weekly Magazine</u>.
Describes the story as a political allegory of whites' treatment of
Indians. Notes that Sarah Morton expanded the work in "Ouabi." See
1977.2.

1977.1   PITCHER, EDWARD W. "James Anderson's Reprinting in <u>The Bee</u>
          <u>of Stories</u> from the <u>American Museum</u>." <u>N&Q</u>, n.s. 24
          (July-August):319-20.
              Briefly describes James Anderson, editor of the <u>Bee</u>
(London), and his sources. Cites specific stories from Matthew
Carey's <u>American Museum</u>, which appeared in the <u>Bee</u> in 1792.

1977.2   _____. "A Note on 'Azakia': Jack B. Moore's Early
          American Short Story." <u>SSF</u> 14 (Fall):395-96.
              Comments on 1976.1. Moore's article would have been
reshaped had he known that "Azakia" was written by Nicholas Bricaire
De La Dixmerie, published in Paris and London. This mistake illus-
trates the pitfalls of analyzing fiction in magazines.

1978.1   MERREN, JOHN. "The Resolute Wife, or a Hazard of New
          Criticism." SSF 15 (Summer):291-300.
          Examines the story "The Captain's Wife," discussed in
1964.1, in light of its analogues. Finds numerous versions of the
tale in literature from all over the world. Concludes that the
author retold an old story, making its setting and frame essay palat-
able for New England readers.

1978.2   PITCHER, EDWARD W. "The Columbian Magazine and Lane's
          Annual Novelist." N&Q, n.s. 25 (June):209-211.
          Reports the recent discovery of a copy of Lane's Annual
Novelist (1786), and finds it a major source of short stories published in the Columbian Magazine between November, 1786 and August,
1788.

1978.3   _____. "A Note on the Source of 'The Child of Snow' and
          'The Son of Snow.'" EAL 8 (Fall):217-18.
          The source of both these stories was a thirteenth-century
French tale in verse published in Paris, 1779-81. This and other
responses to Jack Moore's original study (see 1966.1) show that more
work needs to be done on the early American short story.

1978.4   _____. "Signatures and Sources for Fiction in Webster's
          American Magazine (Dec. 1787-Nov. 1788)." EAL 13
          (Spring):102-6.
          An annotated checklist of nineteen fictional works show-
ing that seventeen definitely originated in British sources and two
probably did.

*1978.5   _____. "Sources for Fiction in the Royal American
          Magazine." AN&Q 17 (September):6-7.

1979.1   _____. "Fiction in the Philadelphia Minerva (1795-1798):
          A Contribution Toward the Establishment of the American
          Canon." RALS 9 (Spring):3-23.
          Provides a catalog of fiction in the Philadelphia Minerva
and answers these questions: "(1) what proportion of fiction was
reprinted from non-fiction sources; (2) which stories clearly or
apparently belong to the American canon; (3) what were some of the
frequently used sources for the fiction in the magazine; (4) to what
extent could one establish authorship for the 227, mostly anonymous,
tales."

1979.2   _____. "The Un-American Fiction of the American Moral
          & Sentimental Magazine, with a comment on the 'Captivity
          Narrative.'" EAL 14 (Winter):312-15.
          The ten stories in the American Moral & Sentimental
Magazine were reprinted from British sources. The parody of a captivity narrative by Alexander Kellet showed that the conventions of
the captivity narrative form were well understood by 1760 and showed

also that "a popular, propagandistic, and sensational genre could be
brought into the mainstream of literature by irony and burlesque."

1979.3   WHARTON, DONALD P. In the Trough of the Sea: Selected
         American Sea-Deliverance Narratives, 1610-1766. Contribu-
         tions in American Studies, no. 44. Westport, Conn.:
         Greenwood Press, p. 24.
             Brief mention of Constantius and Pulchera.

1980.1   PITCHER, EDWARD W. "Anthologized Short Fiction in
         Eighteenth-Century America: The Example of The American
         Bee (1797)." EAL 15 (Winter):247-51.
             A checklist of fiction in the anthology, The American Bee
(1797). The twenty-six items derive primarily from American magazines.

1980.2   _____. "Fiction in the Boston Magazine (1783-1786):
         A Checklist with Notes on Sources." WMQ 37 (July):473-83.
             Traces all reprinted pieces to their first appearance in
British periodicals or miscellanies, collections, and translations.
Has tried to establish authorship. Includes sixty-six entries.

1980.3   _____. "Some Emendations for Lyle B. Wright's American
         Fiction 1774-1850. PBSA 74 (April):143-45.
             Adds authors to Wright's list and shows where several
stories first appeared.

*1980.4 _____. "Some Sources for the Fiction in the Massachusetts
         Magazine." PBSA 74 (4th Quarter):383-86.
             Source: Edward W. Pitcher.

*1981.1 _____. "The Fiction in the American Museum: A Check-
         list with Notes on Sources." AEB 5:100-106.
             Cited in PMLA Bibliography, vol. 1, 1981 (New York:
Modern Language Association of America, 1983), p. 164.

*1981.2 _____. "The Fiction of the Columbian Magazine: An
         Annotated Checklist." AEB 5:16-24.
             Cited in PMLA Bibliography, vol. 1, 1981 (New York:
Modern Language Association of America, 1983), p. 164.

*1981.3 _____. "The Fragment in Early American Literature:
         A Response." SAF 19 (Spring).
             Source: Edward W. Pitcher.

1982.1   DAVIDSON, CATHY N. "Flirting with Destiny: Ambivalence
         and Form in the Early American Sentimental Novel." SAF
         10 (Spring):17-39.
             Cites Fidelity Rewarded, Amelia and others as examples of
novels which masqueraded as nonfiction.

III. Jeremy Belknap (1744-1798)

1792.1   ANON. "Monthly Review of New American Books."
          Massachusetts Magazine 2 (August 1792):513-16.
          The Foresters is a satirical history. The author shows
originality and an easy style in a work designed to criticize "follies in government and religion." Quotes a selection.

1798.1   KIRKLAND, JOHN. A Sermon Delivered at the Interment of
          the Reverend Jeremy Belknap, D.D. June 22, 1798. Boston:
          Manning & Loring, 5 pp.
          High praise for Belknap's preaching and writing.
Includes a bibliography of his publications. Reprinted: 1798.2.

1798.2   _____ . "The Character of the Late Rev. Dr. Belknap."
          Boston Columbian Centinel, 25 June, p. 1.
          Reprint of 1798.1.

1799.1   ANON. Review of The Foresters. New York Monthly Magazine
          and American Register 1 (September-December):434-38.
          Praises the allegory. Notes that the title is incorrect,
as the book is a digression from, rather than a continuation of, The
History of John Bull. Includes a long extract. Finds the work less
vulgar and obscene than the John Bull story and praises its style.

1824.1   ANON. "Collections, Topographical, Historical, and Bio-
          graphical, Relating Principally to New Hampshire." North
          American Review 18:33-40.
          Brief mention of The Foresters. Biography and praise for
The History of New Hampshire.

1847.1   [MARCOW, JANE BELKNAP.] Life of Jeremy Belknap, D.D. The
          Historian of New Hampshire. New York: Harper & Brothers,
          253 pp.
          Biography composed chiefly of letters. Includes a selec-
tion from The Foresters.

1855.1   BRYANT, WILLIAM CULLEN. "Speech presented to the New York
          Historical Society, 20 November [1854]." In Cyclopaedia of
          American Literature: Embracing Personal and Critical
          Notices of Authors, and Selections from Their Writings.
          From the Earliest Period to the Present Day, by Evert
          Duyckinck and George L. Duyckinck. Vol. 1. New York:
          Charles Scribner, pp. 263-68.
          Biography and brief description of The Foresters.
Includes a selection from The Foresters. Reprinted: 1975.1.

1856.1   GOSTWICK, JOSEPH. Handbook of American Literature;
          Historical, Biographical, and Critical. Philadelphia and
          Edinburgh: W. & R. Chambers.
          See 1971.1.

1875.1   TUTTLE. "Remarks Made by Mr. Tuttle to the Society at the
          May Meeting." Massachusetts Historical Society Proceedings
          14 (May):37-38.
                Recollections of Belknap's mansion in Dover, New
Hampshire.

1878.1   HART, JOHN S. A Manual of American Literature.
          Philadelphia: Eldredge & Brother, p. 91.
                A textbook with a brief mention and description of The
Foresters.

1891.1   ELLIS, GEORGE EDWARD. "Jeremy Belknap." Atlantic Monthly
          67 (May, 1891):643-51.
                Biography and description of Dover, New Hampshire. The
Foresters has "many quaint, shrewd, humorous, and satirical touches"
and was popular "with boys in country homes."

1892.1   SMYTH, ALBERT H. The Philadelphia Magazines and Their
          Contributors 1741-1850. Philadelphia: Robert M. Lindsay,
          pp. 63-64.
                Brief mention of The Foresters, written for the Columbian
Magazine.

1898.1   HERRINGSHAW, THOMAS WILLIAM. Herringshaw's Encyclopedia of
          American Biography of the Nineteenth Century. Chicago:
          American Publishers Association, p. 100.
                Biography and brief mention of The Foresters.

1901.1   BRONSON, WALTER COCHRANE. A Short History of American
          Literature. Boston: D.C. Heath, p. 92.
                A textbook that briefly mentions The Foresters as an
example of the fable used as a "political engine" after the Revolution as it had been used before.

1909.1   STANTON, THEODORE, in collaboration with members of the
          faculty of Cornell University. A Manual of American
          Literature. New York and London: G.P. Putnam's Sons,
          Knickerbocker Press, p. 116.
                Brief mention of The Foresters as "an ingenious though
trivial allegorical tale of the colonisation of America and the
rebellion of the colonies."

1912.1   CAIRNS, WILLIAM B. A History of American Literature.
          New York: Oxford University Press, pp. 153-54.
                A textbook that briefly mentions The Foresters as a
"humorous prose sketch."

1912.2   VAN DOREN, CARL. The American Novel. New York:
          Macmillan Co., p. 4.
                Brief description of The Foresters. Revised
edition: 1940.3.

1915.1   ELLIS, HAROLD MILTON. "Joseph Dennie and His Circle.
          A Study in American Literature from 1792 to 1812."
          Bulletin of the University of Texas, no. 40 (July),
          pp. 76, 78n, 102.
               Brief mention of Belknap.

1918.1   BRADSHER, EARL L. "Some Aspects of the Early American
          Novel." Texas Review 3 (April):258.
               ". . . writers who could thus early produce such a witty,
straightforward political satire as The Foresters (1796) . . . are
fit progenitors of even a Hawthorne or a Cooper."

1926.1   MAYO, L.S. "Jeremy Belknap and J.Q. Adams, 1787." PMHS
          59 (February):203-10.
               Belknap must have felt his enthusiasm kindle at Adams's
words at the 1787 Harvard commencement. The Foresters was at that
time appearing in the Columbian.

1926.2   WILLIAMS, STANLEY THOMAS. "The Era of Washington and
          Jefferson." In The American Spirit in Letters. Pageant
          of America Series, edited by Ralph Henry Gabriel. New
          Haven: Yale University Press, p. 89.
               The Foresters is a survival of a fictional form popular
during the Revolution. Includes a portrait of Belknap by Henry
Sargent.

1929.1   HASTINGS, GEORGE E. "John Bull and his American Descend-
          ants." AL 1 (March):40-68.
               "Jeremy Belknap's The Foresters is most decidedly an
imitation of The History of John Bull, of which it professes to be a
sequel, and from which it takes many ideas and one quotation. . . .
Both Belknap and Paulding seem to have read A Pretty Story, but their
indebtedness to Hopkinson is not great."

1929.2   MAYO, LAWRENCE SHAW. "Belknap, Jeremy." In Dictionary of
          American Biography. Edited by Allen Johnson. Vol. 2.
          New York: Charles Scribner's Sons, p. 147.
               Biography including brief mention of The Foresters.
Includes selected bibliography of secondary works.

1929.3   MAYO, L.S. "Jeremy Belknap and Ebenezer Howard." NEQ 11
          (April):183-98.
               Biography, detailing Belknap's relationship with Hazard,
who helped Belknap publish The History of New Hampshire.

1931.1   RICHARDSON, LYON N. A History of Early American Maga-
          zines 1741-1784. New York: Thomas Nelson & Sons, passim.
               Describes the appearance of The Foresters in the
Columbian magazine and Belknap's correspondence about it. Lists
Belknap's other contributions to the same magazine. Recounts inci-
dents in Belknap's life as magazine contributor and editor.

1932.1 FULLERTON, B.M. <u>Selective Bibliography of American Literature 1775-1900: A Brief Survey of the More Important Authors and a Description of Their Works</u>. New York: William Farquhar Payson, pp. 22-33.
Bibliography of primary works. <u>The Foresters</u> was the third American novel. It has literary merit, and in a very tenuous sense is the first American novel.

1933.1 SINGER, GODFREY FRANK. <u>The Epistolary Novel: Its Origin, Development, Decline, and Residuary Influence</u>. Philadelphia: University of Pennsylvania Press, p. 196.
Brief mention of <u>The Foresters</u> as a "rambling affair" that needs footnotes to explain its allusions. Reprinted: 1963.1.

1934.1 GOODMAN, NATHAN G. <u>Benjamin Rush, Physician and Citizen</u>. Philadelphia: University of Pennsylvania Press, p. 80, 159, 277, 278, 279, 283, 318.
Quotations from letters by Rush to Belknap.

1936.1 ELIOT, SAMUEL A. "Jeremy Belknap." <u>PMHS</u> 66:96-106.
Biography, including portrait. A tribute to Belknap as founder of the Massachusetts Historical Society.

1936.2 QUINN, ARTHUR HOBSON. <u>American Fiction: An Historical and Critical Survey</u>. New York: Appleton-Century-Crofts, pp. 4-5.
Briefly describes the story of <u>The Foresters</u>. The style is "lively" and the book is valuable because it is representative of contemporary opinion.

1937.1 COLE, CHARLES WILLIAM. "Jeremy Belknap: Pioneer Nationalist." ·NEQ 10:743-51.
An appreciation of Belknap as an early nationalistic thinker, based on his sermons, his history, and on his life.

1938.1 KUNITZ, STANLEY J., and HOWARD HAYCRAFT. <u>American Authors, 1600-1900</u>. New York: H.W. Wilson Co., pp. 67-68.
Biography, including brief mention of <u>The Foresters</u>. Bibliography of primary and selected secondary works.

1940.1 BLACK, FRANK GEES. <u>The Epistolary Novel in the Eighteenth Century: A Descriptive and Bibliographical Study</u>. Eugene: University of Oregon Press, pp. 64, 70, 109n.
<u>The Foresters</u> is a curiosity in epistolary fiction because the letters are not really letters but "chapters in a retrospective narrative." Magazine fiction of 1787 was not epistolary.

1940.2 BROWN, HERBERT ROSS. <u>The Sentimental Novel in America 1789-1860</u>. Durham: Duke University Press, pp. 70, 70n.
The early magazine version of <u>The Foresters</u> appeared without the epistolary device, but the book form used it. <u>The Foresters</u> used letters as a framework for the political allegory.

1940.3   VAN DOREN, CARL.   The American Novel 1789–1939.
         Rev. and enl. ed.   New York: Macmillan Co., p. 5.
         See 1912.2.

1943.1   BURKE, WILLIAM J., and WILL D. HOWE.   American Authors and
         Books, 1640–1940.   New York: Gramercy Publishing Co., p. 55.
              Bibliography of primary works.   Revised edition: 1962.1.

1945.1   PAINE, GREGORY.   "American Literature a Hundred and Fifty
         Years Ago."   SP 42 (April):387.
              Brief mention of Belknap.

1948.1   COWIE, ALEXANDER.   The Rise of the American Novel.
         New York: American Book Co., p. 29.
              Brief mention of Belknap.

1948.2   WRIGHT, LYLE H.   American Fiction, 1774–1850: A Contri-
         bution toward a Bibliography.   Rev. ed.   San Marino:
         Huntington Library, p. 33.
              Lists The Foresters and its location in thirteen
libraries.

1952.1   BRYAN, WILLIAM ALFRED.   George Washington in American
         Literature, 1775–1865.   New York: Columbia University
         Press, p. 193.
              Brief description of George Washington in The Foresters.

1952.2   WAGENKNECHT, EDWARD.   Cavalcade of the American Novel:
         From the Birth of the Nation to the Middle of the Twentieth
         Century.   New York: Holt, Rinehart, & Winston, p. 7.
              Brief mention of The Foresters as an allegory of "the
whole English adventure in the new world."

1955.1   BLANCK, JACOB.   "Jeremy Belknap."   In Bibliograpy of
         American Literature.   Vol. 1.   New Haven: Yale
         University Press, pp. 185–91.
              Bibliography of primary and secondary works.   Includes
locations.

1956.1   HART, JAMES D.   The Oxford Companion to American Literature.
         3d ed.   New York: Oxford University Press, p. 62.
              Brief biography and mention of The Foresters.

1962.1   BURKE, WILLIAM J., and WILL D. HOWE.   American Authors
         and Books, 1640 to the Present Day.   Rev. ed.   New York:
         Crown Publishers, p. 55.
              See 1943.1.

1962.2   HARZBERG, MAX J., and the staff of the Thomas Y. Crowell Co.
         The Reader's Encyclopedia of American Literature.
         New York: Thomas Y. Crowell Co., p. 74.
              Biography and brief mention of The Foresters.

1963.1   SINGER, GODFREY FRANK. The Epistolary Novel: Its Origin,
          Development, Decline, and Residuary Influence. New York:
          Russell & Russell.
               Reprint of 1933.1.

1968.1   FREE, WILLIAM J. "American Fiction in the Columbian
          Magazine, 1786-1792: An Annotated Checklist." BB
          25:150-51.
               Cites The Foresters in the 1787 and 1788 issues of the
          Columbian Magazine.

1968.2   _____. The Columbian Magazine and American Literary
          Nationalism. The Hague and Paris: Mouton, passim.
               Notes Belknap's contributions to the Columbian Magazine.
          Describes his correspondence with John Quincy Adams and his other
          editorial activities.

1968.3   KETTLER, ROBERT RONALD. "The Eighteenth-Century American
          Novel: The Beginnings of a Fictional Tradition." Ph.D.
          Dissertation, Purdue University, pp. 80-83 and passim.
               The Foresters is an example of early American writers'
          conflicts with Europe. Belknap expressed the conventional idea that
          Americans were doing just a little better than other people, making
          the most of their "grand piece of real estate."

1969.1   TURLISH, LEWIS A. Introduction to The Foresters, An
          American Tale (1792), by Jeremy Belknap. Gainesville:
          Scholars' Facsimile & Reprint Society, 8 pp.
               The Foresters is not a "historical allegory" as Belknap
          called it; it is a satiric history more closely allied to Swift than
          to literal allegory. The work is, in Northrop Frye's term, an anat-
          omy, "an outgrowth of the Menippean or Varronian Satire." Belknap's
          "treatment of his pseudo-historical material reflects his anti-
          Jacobin sentiments," and his treatment of Indians is interesting.
          The work is flawed but significant.

1971.1   GOSTWICK, JOSEPH. Handbook of American Literature:
          Historical, Biographical and Critical. Port Washington,
          New York: Kennikat Press, p. 67.
               Brief mention of The Foresters. Reprint of 1856.1.

1971.2   PETTER, HENRI. The Early American Novel. Columbus:
          Ohio State University Press, pp. 87-88, 90, 153 n. 3.
               Compares The Foresters to Arbuthnot's John Bull.

1972.1   HAYCOCK, STEPHEN WALTER. "Jeremy Belknap and Early American
          Nationalism: A Study in the Political and Theological Foun-
          dations of American Literature." Ph.D. Dissertation, Uni-
          versity of Oregon, 1971.
               Belknap believed the love of liberty was characteristic
          of American society but that limitations needed to be placed on the

exercise of liberty. He dedicated his career to teaching Americans
that an individual's freedom to exploit and cheat others of their
freedom must be restrained.

1975.1   DUYCKINCK, EVERT A., and GEORGE L. DUYCKINCK. Cyclopaedia
          of American Literature: Embracing Personal and Critical
          Notices of Authors, and Selections from Their Writings.
          From the Earliest Period to the Present Day. Vol. 1.
          Detroit: Gale Research Co., pp. 263-68.
               Reprint of 1855.1.

1977.1   ROBBINS, J. ALBERT et al., comps. American Literary Manu-
          scripts: A Checklist of Holdings in Academic, Historical,
          and Public Libraries, Museums, and Authors' Homes in the
          United States. 2d ed. Athens: University of Georgia
          Press, p. 27.
               Cites twenty-two places containing documents.

1979.1   EITNER, WALTER H. "The Names for the American Colonies in
          Jeremy Belknap's The Foresters." BSUF 20 (Spring):22-27.
               Explains the biographical, geographical, and economic
sources Belknap drew upon when he created his fictional characters.
Discusses each name separately.

1979.2   _____. "Jeremy Belknap's The Foresters: A Thrice-Told
          Tale." EAL 14 (Fall):156-62.
               Criticizes the introduction to the only edition of The
Foresters in print. Describes the first serialized publication and
the ways it differed from the first book edition. Describes some of
the revisions and expansions of the second edition.

IV. Ann Eliza Bleecker (1752-1783)

1805.1   ANON. "Ann Eliza Bleecker." Boston Weekly Magazine 3
          (28 September):194.
              Biography and note of Bleecker's posthumously published
works.

1838.1   STONE, WILLIAM LEETE. Life and Times of Joseph Brant
          (Thayendanegen). Vol. 1. New York: A.V. Blake, p. 207.
              "The memoirs of Mrs. Bleecker and her Poems, were pub-
lished many years ago, but I have sought in vain among the libraries
and the Bleeckers, to obtain a copy."

1850.1   ELLET, ELIZABETH F. The Women of the American Revolution.
          Vol. 2. New York: Baker & Scribner, n.p.
              Biography. Reprinted: 1969.1.

1854.1   ALLIBONE, S. AUSTIN. A Critical Dictionary of English
          Literature and British and American Authors Living and
          Deceased from the Earliest Accounts to the Latter Half of
          the Nineteenth Century. Vol. 1. Philadelphia: Childs &
          Peterson, p. 205.
              Biography.

1855.1   DUYCKINCK, EVERT A., and GEORGE L. DUYCKINCK. Cyclopaedia
          of American Literature: Embracing Personal and Critical
          Notices of Authors, and Selections from Their Writings.
          From the Earliest Period to the Present Day. Vol. 1.
          New York: Charles Scribner, pp. 356-66.
              Biography. Brief mention of Bleecker's writings.
Includes a selection of her poetry.

1855.2   SCHUYLER, GEORGE W. Colonial New York: Philip Schuyler and
          His Family. Vol. 2. New York: C. Scribner's Sons,
          pp. 173-79.
              Detailed biography.

1901.1   BRONSON, WALTER COCHRANE. A Short History of American
          Literature. Boston: D.C. Heath & co., p. 92.
              A textbook. The History of Maria Kittle has an American
subject but shows European influences in its sentimental style. It
purports to be true, but much of it is evidently fictitious.

1907.1   LOSHE, LILLIE DEMING. The Early American Novel. New York:
          Columbia University Press, pp. 66-67.
              Describes the story of Maria Kittle. Finds that it
hesitates "between the novel and the short story." Notes the
author's interest in Indians, based on her husband's experiences
in an Indian raid. Reprinted: 1958.1.

1909.1 STANTON, THEODORE, in collaboration with members of the faculty of Cornell University. A Manual of American Literature. New York and London: G. P. Putnam's Sons, Knickerbocker Press, p. 116.
A textbook that briefly mentions The History of Maria Kittle and "The Story of Henry and Anne."

1911.1 BATES, KATHARINE LEE. American Literature. New York: Macmillan Co., p. 80.
Brief mention of Bleecker.

1918.1 BRADSHER, EARL L. "Some Aspects of the Early American Novel." Texas Review 3 (April):258.
Maria Kittle anticipates "John Neal's Logan" of 1822.

1926.1 WILLIAMS, STANLEY THOMAS. "The Era of Washington and Jefferson." In The American Spirit in Letters. Pageant of America Series, edited by Ralph Henry Gabriel. New Haven: Yale University Press, pp. 77, 89, 91.
Cites Bleecker as an example of an early American sentimental writer.

1927.1 McDOWELL, TREMAINE. "Sensibility in the Eighteenth-Century American Novel." SP 24 (July):387, 391.
Brief mention of examples of sensibility in The History of Maria Kittle.

1928.1 CLARK, DAVID LEE. Introduction to Edgar Huntley, by Charles Brockden Brown. New York: Macmillan Co., p. xix.
Brief mention of Bleecker.

1929.1 BATES, ERNEST SUTHERLAND. "Bleecker, Ann Eliza." In Dictionary of American Biography. Edited by Allen Johnson. Vol. 2. New York: Charles Scribner's Sons, pp. 365-66.
Biography. Selected bibliography of secondary works.

1929.2 LEISY, ERNEST E. American Literature: An Interpretative Survey. New York: Thomas Y. Crowell Co., p. 50.
Brief mention of The History of Maria Kittle.

1933.1 KEISER, ALBERT. The Indian in American Literature. New York: Oxford University Press, p. 33.
The History of Maria Kittle is an ambitious tale without literary significance.

1933.2 SINGER, GODFREY FRANK. The Epistolary Novel: Its Origin, Development, Decline, and Residuary Influence. Philadelphia: University of Pennsylvania Press, p. 198.
Brief mention of Bleecker. Reprinted: 1963.1.

*1935.1   HENDRICKSON, JAMES C.   "Ann Eliza Bleecker: Her Life and
           Works." M.A. Thesis, Columbia University.
                Cited in 1971.1.

1936.1   QUINN, ARTHUR HOBSON. American Fiction: An Historical and
          Critical Survey. New York: Appleton-Century-Crofts, p. 5.
               Maria Kittle is a tale rather than a novel, and it con-
tains a blood-curdling realism. It is interesting for its autobiographical account of incidents.

1938.1   KUNITZ, STANLEY J., and HOWARD HAYCRAFT. American Authors
          1600-1900. New York: H.W. Wilson Co., p. 83.
               Biography, with no mention of Bleecker's fiction.
Includes bibliography of primary and secondary works.

1939.1   REDDEN, Sister MARY M. The Gothic Fiction in the American
          Magazines (1765-1800). Washington, D.C.: Catholic Univer-
          sity Press, pp. 44-45.
               Summarizes Maria Kittle and describes various Gothic
devices and the way they are presented. Notes that the deeds of the
Indians in Maria Kittle are Gothic, and a remark early in the novel
suggests an imitation of English Gothic novels.

1940.1   BLACK, FRANK GEES. The Epistolary Novel in the Late
          Eighteenth Century: A Descriptive and Bibliographical
          Study. Eugene: University of Oregon Press, pp. 6, 34, 128.
               Brief mention of Bleecker.

1940.2   BROWN, HERBERT ROSS. The Sentimental Novel in America 1789-
          1860. Durham: Duke University Press, pp. 10, 64, 84, 87, 89.
               Quotes from The History of Maria Kittle to show
Bleecker's artificial epistolary device and scenes of extravagant
sensibility.

1943.1   BURKE, WILLIAM J., and WILL D. HOWE. American Authors
          and Books, 1640-1940. New York: Gramercy Publishing Co.,
          p. 69.
               Bibliography of primary works.

1943.2   CARLETON, PHILLIPS D. "The Indian Captivity." AL 15 (May):
          179.
               Brief description of the vivid imagination" and "exhorbi-
tant rhetoric" of Maria Kittle.

1948.1   COWIE, ALEXANDER. The Rise of the American Novel. New
          York: American Book Co., p. 29.
               Brief mention of Bleecker.

1948.2   SPILLER, ROBERT E., WILLARD THORP, THOMAS H. JOHNSON, HENRY
          SEIDEL CANBY, HOWARD MUMFORD JONES, DIXON WECTER, and
          STANLEY T. WILLIAMS, eds. "Indian Captivities." In

Literary History of the United States. Vol. 3. New York:
Macmillan Co., p. 274.
Brief mention of The History of Maria Kittle.

1950.1   HART, JAMES D. The Popular Book: A History of America's
Literary Taste. New York: Oxford University Press, p. 59.
Brief mention of the confusion in the plot of Maria
Kittle.

1952.1   WAGENKNECHT, EDWARD. Cavalcade of the American Novel:
From the Birth of the Nation to the Middle of the Twentieth
Century. New York: Henry Holt & Co., p. 1.
Brief mention of Bleecker.

1953.1   PEARCE, ROY HARVEY. The Savages of America: A Study of the
Indian and the Idea of Civilization. Baltimore: Johns
Hopkins Press, p. 198.
Bleecker uses Indians as a means to literary terror.
Maria Kittle is a captivity narrative turned novel of sensibility.

1956.1   HART, JAMES D. The Oxford Companion to American Literature.
3d ed. New York: Oxford University Press, p. 74.
Brief biography and mention of primary works.

1958.1   LOSHE, LILLIE DEMING. The Early American Novel 1789-1830.
New York: Frederick Ungar Publishing Co., pp. 66-67.
Reprint of 1907.1.

1961.1   MARTIN, TERENCE. The Instructed Vision: Scottish Common
Sense Philosophy and the Origins of American Fiction.
Indiana Humanities Series, no. 48. Bloomington: Indiana
University Press, p. 82.
Brief mention of Maria Kittle as an example of criticism
of the novel based on the metaphysics of actuality.

1962.1   HERZBERG, MAX J., and the staff of the Thomas Y. Crowell Co.
The Reader's Encyclopedia of American Literature. New York:
Thomas Y. Crowell Co., p. 9.
Bleecker's hardships during the Revolution were reflected
in her poems and in her novel.

1963.1   SINGER, GODFREY FRANK. The Epistolary Novel: Its Origin,
Development, Decline, and Residuary Influence. New York:
Russell & Russell, p. 198.
Brief mention of Bleecker. Reprint of 1933.2.

1968.1   FREE, WILLIAM. The Columbian Magazine and American Literary
Nationalism. The Hague and Paris: Mouton, p. 94.
Brief mention of Bleecker as one of the women novelists
more skilled than their predecessors in the Columbian Magazine.

1968.2   KETTLER, ROBERT RONALD. "The Eighteenth-Century American
          Novel: The Beginning of a Fictional Tradition." Ph.D.
          Dissertation, Purdue University, p. 112–115, 135.
               Defines the Americanness of the American novel and shows
how Bleecker fits the definition. Finds that The History of Maria
Kittle provides an example of the new man, a typical character in
early American fiction, and that the book also exemplifies the theme
of terror in early American novels.

1969.1   ELLET, ELIZABETH F. The Women of the American Revolution.
          Vol. 2. New York: Haskell House, pp. 243–45.
               Reprint of 1850.1

1969.2   WRIGHT, LYLE H. American Fiction, 1774–1805: A Contri-
          bution toward a Bibliography. 2d rev. ed. San Marino:
          Huntington Library, pp. 37–38.
               Lists editions and their locations.

1971.1   LEARY, LEWIS. "Bleecker, Ann Eliza." In Notable American
          Women, 1607–1950: A Biographical Dictionary. Edited by
          Edward T. James, Janet Wilson James, and Paul S. Boyer.
          Vol. 1. Cambridge, Mass.: Harvard University Press,
          Belknap Press, pp. 77–78.
               Biography and account of Bleecker's writings. The His-
tory of Maria Kittle "retells in graphical though sentimental detail"
what the author had learned of the French and Indian Wars. The
twenty-four letters in the Posthumous Works are more realistic.

1971.2   PETTER, HENRI. The Early American Novel. Columbus: Ohio
          State University Press, pp. 373–76.
               Compares the fictional Maria Kittle to the real Mary
Rowlandson. Contrasts the emotional content of Bleecker's language
to Rowlandson's.

1974.1   TILLINGHAST, CHARLES ALLEN. "The Early American Novel: A
          Critical Revaluation." Ph.D. Dissertation, Syracuse Univer-
          sity, pp. 81–82.
               Notes the use of the theme of terror, described without
the emotional language usually used.

1975.1   BARNETT, LOUISE K. The Ignoble Savage: American Literary
          Racism, 1790–1890. Contributions to American Studies, no.
          18. Westport, Conn.: Greenwood Press, pp. 56–58, 62, 68n,
          82.
               Describes The History of Maria Kittle as a narrative
without the trappings of romance or history, and notes its departure
from the typical captivity narrative.

V. Hugh Henry Brackenridge (1748-1816)

1792.1   ANON.   Review of <u>Modern</u> <u>Chivalry</u>, vol. 1. <u>Universal</u>
         <u>Asylum</u> <u>and</u> <u>Columbian</u> <u>Magazine</u> 5 (February):123-25.
             Sees the work as a good-humored satire, at which no one
can take offense, and finds "some striking reflections" interspersed
among the hero's ludicrous adventures. Finds the style "easy and
natural, sometimes rather loose; and at times bordering on vulgarity."
Expresses hope for more publications from the author. See 1972.1.

1792.2   ANON.   Review of <u>Modern</u> <u>Chivalry</u>, vol. 2. <u>Universal</u>
         <u>Asylum</u> <u>and</u> <u>Columbian</u> <u>Magazine</u> 6 (August):115-16;
         (September):169-74.
             "Mr. B. affects to write merely for the sake of style,
but no person, who has perused the work, can, for a moment, look upon
this pretension in a serious light."
             Summarizes each of the books and quotes extensively.
Praises Brackenridge's sense of humor. See 1972.1.

1808.1   ANON.   Review of <u>Modern</u> <u>Chivalry; or, The</u> <u>Adventures</u> <u>of</u>
         <u>Captain</u> <u>Farrago</u> <u>and</u> <u>Teague</u> <u>O'Regan</u>. <u>Monthly</u> <u>Anthology</u> <u>and</u>
         <u>Boston</u> <u>Review</u> 5 (September):498-508; (October):554-58.
             Feels pleased to find a work of humor. Discusses bur-
lesque in general and notes that <u>Modern</u> <u>Chivalry</u> at first appears to
be similar to <u>Don</u> <u>Quixote</u>. Complains of the uniformity of Teague's
adventures, but finds much to favor in the book. Praises the characterization of Teague as hero of the book. Quotes extensively.
             Describes Brackenridge's democracy and the objects of
his satire. Takes issue with his position on immigration and immi-
grants' rights. Commends Brackenridge's style as plain, perspicuous,
and simple. Prefers his vulgar to his elevated style.

1835.1   PAULDING, JAMES KIRK.   <u>A</u> <u>Life</u> <u>of</u> <u>Washington</u>. Vol. 2.
         New York: Harper & Brothers, p. 194.
             Biographical anecdotes.

*1846.1   ANON.   "Biographical Notice." In <u>Modern</u> <u>Chivalry; or The</u>
         <u>Adventures</u> <u>of</u> <u>Captain</u> <u>Farrago</u> <u>and</u> <u>Teague</u> <u>O'Regan</u>, by H.H.
         Brackenridge. 2d ed. since the author's death. With a
         Biographical Notice, a Critical Disquisition on the Work,
         and Explanatory Notes. Philadelphia: Carey & Hart.
             Cited in 1926.1.

1854.1   ALLIBONE, S. AUSTIN.   <u>A</u> <u>Critical</u> <u>Dictionary</u> <u>of</u> <u>English</u>
         <u>Literature</u> <u>and</u> <u>British</u> <u>and</u> <u>American</u> <u>Authors</u> <u>Living</u> <u>and</u>
         <u>Deceased</u> <u>from</u> <u>the</u> <u>Earliest</u> <u>Accounts</u> <u>to</u> <u>the</u> <u>Latter</u> <u>Half</u> <u>of</u>
         <u>the</u> <u>Nineteenth</u> <u>Century</u>. Vol. 1. Philadelphia: Childs &
         Peterson, p. 234.
             Bibliography of primary works.

1855.1   DUYCKINCK, EVERT A., and GEORGE L. DUYCKINCK.   <u>Cyclopaedia</u>
         <u>of</u> <u>American</u> <u>Literature</u>: <u>Embracing</u> <u>Personal</u> <u>and</u> <u>Critical</u>

Notices of Authors, and Selections from Their Writings.
From the Earliest Period to the Present Day. Vol. 1.
New York: Charles Scribner, p. 288.
Biography, including portrait. Views Modern Chivalry as
an "aboriginal classic." Praises its style and didacticism. Includes
a selection. Reprinted: 1975.2.

1856.1   BROWN, DAVID PAUL. The Forum; or Forty Years at the
          Philadelphia Bar. Philadelphia: Robert H. Small,
          pp. 396–417.
          Brief mention of Governor McKean's refusal to remove
"Judge Breckenridge" [sic].

1876.1   JENKINS, OLIVER L. The Student's Handbook of British and
          American Literature Containing Sketches Biographical and Criti-
          cal of the Most Distinguished Authors From the Earliest Times to
          the Present Day. Baltimore: John Murphy & Co., pp. 437–38.
          A textbook containing a brief biography and a description
of Brackenridge's writings as introduction to a brief selection from
Modern Chivalry.

1878.1   HART, JOHN S. A Manual of American Literature. Philadel-
          phia: Eldredge & Brother, pp. 74–75.
          Biography and brief selection from Modern Chivalry.

1884.1   SCHARF, J. THOMAS, and THOMPSON WESTCOTT. History of
          Philadelphia 1609–1884. Vol. 2. Philadelphia: L.H. Everts
          & Co., p. 1530.
          Biography of Brackenridge as judge.

1892.1   SMYTH, ALBERT H. The Philadelphia Magazines and Their
          Contributors 1741–1850. Philadelphia: Robert M. Lindsay,
          pp. 53–60.
          On Brackenridge as editor of the Philadelphia Magazine.
"As might be expected from Brackenridge's management, the magazine was
full of wit and scurrility." Describes works that appeared under his
editorship and describes his quarrel with General Charles Lee.

1898.1   HERRINGSHAW, THOMAS WILLIAM. Herringshaw's Encyclopedia of
          American Biography of the Nineteenth Century. Chicago:
          American Publishers Association, p. 138.
          Brief mention of Brackenridge.

1901.1   BRONSON, WALTER COCHRANE. A Short History of American
          Literature. Boston: D.C. Heath, p. 98.
          A textbook noting that Modern Chivalry is "a vigorous
satire on American life. The satire and humor are broad but vigorous
and genuine."

1902.1   PATTEE, FRED LEWIS. The Poems of Philip Freneau: Poet of
          the American Revolution. Vol. 1. Princeton: Princeton
          University Press, pp. xviii–xix.
          Brief mention of Brackenridge and Freneau at Princeton.

1903.1   TRENT, WILLIAM PETERFIELD. <u>A History of American Literature</u>
         <u>1607-1865</u>. New York: D. Appleton & Co., p. 204.
         <u>Modern Chivalry</u> is a "rambling satirical extravaganza."
The author's change from Hudibrastic poem to novel "may indicate a
certain amount of literary prescience." The book does not do justice
to the author's real powers.

1906.1   OBERHOLTZER, ELLIS PAXSON. <u>The Literary History of Phila-</u>
         <u>delphia</u>. Philadelphia: George W. Jacobs & Co., p. 116n.
         Brief mention of <u>Modern Chivalry</u>.

1907.1   LOSHE, LILLIE DEMING. <u>The Early American Novel</u>. New York:
         Columbia University Press, pp. 22-23.
         Summarizes the plot of <u>Modern Chivalry</u> and concludes that
Brackenridge had great satiric power and a clear and vigorous style.
<u>Modern Chivalry</u> displays more ability than any other tale before the
writings of Charles Brockden Brown. The novel is closer in spirit to
Butler than to Cervantes. Reprinted: 1958.1.

1907.2   MARBLE, ANNIE. <u>Heralds of American Literature: A Group of</u>
         <u>Patriot Writers of the Revolution and National Periods</u>.
         Chicago: University of Chicago Press, pp. 281-82.
         Brief mention of <u>Modern Chivalry</u>.

1909.1   SIMONDS, WILLIAM EDWARD. <u>A Student's History of American</u>
         <u>Literature</u>. Boston: Houghton Mifflin Co.; Cambridge:
         Riverside Press, p. 86.
         <u>Modern Chivalry</u> has neither the interest nor the import
of Susanna Rowson's and Hannah Foster's works.

1909.2   STANTON, THEODORE, in collaboration with members of the
         faculty of Cornell University. <u>A Manual of American</u>
         <u>Literature</u>. New York and London: G. P. Putnam's Sons,
         Knickerbocker Press, p. 117.
         A textbook noting that <u>Modern Chivalry</u> is the story of a
"modern 'Don Quixote' narrating the author's experiences in the
Whiskey Insurrection of 1794."

1912.1   CAIRNS, WILLIAM B. <u>A History of American Literature</u>.
         New York: Oxford University Press, pp. 146-47.
         <u>Modern Chivalry</u> is a "rambling prose burlesque" with a
half-hidden satire on democracy. The first part succeeds better than
the second. Reprinted: 1969.1.

1912.2   HOLLIDAY, CARL. <u>The Wit and Humor of Colonial Days (1607-</u>
         <u>1800)</u>. Philadelphia: J.B. Lippincott, pp. 272-287.
         Biography, presenting the facts of Brackenridge's life as
"unconscious preparation for his masterpiece." <u>Modern Chivalry</u> is
"positive and manly in its sentiments." Its main purpose is to show
the follies of a young democracy. "In its day the book was really
needed; for there seemed to be imminent danger of our nation's

becoming freedom-mad and filling the halls of congress with the
butcher, the baker, and the candlestick maker, instead of with oil-
magnates, coal-barons, and railroad-manipulators." Reprinted:
1970.2.

1912.3   VAN DOREN, CARL. The American Novel. New York: Macmillan
         Co., pp. 4-6.
             Modern Chivalry evolved from a hudibrastic poem. It is a
description of eighteenth-century manners "unapproached by any other."
It satirizes doctrines and demagogues, follies and affectations.
Brackenridge is a more forceful satirist than Hopkins or Belknap.
Revised edition: 1940.1.

1914.1   METCALF, JOHN C. American Literature. Atlanta: B.F.
         Johnson Publishing Co., p. 102.
             A textbook briefly mentioning Brackenridge.

1915.1   ELLIS, HAROLD MILTON. "Joseph Dennie and his Circle: A
         Study in American Literature from 1792 to 1812." Bulletin
         of the University of Texas, no. 40, p. 138.
             Brief mention of Brackenridge.

1917.1   HEARTMAN, CHARLES F. A Bibliography of the Writings of
         Hugh Henry Brackenridge Prior to 1825. New York: for the
         compiler, 37 pp.
             An annotated bibliography indicating locations. Does not
attempt to distinguish between various editions of Modern Chivalry.

1917.2   VAN DOREN, CARL. "Fiction I: Brown, Cooper." In The
         Cambridge History of American Literature. Edited by
         William Peterfield Trent, John Erskine, Stuart P. Sherman,
         and Carl Van Doren. Vol. 1, Colonial and Revolutionary
         Literature. Early National Literature. New York: G.P.
         Putnam's Sons, pp. 286-87.
             Modern Chivalry is chiefly directed at political cant and
excess ambition. The second part is badly constructed.

1922.1   DUBREUIL, ALICE JOUVEAU. The Novel of Democracy in America.
         Darby, Pa.: Darby Books, 6 pp.
             Calls Modern Chivalry our first novel of satire and the
first picaresque novel. Summarizes the plot and calls it "a burlesque of political, religious, and educational institutions of the
author's own time."

1926.1   WILLIAMS, STANLEY THOMAS. "The Era of Washington and
         Jefferson." In The American Spirit in Letters. Pageant
         of America Series, edited by Ralph Henry Gabriel. New
         Haven: Yale University Press, pp. 90-91.
             Brackenridge was "the merriest" of the early novelists.
Modern Chivalry was "a wild, rollicking satire on democracy." If it
lacked delicacy, it had vigor.

Includes a portrait by Gilbert Stuart and three drawings
from the 1846 edition of Modern Chivalry.

1927.1   McDOWELL, TREMAINE.   "Sensibility in the Eighteenth-Century
         American Novel."   SP 24 (July):382-402, passim.
         Cites various examples of sensibility and burlesques of
sensibility in Modern Chivalry.

1927.2   PARRINGTON, VERNON LOUIS.   Main Currents in American
         Thought.   Vol. 1, The Colonial Mind 1620-1800.   New York:
         Harcourt, Brace & Co., pp. 390-93.
         Modern Chivalry is "our first backcountry book," one
which gave voice to the widespread dissatisfaction with political
leadership in the early years of the new government.   The book is
refreshing when one is satiated with the heroic.   The aim of the book
is to criticize the unseemly office-hunting by coonskin candidates.
In the nineteenth century Brackenridge was praised as a defender of
democracy.

1928.1   CAIRNS, WILLIAM B.   "British Republication of American
         Writings, 1783-1833."   PMLA 43 (March):306-7.
         Brief mention of the republication of Modern Chivalry.

1929.1   LEISY, ERNEST E.   American Literature: An Interpretive
         Survey.   New York: Thomas Y. Crowell, p. 50.
         Brief mention of Brackenridge.

*1929.2 NEWLIN, CLAUDE.   "The Life and Writings of Hugh Henry
         Brackenridge."   Ph.D. Dissertation, Harvard University.
         Cited in 1932.3.   Published: 1932.3.

1931.1   ANGOFF, CHARLES.   A Literary History of the American People.
         Vol. 2.   New York: Alfred A. Knopf, pp. 315-19.
         Traces the beginnings of the American novel to
Brackenridge rather than to Charles Brockden Brown.   Describes
the plot and form of Modern Chivalry and calls it tiresome.

1931.2   BLANKENSHIP, RUSSELL.   American Literature as an Expres-
         sion of the National Mind.   New York: Henry Holt & Co.,
         pp. 189-90.
         A textbook noting that Modern Chivalry is not an attack
on democracy; it points out weaknesses in democracy.

1931.3   RICHARDSON, LYON N.   A History of Early American Magazines
         1741-1784.   New York: Thomas Nelson & Sons, pp. 196-210.
         Brackenridge worked as editor of the United States Maga-
zine to attract notable writers while pouring his own "patriotic,
religious, tutorial fervor" into the pages.   During his year as
editor, Brackenridge developed into a satirist.
         Identifies unsigned pieces by Brackenridge.   Notes that
the magazine reflected a softening of attitude toward the French.

Evaluates the historical, political, and military essays. Notes the secondary importance of literature.

1932.1   FULLERTON, BRADFORD M.   Selective Bibliography of American
         Literature 1775-1900.   New York: William Farquhar Payson,
         pp. 28-29.
             Brief biography and list of primary works.   Calls Modern
Chivalry the first important novel.

1932.2   JOHNSON, MERLE.   American First Editions: Bibliographic
         Check Lists of the Works of 146 American Authors.   Rev. and
         enl. ed.   New York: R.R. Bowker Co., pp. 34-35.
             Bibliography of primary sources.

*1932.3 NEWLIN, CLAUDE.   The Life and Writings of Hugh Henry
         Brackenridge.   Princeton: Princeton University Press.
             Publication of 1929.2.

1934.1   DUNLAP, GEORGE ARTHUR.   "The City in the American Novel
         1789-1900:   A Study of American Novels Portraying Contempo-
         rary Conditions in New York, Philadelphia, and Boston."
         Ph.D. Dissertation, University of Pennsylvania, pp. 8, 45,
         149.
             A survey of aspects of city life in selected American
novels.   Brackenridge and Charles Brockden Brown are the only early
novelists mentioned.
             Modern Chivalry contains the first definite indication of
the city in an American novel, the first discussion of duelling in
the American novel, and one of the first references to political
affairs.

1935.1   WINTERICH, JOHN TRACEY.   Early American Books and Printing.
         Boston: Houghton Mifflin Co., pp. 146, 152, 153, 157.
             Brief references to Modern Chivalry.

1936.1   BOYNTON, PERCY H.   Literature and American Life.   Boston:
         Ginn & Co., pp. 174-76.
             Describes the structure and plot of Modern Chivalry.
Views the book as an elephantine jumbled thesaurus of Americana.

1936.2   FLORY, CLAUDE REHERD.   "Economic Criticism in American Fic-
         tion 1792-1900."   Ph.D. Dissertation, University of Pennsyl-
         vania, pp. 5-36, 40.
             Quotes from Modern Chivalry as an early satirical comment
on the way our promises to the Indians were being nullified by our
practices.   Also quotes Brackenridge's position on slavery.

1936.3   LEISY, ERNEST E.   "The Novel in America: Notes for a
         Survey."   SWR 22 (Autumn):89.
             Modern Chivalry was one of very few choices for readers
of early American fiction.

1936.4   QUINN, ARTHUR HOBSON. <u>American</u> <u>Fiction:</u> <u>An</u> <u>Historical</u> <u>and</u>
          <u>Critical</u> <u>Survey</u>. New York: Appleton–Century–Crofts,
          pp. 8–11.
              <u>Modern</u> <u>Chivalry</u> is a picaresque romance. The first
part satirizes various institutions, and the second part satirizes
the excesses of democracy. The second part is the weaker.
Brackenridge's style was "far above that of his feminine rivals," and
he was a conscious artist. Brackenridge's model was <u>Don</u> <u>Quixote</u>.

*1937.1   NEWLIN, CLAUDE M., ed. Introduction to <u>Modern</u> <u>Chivalry;</u> <u>or,</u>
          <u>The</u> <u>Adventures</u> <u>of</u> <u>Captain</u> <u>Farrago</u> <u>and</u> <u>Teague</u> <u>O'Regan</u>, by
          Hugh Henry Brackenridge. New York: American Book Co.,
          pp. ix–xli.
              See 1968.3.

1939.1   JACKSON, JOSEPH. <u>Literary</u> <u>Landmarks</u> <u>of</u> <u>Philadelphia</u>.
          Philadelphia: David McKay Co., pp. 37–38.
              Brief biography of "Judge Breckenridge" [<u>sic</u>].

1940.1   VAN DOREN, CARL. <u>The</u> <u>American</u> <u>Novel</u> <u>1789–1939</u>. Rev. and
          enl. ed. New York: Macmillan Co., pp. 4–6.
              Slight changes in wording from 1912.3.

1941.1   DOS PASSOS, JOHN. <u>The</u> <u>Ground</u> <u>We</u> <u>Stand</u> <u>On:</u> <u>Some</u> <u>Examples</u>
          <u>from</u> <u>the</u> <u>History</u> <u>of</u> <u>a</u> <u>Political</u> <u>Creed</u>. New York: Harcourt,
          Brace & Co., pp. 381–401.
              Biography, with emphasis on the whiskey rebellion.

1942.1   LEARY, LEWIS. "Father Bombo's Pilgrimage." <u>PMHB</u> 66
          (October):459–78.
              Prints the full surviving manuscript. Though "exag-
gerated, ridiculous, and full of youthful bombast," "Father Bombo's
Pilgrimage" deserves preservation because it is the earliest known
writing of two of our earliest men of letters.

1944.1   BROOKS, VAN WYCK. <u>The</u> <u>World</u> <u>of</u> <u>Washington</u> <u>Irving</u>. New
          York: E.P. Dutton & Co., pp. 91–93.
              In a chapter on "The West," surveys Brackenridge's life
and novel. <u>Modern</u> <u>Chivalry</u> was meant to educate the gullible frontier in order that democracy might succeed and endure.

1945.1   PAINE, GREGORY. "American Literature a Hundred and Fifty
          Years Ago." <u>SP</u> 17 (April):385–402.
              <u>Modern</u> <u>Chivalry</u> is the best novel of its time.

1948.1   COWIE, ALEXANDER. <u>The</u> <u>Rise</u> <u>of</u> <u>the</u> <u>American</u> <u>Novel</u>. New
          York: American Book Co., pp. 43–60.
              Brackenridge uses episode, conference and reflection to
deliver a series of ironical commentaries throughout part one. The
book lacks plot construction but has a "fairly coherent centre of
thought." To call the book a "satire on democracy" does not do

justice to the author's political position; he cherished republican
principles regardless of party. Despite his stated aims, Modern
Chivalry is a book for the intelligentsia.

1948.2   SPILLER, ROBERT E., WILLARD THORP, THOMAS H. JOHNSON,
         HENRY SEIDEL CANBY, HOWARD MUMFORD JONES, DIXON WECTER, and
         STANLEY T. WILLIAMS, eds. "The Beginnings of Fiction and
         Drama." In Literary History of the United States. Vol. 1.
         New York: Macmillan Co., pp. 178–80.
         Modern Chivalry contains stock elements of the picaresque
novel. Its targets are incompetence and corruption in democracy.
Brackenridge was a deliberate craftsman, acutely aware of his
audience.

1949.1   ROADES, Sister MARY THERESA. "Don Quixote and Modern
         Chivalry." Hispania 32 (August):320–25.
         Draws parallels between characters and episodes in the
two works.

1950.1   HART, JAMES D. The Popular Book: A History of America's
         Literary Taste. New York: Oxford University Press, p. 56.
         Brief mention of Modern Chivalry as the only early novel
indebted to Fielding.

1950.2   JONES, ARTHUR E. "Early American Literary Criticism: A
         Study of American Literary Opinions and Attitudes 1741 to
         1820." Ph.D. Dissertation, Syracuse University, pp. 196–
         209.
         Examines influences of John Winterspoon, President of
Princeton, on Brackenridge. Examines Brackenridge's literary theo-
ries in the United States Magazine. Finds Modern Chivalry a novel
only by our definition, not by the author's. To call the book satire
is to falsify Brackenridge's political position. The purpose of the
book was to comment on Brackenridge's observation of social and
political situations in the U.S.
         Brackenridge's concept of style is that of eighteenth-
century neoclassical writers, reinforced by the Scottish doctrine of
sublimity in simplicity and by the stylistic school Brackenridge
found in ancient classics. Brackenridge attacked Johnson and praised
Hume, combining his view of style with patriotism and Scottish
criticism.

1956.1   HART, JAMES D. The Oxford Companion to American Literature.
         3d ed. New York: Oxford University Press, p. 87.
         Biography and description of Brackenridge's writings.

1958.1   LOSHE, LILLIE DEMING. The Early American Novel 1789–1830.
         New York: Frederick Ungar Publishing Co., pp. 22–23.
         Reprint of 1907.1.

1960.1   HOWARD, LEON. Literature and the American Tradition.
         Garden City, New York: Doubleday & Co., p. 81.

Modern Chivalry is more alive than the writings of
Charles Brockden Brown because it is social history. Brackenridge
saw his dream of a national future being frustrated and found relief
in satiric laughter.

1960.2   JONES, JOSEPH, E. MARCHAND, H.D. PIPER, J.A. ROBBINS, and
         H.E. SPIVEY, comps. American Literary Manuscripts: A
         Checklist of Holdings in Academic, Historical and Public
         Libraries in the United States. Compiled and published
         under the auspices of the American Literature group of the
         Modern Language Association. Austin: University of Texas
         Press, p. 50.
         Lists locations of primary source materials.

1962.1   BURKE, WILLIAM J., and WILL D. HOWE. American Authors
         and Books, 1640 to the Present Day. Augmented and revised
         by Irving R. Weiss. New York: Crown Publishing, p. 83.
         Bibliography of primary and secondary works.

1963.1   WEBER, ALFRED. "Hugh Henry Brackenridges Epistel an Sir
         Walter Scott." Jahrbuch für Amerikastudien 8 (March):
         267-275.
         In German. Modern Chivalry and this Epistle to Walter
Scott are Brackenridge's last poetic efforts. The poem is usually
ignored by critics because Modern Chivalry receives so much interest.
The poem deserves consideration because it is revealing as literary
history, and it shows how Brackenridge appreciated the epic form.

1965.1   LEARY, LEWIS, ed. Introduction to Modern Chivalry. New
         Haven: College & University Press, pp. 7-19.
         The object of Brackenridge's satire is not narrowly
political; it is human greed and stupidity. Modern Chivalry is
distinctively American, with Farrago a caricature of the Jeffersonian
agrarian ideal. The book is kept alive not by its ideas, but with
the humor and humane episodes and lively, plain-spoken words. The
language, especially before it was cleaned up for the 1819 edition,
was simple, direct, colloquial, and sometimes coarse. Includes a
biography to page 15. Revised: 1975.5.

1965.2   SPILLER, ROBERT E. "New Wine in Old Bottles." In The Third
         Dimension: Studies in Literary History. New York:
         Macmillan Co., p. 84.
         In a discussion of the literary movement following the
Revolution, cites Modern Chivalry as an example of burlesque trans-
planted from the Old World.

1967.1   CRADDOCK, WILLIAM BRUCE. "A Structural Examination of Hugh
         Henry Brackenridge's Modern Chivalry." DA 27:3040A.
         Part one of the novel has a clear, picaresque structure,
but in part two Brackenridge grew away from the picaresque, probably
unintentionally, toward a more novelistic development. Part two is

badly disorganized. The 1815 edition was not a finished product but
a collection of incidents linked by plot, character, and theme. Even
the revision of 1819 is not a completely finished work.

1967.2   MARDER, DANIEL. Hugh Henry Brackenridge. Twayne United
          States Authors Series. New York: Twayne Publishers,
          140 pp.
          Biography and critical descriptions of writings. Finds
Brackenridge's satire morally instructive. Notes that "Father
Bombo's Pilgrimage" shows the author's early concern with cultural
values in a democracy. Discusses the development of Modern Chivalry
and the author's purposes. Describes his humor as in the same vein
as the Western tall story. Finds Brackenridge's sentiment qualified
with realism.

1967.3   MATTFIELD, MARY. "Modern Chivalry: The Form." Western
          Pennsylvania Historical Magazine 50 (October):305-26.
          Identifies Modern Chivalry as the first long fictional
work to depend on an American scene and the first kind of literature
having "symbolic illumination." Notes the similarities and differences between Modern Chivalry and Fielding, and finds the key to the
classification of Modern Chivalry in its affinity to other writers:
Swift and writers of Menippean satire. Shows how Brackenridge
naturalized the classical and European form of the "anatomy" and
adapted it to the American situation. Quotes the theme of the novel:
"There is freedom enough in the constitution; why need we be afraid
of aristocracy in practice?"
          Attributes what is usually called the chaos of the novel
to Brackenridge's use of the classic formula for narrative frame.
Examines the rhetorical techniques, point of view, and ironic masks.
Continued in 1968.2.

1967.4   NANCE, WILLIAM L. "Satiric Elements in Brackenridge's Modern
          Chivalry." TSLL 9 (Autumn):381-89.
          Examines Modern Chivalry for its purposes and for its
uses of burlesque and irony in order to demonstrate the author's
artistic strength.

1968.1   CAPLAN, RON. Review of Hugh Henry Brackenridge, by Daniel
          Marder. Western Pennsylvania Historical Magazine 51
          (April):192-94.
          Criticizes Marder's book (1967.2) for its emphasis on
literature to the exclusion of history, for his handling of the facts
of Brackenridge's personal life, and for his lack of familiarity with
the period in which Brackenridge lived.

1968.2   MATTFIELD, MARY S. "Modern Chivalry: The Form."
          Western Pennsylvania Historical Magazine 51 (January):17-29.
          A continuation of 1967.3. The narrative frame of Modern
Chivalry provides a mechanism for bringing together a number of
conflicting viewpoints. Another element of classical verse satire

used by Brackenridge is the formal set-piece of parody. The
burlesque also plays an important part, as does the allegory.
          Since the time of Brackenridge, American satire as
a formal method has all but disappeared.

1968.3   NEWLIN, CLAUDE M., ed.   Introduction to Modern Chivalry; or,
         The Adventures of Captain Farrago and Teague O'Regan, by
         Hugh Henry Brackenridge.   New York and London: Hafner Pub-
         lishing Co., pp. ix-xli.
          Traces the relationship between the book and the life
of its author and the history of the country.   Finds that Brackenridge
represents the eighteenth-century ideals of sanity and moderation.
Describes Brackenridge's political ideas, derived from the classics, and his literary ideas, derived from the classics and from
seventeenth- and eighteenth-century satirists.   Contains a biography
to page xix.   Reprint of 1937.1.

1968.4   REDEKOP, ERNEST.   "The Redmen: Some Representations of
         Indians in American Literature before the Civil War."
         Canadian Association for American Studies 3 (Winter):1-44.
          Early American fiction shows "the fascination of race for
ante-bellum writers."   Brackenridge satirizes the romantic view of
Indians as well as the white man's view, but his interest in Indians
is only part of his larger structure of social satire.

1969.1   CAIRNS, WILLIAM B.   A History of American Literature.
         New York and London: Johnson Reprint Corp., pp. 146-47.
         Reprint of 1912.1.

1969.2   KENNEDY, W. BENJAMIN.   "Hugh Henry Brackenridge: Thoughts
         and Acts of a Moderate Democrat."   WGCR 2:26-38.
          Brackenridge was a moderate, fully committed to democracy
yet critically sensitive to its excesses.   The satirical themes of
Modern Chivalry were simple: "the ambition of unqualified persons to
climb to high places and the lack of intelligent action by people in
general and voters in particular."   Brackenridge did not believe in
perfect equality, and he relied little on political theory.   He
viewed Indians as brutes but held more sympathy for blacks.   He
opposed Hamilton's financial program.   He participated in the Whiskey
Rebellion, for which he was politically attacked but which he used as
a basis for further writing.

1969.3   KULIASHA, FRANCES HOAG.   "Form and Patterning in Modern
         Chivalry by Hugh Henry Brackenridge."   DA 29, n. 12,
         p. 4494A.
          A study made by reading and comparing the works mentioned
within Modern Chivalry with the structure of Modern Chivalry itself.
Examines the forms of the anatomy, the picaresque novel, and the
satiric epic, and finds patterns common to these forms and to the
form of Modern Chivalry.   Also examines the types of humor used as
satiric masks and the beast image which unites the work through

structural metaphor. Concludes that "unity and consistency do exist
in Modern Chivalry and that understanding of the various traditions
explain and enrich its total meaning."

1969.4   MARTIN, WENDY. "The Chevalier and the Charlatan: A
          Critical Study of Hugh Henry Brackenridge's Modern
          Chivalry." DA 29, no. 7A, p. 2220A.
              Evaluates the ways form and content comment on the polit-
ical, social, and economic values of post-Revolutionary America.
Demonstrates that the novel's "formlessness" and Brackenridge's authorial intrusions do not constitute a lapse in artistic control,
"but that the digressions and didactic materials are suited to ex-
ploring the subjective reality of the artist or social philosopher in
a democracy, as well as expressing the fluidity of post-Cartesian and
Lockean associative experience." Also asserts that the loose form
and episodic structure of the novel is suited to the narration of the
exploits of the profiteer or man on the make.

1969.5   WRIGHT, LYLE H. American Fiction, 1774-1850: A Contri-
          bution toward a Bibliography. 2d rev. ed. San Marino:
          Huntington Library, p. 40.
              Lists editions of Modern Chivalry and locates them.

1970.1   GERSTENBERGER, DONNA, and GEORGE HENDRICK. The American
          Novel: A Checklist of Twentieth Century Criticism on Novels
          Written Since 1789. Vol. 2, Criticism Written 1960-1968.
          Chicago: Swallow Press, pp. 28-29.
              Bibliography of secondary works, divided into full-length
books, parts of books, and articles.

1970.2   HOLLIDAY, CARL. The Wit and Humor of Colonial Days (1607-
          1800). Detroit: Gale Research Co., pp. 272-87.
              Reprint of 1912.2

1970.3   MARDER, DANIEL, ed. Introduction to A Hugh Henry
          Brackenridge Reader 1770-1815. Pittsburgh: University
          of Pittsburgh Press, pp. 3-46.
              Traces Brackenridge's literary development from an immi-
grant boy to a Pennsylvania Supreme Court judge. Analyzes the major
satires and narratives in terms of thought, style, and mood, and
relates them to the work of his time. Avoids "the usual probing for
archetypes and symbolic significations." Shows Brackenridge to be a
literary pioneer by "revealing the ways in which he is atypical of
his times and in which he may pre-figure later literary modes such as
local color and realism."
              Shows how "Father Bombo's Pilgrimage" anticipates
Brackenridge's later themes and epitomizes American western humor.
Describes the satire in Modern Chivalry as "almost good-natured."
Finds that the book lacks thematic development; instead it has
thematic elaborations as in an essay. Finds little resemblance to

<u>Don Quixote</u> but some comparison to later western literature. See
1971.4.

1971.1   MARTIN, WENDY. "In the Road with the Philosopher and
          Profiteer: A Study of Hugh Henry Brackenridge's <u>Modern</u>
          <u>Chivalry</u>." ECS 4:241-56.
          Sees <u>Modern Chivalry</u> as foreshadowing many nineteenth and
twentieth-century novelists' use of artistic isolation, subjectivity,
and alienation. Describes Brackenridge's philosopy as it affected
his technique.

1971.2   LEARY, LEWIS. <u>That Rascal Freneau: A Study in Literary</u>
          <u>Failure</u>. New York: Octagon Books, passim.
          Accounts of Brackenridge's youthful writings and collabo-
rations with Freneau. Notes that Mr. Bombo in "Father Bombo's Pilgrimage" uses an Irish brogue which Brackenridge later used in <u>Modern</u>
<u>Chivalry</u>.

1971.3   PETTER, HENRI. <u>The Early American Novel</u>. Columbus: Ohio
          State University Press, pp. 126-136.
          <u>Modern Chivalry</u> is even more episodic than <u>Don Quixote</u>.
Captain Farrago is essentially sane, but idealistic; it is his world
which has become crazy. Teague represents the public level of erratic
impulsiveness and is the narrative hero of the book. He ensures the
liveliness and three-dimensional effect of comedy.
          The problem with the second part of the book lies with
Brackenridge's management of it and with the subject matter. The
book is made up of individual episodes and lacks a proper plot. Its
main theme is democracy in theory and practice, but its most lively
parts arise from its illustration of perfectible human standards and
attributes.

1971.4   TANSELLE, G. THOMAS. "Two Editions of Eighteenth-Century
          Fiction." EAL 6 (Winter):274-83.
          A review of Marder's <u>A Hugh Henry Brackenridge Reader</u>
(1970.3). Questions Marder's selections. Criticizes him for not
indicating the copies from which the texts are taken. Finds inaccu-
racies in the text of <u>Modern Chivalry</u> and questions the moderniza-
tion. Finds that the edition fails, even on its own terms.

1971.5   WHITTLE, AMBERYS R. "<u>Modern Chivalry</u>: The Frontier as
          Crucible." EAL 6 (Winter):263-70.
          "<u>Modern Chivalry</u> is fundamentally an examination of basic
human nature in an ideal test situation, the American frontier."
Politics is less important in the novel than has been claimed, and
madness is a theme of the novel.

1972.1   BUSH, SARGENT, Jr. "<u>Modern Chivalry</u> and 'Young's
          Magazine.'" AL 44 (May):292-99.
          The review to which Brackenridge refers in volume three
of <u>Modern Chivalry</u> is not, as it claims, in <u>Young's Magazine</u>, but in

fact occurs as two reviews in the Universal Asylum and Columbian
Magazine, though Brackenridge greatly elaborated on the originals.
The reviews influenced Brackenridge's writing of volumes two and
three. See 1792.1-2.

1972.2   COLOMBO, ROSA MARIA. "Hugh Henry Brackenridge e la
          frontiera americana." Studi americani 18:7-28.
               In Italian. An examination of Brown's essays and other
writings before Modern Chivalry. A main theme of these writings is
the frontier. Brackenridge saw the reality of the world of the
frontier and its political influences in American life. "Father
Bombo's Pilgrimage" deals with this theme and anticipates several
aspects of Modern Chivalry. Brackenridge's writings for the United
States Magazine show that he was not sympathetic to popular demands.
He departed from literary models in these essays and used direct
argumentation, especially in discussions of slavery.
               The conceived world of Modern Chivalry is connected to
Brackenridge's view of Pittsburgh as a utopia. Various aspects of
structure and theme in Modern Chivalry can be analyzed in light of
these earlier essays.

1973.1   BROOKS, CLEANTH, W.B. LEWIS, and ROBERT PENN WARREN.
          American Literature: The Makers and the Making. Vol. 1.
          New York: St. Martin's Press, pp. 230-31.
               A textbook noting that Brackenridge developed the "real-
istic, satirical objective bent" in American literature. Modern
Chivalry derived from Don Quixote, Tristram Shandy, and Tom Jones,
and its fundamental motive is the satirical investigation of American
society.

1973.2   HARKEY, JOSEPH H. "The Don Quixote of the Frontier:
          Brackenridge's Modern Chivalry." EAL 8 (Fall):193-203.
               Finds many similarities between Don Quixote and Modern
Chivalry but finds the differences significant. Instead of intending
"to laugh chivalry away," Brackenridge wanted to maintain his aristo-
cratic ideals.

1973.3   GREEN, MARTIN. "The God that Neglected to come: American
          Literature 1780-1820." In History of Literature in the
          English Language. Vol. 8. American Literature to 1900,
          edited by Marcus Cunliffe. London: Barrie & Jenkins,
          pp. 89-90.
               Brackenridge's main satiric themes are "the excesses of
democratic behavior, the inordinate ambition of the unqualified, and
the unintelligent choice the voters usually make." Brackenridge's
attitude is largely conservative and he resembles Cooper in attitude.
The book reflects his personality.

1973.4   MARTIN, WENDY. The Rogue and the Rational Man: Hugh Henry
          Brackenridge's Study of a Con Man in Modern Chivalry." EAL
          8 (Fall):179-92.

Brackenridge creates Teague, the first American fictional con man, and Farrago, the rational man, both to reflect tensions created by shifts in the politics, society and economy of late eighteenth-century America and to try to establish values transcending those changes.

1975.1   BARNETT, LOUISE K. The Ignoble Savage: American Literary Racism, 1790-1890. Contributions to American Studies, no. 18. Westport, Conn.: Greenwood Press, pp. 17-18.
          Quotes Brackenridge's Indian treaty-maker.

1975.2   DUYCKINCK, EVERT A., and GEORGE L. DUYCKINCK. Cyclopaedia of American Literature: Embracing Personal and Critical Notices of Authors, and Selections from Their Writings. From the Earliest Period to the Present Day. Vol. 1. New York: Gale Research Co., p. 288.
          Reprint of 1855.2.

1975.3   HAIMS, LYNN. "Of Indians and Irishmen: A Note on Brackenridge's Use of Sources for Satire in Modern Chivalry. EAL 10 (Spring):88-91.
          Brackenridge had verifiable sources for his Indian speech and for his characterization of Teague.

1975.4   KIRBY, DAVID K. American Fiction to 1960: A Guide to Information Sources. Detroit: Gale Research Co., pp. 35-36.
          Annotated bibliography of primary and secondary works.

1975.5   LEARY, LEWIS. "Hugh Henry Brackenridge's Modern Chivalry." In Soundings: Some Early American Writers. Athens: University of Georgia Press, pp. 161-74.
          Modern Chivalry is a formless story written by a loyal but independent-minded democrat who saw the enemy as human greed and stupidity and failure to recognize talents. "Captain Farrago is a good-natured caricature of the Jefferson agrarian ideal." Brackenridge is "wily and unreliable" and should not be taken literally. His satire should be accepted in the spirit it is offered, but it will not please all readers. Revision of 1965.1.

1975.6   McALEXANDER, PATRICIA JEWELL. "The Creation of the American Eve: The Cultural Dialogue on the Nature and Role of Women in Late Eighteenth-century America." EAL 9 (Winter):260.
          Brief mention of Brackenridge.

1975.7   MONTESER, FREDERIC. The Picaresque Element in Western Literature. Studies in the Humanities, no. 5. University: University of Alabama Press, p. 77.
          The critical consensus is that Modern Chivalry is a picaresque novel. The book is significant for showing that the picaresque had crossed the Atlantic.

1976.1   CALLOW, JAMES T., and ROBERT J. REILLY. Guide to American
          Literature from Its Beginnings through World War II. New
          York: Harper & Row, pp. 68-69.
             The purpose of Modern Chivalry was "to explain democracy
to Americans, and each installment had its own theme toward this
aim." Brackenridge satirized many groups, occupations, and customs
but he did not satirize democracy "because he considered it a desir-
able and workable system of government."

1976.2   GRANGER, BRUCE. "The Addisonian Essay in the American Revo-
          lution." SLitI 9:43-52.
             Summarizes and comments on Brackenridge's political arti-
cles in the United States Magazine.

1976.3   KAY, DONALD, and CAROL McGINNIS KAY. "American Satire in
          the Early National Period, 1791-1830." BB 33 (January):
          19-23.
             A list of primary materials and major secondary sources
including biographies and general works and articles.

1976.4   PEROTIN, CLAUDE. "Un témoin de l'Amérique révolutionnaire:
          Hugh Henry Brackenridge." Études Anglaises 29
          (July-September):371-78.
             In French. Describes Brackenridge as well qualified to
write Modern Chivalry. Notes that Brackenridge satirized various
dangers to the new republic while describing the people and the
times. Notes his use of dialect. Criticizes the lack of coherence
between scenes. Sees Brackenridge as an important figure in the
democratic education of the western frontier.

1977.1   GALVIN, MARTIN GEORGE. "Hugh Henry Brackenridge and the
          Popular Press." DAI 38, no. 7A, p. 4166A.
             Examines Brackenridge's principal journalistic activi-
ties, his summary of his journalistic work in Gazette publications,
his writings about American Indians, and his use of the popular press
as a motif in Modern Chivalry. The purpose is to "demonstrate that
Brackenridge progressively modified the European notions of balance,
harmony, and reason as he applied the principles of the Enlightenment
to American life.
             Brackenridge's use of the press as motif in Modern
Chivalry underscores his belief that the press could be a major
balancing force in the society. He used his experiences with the
press to write the novel.

1977.2   MESERVE, WALTER J. An Emerging Entertainment: The Drama of
          The American People to 1828. Bloomington: Indiana Univer-
          sity Press, pp.81-83.
             Describes Brackenridge as a propagandist and dramatist at
the Maryland Academy. Describes his two plays.

1977.3   ROBBINS, J. ALBERT et al., comps. American Literary Manu-
          scripts: A Checklist of Holdings In Academic, Historical,
          and Public Libraries, Museums, and Authors' Homes in the
          United States. 2d ed. Athens: University of Georgia
          Press, p. 38.
              Lists eighty items in twelve locations.

1977.4   SPENGEMANN, WILLIAM C. The Adventurous Muse: The Poetics
          of American Fiction, 1789-1900. New Haven: Yale University
          Press, pp. 94-96.
              The domestic picaresque form was amenable to
Brackenridge's political purposes because of its satirical bent and
because of the social dimension implicit in domestic moral geography.
The moral of the book is that government should rest in the hands of
men like the captain, not in the will of the brutish mob or traditional aristocracy. The novel addresses all issues from an unvarying
social and political middle ground.

1979.1   SCHULTZ, LUCILLE M. "Uncovering the Significance of the
          Animal Imagery in Modern Chivalry." EAL 14 (Winter):306-311.
              To reconcile Brackenridge's animal satire of O'Regan and
the novel's endorsement of the new democracy, one must look to
Scottish Common Sense philosophers Reid and Witherspoon.
Brackenridge believed, as they did, that most of humankind possesses
common sense, but it is not possessed by all, and education and
experience will not create it.

1979.2   TICHI, CECELIA. New World, New Earth: Environmental Reform
          in American Literature from the Puritans through Whitman.
          New Haven: Yale University Press, pp. 106-7.
              Quotes from Modern Chivalry to show a writer who under-
stood the power of geography as an influence on American development.

1979.3   TREADWAY, JAMES LEWIS. "The American Picaresque: 1792-
          1857." DAI 39, no. 12A, p. 7350A.
              Examines selected American novels to demonstrate that
prior to the Civil War a number of American novels were consciously
written within the European picaresque tradition. Finds
Brackenridge's Modern Chivalry, among others, varies little from the
traditional picaresque novel.

1980.1   GRANT, BARRY K. "Literary Style as Political Metaphor in
          Modern Chivalry." CRevAS 11 (Spring):1-11.
              Examines Brackenridge's comments on literary style as a
reflection of his political ideas. Finds Brackenridge's satire bit-
ter and his affirmation of democracy less than firm.

1980.2   KAISER, LEO M. "An Aspect of Hugh Henry Brackenridge's
          Classicism." EAL 15 (Winter):260-70.

Discusss Brackenridge's quotations from Latin classics in
<u>Modern</u> <u>Chivalry</u>. Identifies some 150 Latin quotations for the first
time.

1980.3   TAUB, ANDREW. "Laughing at the Law: An Examination of
          Legal Criticism in the Works of Selected American Humorists,
          1790–1900." <u>DAI</u> 40, no. 10A, p. 5445A.
          An analysis of criticism of the American legal system as
found in the literary works of American humorists. Examines
Brackenridge and others, noting their accuracy of case law and the
validity of their legal philosophies. Finds that Brackenridge used
legal themes both for humor and as criticism of defects in the legal
system.

VI. Ebenezer Bradford (c. 1746-1801)

1795.1   ANON. Review of The Art of Courting. Massachusetts
          Magazine 8:68.
          This book is a "vapid narration," which lacks genuine feeling.

1898.1   HERRINGSHAW, THOMAS WILLIAM. Herringshaw's Encyclopedia of
          American Biography of the Nineteenth Century. Chicago:
          American Publishers Association, p. 139.
              Brief mention of Bradford.

1907.1   LOSHE, LILLIE DEMING. The Early American Novel. New York:
          Columbia University Press, pp. 21-22.
              Describes the novel and locates its inspiration in
Defoe's Religious Courtship. Reprinted: 1958.1.

1932.1   FULLERTON, BRADFORD M. Selective Bibliography of American
          Literature 1775-1900: A Brief Survey of the More Important
          Authors and a Description of Their Works. New York:
          William Farquhar Payson, pp. 29-30.
              The Art of Courting exemplifies didacticism in our early
novels.

1940.1   BROWN, HERBERT ROSS. The Sentimental Novel in America 1789-
          1860. Durham: Duke University Press, pp. 11, 53-54, 64,
          108.
              Bradford claimed his Art of Courting was based on
genuine letters, and he recommended the avantages of epistolary
correspondence.

1956.1   HART, JAMES D. The Oxford Companion to American Literature.
          3d ed. New York: Oxford University Press, p. 88.
              Brief mention of Bradford.

1958.1   LOSHE, LILLIE DEMING. The Early American Novel 1789-1830.
          New York: Frederick Ungar Publishing Co., pp. 21-22.
              Reprint of 1907.1

1971.1   PETTER, HENRI. The Early American Novel. Columbus: Ohio
          State University Press, pp. 70-71, 81, 83n, 229n.
              In a chapter on didactic fiction, describes the novel and
its insistence on its authenticity. Finds it unappealing for a
modern reader.

VII. William Hill Brown (1765-1793)

1789.1   ANON. "Beauties of The Power of Sympathy." Massachusetts
          Magazine 1 (January):50-54.
              Extracts from the novel, sent in by a subscriber.

1789.2   CIVIL SPY [pseud.]. Review of The Power of Sympathy."
          Massachusetts Centinel, 7 February 1789, p. 1.
              Feels disappointed that "it is not until we arrive near
the end of the work, that we find anything to authorize the title."
See 1789.3-4.

1789.3   ANTONIA [pseud.]. "Reply." Herald of Freedom, 10 February,
          p. 1.
              Reply to 1789.2. Calls The Power of Sympathy an "elegant
composition," the first American attempt "in this stile." Refers to
"the amiable youth who is the reputed author." Calls him "a champion
of feminine innocence, a promoter of religion and chastity, and a
pleasing moniter of inexperienced minds."

1789.4   CIVIL SPY [pseud.]. "Reply." Massachusetts Centinel,
          18 February 1789, p. 1.
              Reply to 1789.3. Apologizes and says he now sees the
morality and excellence of the two little volumes he had earlier
criticized.

1812.1   PAINE, ROBERT TREAT. "A Monody, to the Memory of W.H.
          Brown." In The Works and Prose of the Late Robert Treat
          Paine. Boston: J. Belcher, pp. 118-121.
              Poetic tribute to the author.

1850.1   BUCKINGHAM, JOSEPH TINKER. Specimens of Newspaper
          Literature. Vol. 1. Boston: Little & Brown, p. 323.
          The Power of Sympathy was "no sooner announced as published,
than an attempt was made to suppress it, by purchasing and destroying
all the copies that could be found. Few, if any, are now in
existence."

1854.1   ALLIBONE, S. AUSTIN. A Critical Dictionary of English
          Literature and British and American Authors Living and
          Deceased from the Earliest Accounts to the Latter Half of
          the Nineteenth Century. Vol. 1. Philadelphia: Childs &
          Peterson, p. 260.
              Brief mention of Brown.

1861.1   ANON. "The First American Novel." Boston Evening
          Transcript, 2 May, p. 2.
              Letter from a reader requesting information about The
Power of Sympathy.

1878.1   DRAKE, FRANCIS SAMUEL. The Town of Roxbury: Its Memorable
         Persons and Places, Its History and Antiquities, with Numer-
         ous Illustrations of Its Old Landmarks and Noted Personages.
         Roxbury: by the author, p. 134.
               Mentions the home of Mrs. Perez Morton, who wrote The
         Power of Sympathy (sic) which was "so effectively suppressed that
         scarcely a copy remains." Describes the main plot of the novel.

1894.1   BRAYLEY, ARTHUR W. "The Real Author of The Power of
         Sympathy." Bostonian, 1 (December):224-233.
               Quotes from 1789.2. Denies that Sarah Morton was the
         author of The Power of Sympathy and attributes the novel to William
         Hill Brown.

1894.2   LITTLEFIELD, WALTER, ed. Introduction to The Power of
         Sympathy. Boston: Isaiah Thomas & Co., pp. ix-xv.
               The values of this book are antiquarian, historical,
         literary, and artistic.
               Attributes the book to Sarah Morton, the "self-
         acknowledged author." Repeats Drake's assertion (1878.1) that the
         first edition was destroyed. Describes the post-Revolutionary aris-
         tocracy and its movement toward a more realistic literature of social
         commentary. Praises The Power of Sympathy for its omitted detail and
         for its diction.

1898.1   HERRINGSHAW, THOMAS WILLIAM. Herringshaw's Encyclopedia of
         American Biography of the Nineteenth Century. Chicago:
         American Publishers Association, p. 160.
               Brief mention of Brown.

1907.1   LOSHE, LILLIE DEMING. The Early American Novel.
         New York: Columbia University Press, pp. 7-9.
               Attributes The Power of Sympathy to Sarah Wentworth
         Morton. Summarizes the story and criticizes its construction,
         characterization, and style. Reprinted: 1958.1.

1907.2   MARBLE, ANNIE. Heralds of American Literature: A Group of
         Patriot Writers of the Revolutionary and National Periods.
         Chicago: University of Chicago Press, p. 280.
               Describes the plot of The Power of Sympathy and assumes
         Morton was its author.

1909.1   JOHNSON, J.G. Southern Fiction Prior to 1860: An Attempt
         at a First-Hand Bibliography. Charlottesville: Michie Co.,
         p. 13.
               Bibliography of primary and secondary works.

1911.1   HALLECK, REUBEN POST. History of American Literature. New
         York: American Book Co., p. 85.
               The Power of Sympathy by Sarah Morton was probably the
         "first novel to appear in print."

1912.1   VAN DOREN, CARL. The American Novel. New York: Macmillan
          Co., pp. 3, 7.
              Brief mention of Sarah Morton's The Power of Sympathy,
one of the two most important novels of the Richardsonian type.
Revised edition: 1940.3.

1917.1   VAN DOREN, CARL. "Fiction I: Brown, Cooper." In The
          Cambridge History of American Literature. Edited by
          William Peterfield Trent et al. Vol. 1, Colonial and Revo-
          lutionary Literature. Early National Literature. New York:
          G.P. Putnam's Sons, p. 285.
              Mrs. Sarah Wentworth Morton produced the first "regular"
novel, The Power of Sympathy. Its two volumes of stilted letters
caused a scandal, and the book was suppressed. The Coquette is a
better novel.

1919.1   BOYNTON, PERCY H. A History of American literature.
          Boston: Ginn & Co., p. 85.
              Brief mention of The Power of Sympathy by Mrs. Morton.

1922.1   HALL, ERNEST JACKSON. The Satirical Element in the American
          Novel. Philadelphia: University of Pennsylvania Press.
              Reprinted: 1966.1.

1925.1   COAD, ORAL SUMNER. "The Gothic Element in American Litera-
          ture Before 1825." JEGP 24:80.
              Brief mention of The Power of Sympathy as the earliest
trace of Gothic horror in American fiction.

1926.1   WILLIAMS, STANLEY THOMAS. "The Era of Washington and
          Jefferson." In The American Spirit in Letters. Pageant
          of America Series, edited by Ralph Henry Gabriel. New Haven:
          Yale University Press, p. 91.
              The Power of Sympathy by Sarah Morton indulges the
"divine sensibilities."

1927.1   McDOWELL, TREMAINE. "Sensibility in the Eighteenth-Century
          American Novel." SP 24 (July):397 and passim.
              Cites various examples of sensibility in The Power of
Sympathy by Mrs. Morton.

1928.1   CLARK, DAVID LEE, ed. Introduction to Edgar Huntley,
          by Charles Brockden Brown. New York: Macmillan Co.,
          pp. xiii-xiv.
              The Power of Sympathy by Sarah Morton was "too seductive,
and it was promptly and deservedly suppressed."

1929.1   BROWN, HERBERT ROSS. "Elements of Sensibility in the
          Massachusetts Magazine." AL 1:290.
              Quotes from Mrs. Morton's The Power of Sympathy to show
the emphasis on sensibility.

1931.1   PENDLETON, EMILY, and MILTON ELLIS. Philenia: The Life and
          Works of Mrs. Sarah Wentworth Morton. University of Maine
          studies, 2d ser., no. 20. Orono: Maine University Press,
          pp. 109–112.
                  Offers evidence to show that Sarah Morton did not write
The Power of Sympathy.

1932.1   FULLERTON, BRADFORD M. Selective Bibliography of American
          Literature 1775–1900: A Brief Survey of the More Important
          Authors and a Description of Their Works. New York:
          William Farquhar Payson, p. 316.
                  The Power of Sympathy by William Hill Brown lacks liter-
ary merit but is significant as a first attempt at fiction and the
first novel written in America.

1932.2   McDOWELL, TREMAINE. "Last Words of a Sentimental Heroine."
          AL 4 (May):174–77.
                  Quotes from manuscript copies of the last letters of
Frances Apthorp, the seduced woman on whom The Power of Sympathy was
supposed to have been based. "In this tragic and moving document,
there will be found more acute sensibility and more frantic passion
than are set down in any early American novel."

1933.1   ELLIS, MILTON. "Author of the First American Novel." AL 4
          (January):359–68.
                  Considers further the claim for William Hill Brown as
author of The Power of Sympathy. Gives background of the Morton-
Apthrop affair and surveys the published comments about the novel.
Bases the attribution to Brown on the account of Mrs. Thompson who
reported the Brown authorship to Brayley (see 1894.1). Offers other
evidence for Brown's authorship.

1933.2   McDOWELL, TREMAINE. "The First American Novel." American
          Review 3 (November):73–81.
                  Relates the story of The Power of Sympathy, its appear-
ance and suppression. Attributes its suppression to its seduction
theme, its advocacy of sensibility, and most importantly, to its
being based on literal truth. Notes that Milton Ellis has recently
identified the author as William Hill Brown. See 1933.1.

1933.3   SINGER, GODFREY FRANK. The Epistolary Novel: Its Origin,
          Development, Decline, and Residuary Influence. Philadelphia:
          University of Pennsylvania Press, pp. 195–96.
                  Lists The Power of Sympathy as an early epistolary novel,
"now doubted to be" by Sarah Morton. Reprinted: 1963.1.

1935.1   BENSON, MARY SUMNER. Women in Eighteenth-Century America:
          A Study of Opinion and Social Usage. New York: Columbia
          University Press, pp. 189–92.
                  Examines The Power of Sympathy and two other novels for
examples of "women in early American literature."

1935.2   PATTEE, FRED LEWIS. The First Century of American Litera-
          ture 1770-1870. New York and London: D. Appleton-Century
          Co., pp. 83-86.
              The Power of Sympathy is "typical of everything a novel
should not be. . . . Its sentimentality, its Della Cruscan floridity
of style, its total absence of actuality and verisimilitude make it
everything a novel should not be."

1935.3   WINTERICH, JOHN TRACEY. Early American Books and Printing.
          Boston: Houghton Mifflin, p. 151.
              Brief mention of The Power of Sympathy, its origin in
scandal and the rarity of the book today.

1936.1   BOYNTON, PERCY H. Literature and American Life. Boston:
          Ginn & Co., pp. 188, 190, 191.
              Brief mention of The Power of Sympathy.

1936.2   LEISY, ERNEST E. "The Novel in America: Notes for a
          Survey." SWR 22 (Autumn):89.
              Brief mention of The Power of Sympathy as one of a host
of seduction stories.

1936.3   QUINN, ARTHUR HOBSON. American Fiction: An Historical and
          Critical Survey. New York: Appleton-Century Crofts,
          p. 190.
              Brief mention. Finds the controversy over the authorship
of The Power of Sympathy inconclusive.

1937.1   ELLIS, MILTON. Bibliographical note to The Power of
          Sympathy, by William Hill Brown. New York: Columbia
          University press, pp. i-iv.
              Describes the first edition of 1789. Finds few contempo-
rary reviews, contrary to the assertion that the book aroused a storm
of protest. Traces the controversy over authorship.

1940.1   BLACK, FRANK GEES. The Epistolary Novel in the Late Eight-
          eenth Century: A Descriptive and Bibliographical Study.
          University of Oregon Monograph Studies in Literature and
          Philology, no. 2. Eugene: University of Oregon Press,
          pp. 6, 21n, 22, 24n, 129.
              Brief mention of The Power of Sympathy.

1940.2   RADDIN, GEORGE GATES. An Early New York Library of Fiction
          with a Checklist of the Fiction in H. Caritat's Circulating
          Library, No. 1 City Hotel, Broadway, New York 1804. New
          York: H.W. Wilson Co., p. 27.
              Includes works by William Hill Brown in the checklist.

1940.3   VAN DOREN, CARL. The American Novel 1789-1939. Rev. and
          enl. ed. New York: Macmillan Co., p. 3, 7.
              See 1912.1.

1943.1   BURKE, WILLIAM J., and WILL J. HOWE. American Authors
         and Books, 1640-1940. New York: Gramercy Publishing Co.,
         p. 99.
              Bibliography of primary works. Lists Brown as "supposed
author" of The Power of Sympathy.

1944.1   BROOKS, VAN WYCK. The World of Washington Irving. New
         York: E.P Dutton & Co., p. 3n.
              Brief mention of Brown.

1944.2   HAVILAND, THOMAS P. "Precosité Crosses the Atlantic." PMLA
         59 (March):131-41.
              The French heroic romance, consciously or unconsciously,
heavily influenced The Power of Sympathy and the novels of Charles
Brockden Brown.

1945.1   PAINE, GREGORY. "American Literature a Hundred and Fifty
         Years Ago." SP 42 (July):387-88.
              The Power of Sympathy is "a sickening tale of deceit and
narrowly-avoided incest." The novel imitates the Richardson-Sterne-
Mackenzie school at its worst and has no American elements.

1948.1   SPILLER, ROBERT S., WILLARD THORP, THOMAS H. JOHNSON,
         HENRY SEIDEL CANBY, HOWARD MUMFORD JONES, DIXON WECTER, and
         STANLEY T. WILLIAMS, eds. "The Beginnings of Fiction and
         Drama." In The Literary History of the United States. Vol. 1.
         New York: Macmillan Co., p. 177.
              Describes The Power of Sympathy, "usually reckoned as the
first indubitably American novel."

1948.2   WRIGHT, LYLE H. American Fiction, 1774-1850: A Contri-
         bution toward a Bibliography. Rev. ed. San Marino:
         Huntington Library, p. 49.
              Lists The Power of Sympathy and its location in twelve
libraries.

1950.1   HART, JAMES D. The Popular Book: A History of America's
         Literary Taste. New York: Oxford University Press, pp. 54,
         62.
              Brief mention of The Power of Sympathy as a novel of
sensibility.

1951.1   COWIE, ALEXANDER. Rise of the American Novel. New York:
         American Book Co., pp. 10-12, 90.
              Criticizes The Power of Sympathy for its unsuitability
for young readers, its "poor characterization, loose motivation,
graceless digressions," and careless structure.

1951.2   WALSER, RICHARD. "The North Carolina Sojourn of the First
         American Novelist." NCHR 28:138-55.
              Biography of Brown. Includes lettes and poems and obit-
uary from the North Carolina Journal.

1952.1   WAGENKNECHT, EDWARD. Cavalcade of the American Novel:
         From the Birth of the Nation to the Middle of the
         Twentieth Century. New York: Henry Holt & Co., pp. 2-3.
             The Power of Sympathy is "a morbid, nasty book," an
example of the provocative themes of early American fiction.

1952.2   WALSER, RICHARD. "More About the First American Novel." AL
         24 (November):352-57.
             Links two dramatic pieces, Occurrences of the Times, and
The Better Sort, with The Power of Sympathy.

1954.1   _____. "The Fatal Effects of Seduction (1789)." MLN
         69:574-76.
             Describes the plot of an eighteenth-century play, The
Fatal Effects of Seduction, which is similar to the story of The
Power of Sympathy.

1956.1   HART, JAMES D. The Oxford Companion to American Literature.
         3d ed. New York: Oxford University Press, p. 98.
             Brief mention of Brown's works.

1957.1   POCHMANN, HENRY A. German Culture in America: Philosoph-
         ical and Literary Influence 1600-1900. Madison: University
         of Wisconsin Press, pp. 356, 364.
             The Gothic element was present in American fiction from
the first, as demonstrated by The Power of Sympathy, which initiated
"the American fashion of explaining mysteries and supernatural happenings
naturally or rationally."

1957.2   SPENCER, BENJAMIN T. The Quest for Nationality. Syracuse:
         Syracuse University Press, pp. 30, 31, 134, 135.
             Quotes from The Power of Sympathy to demonstrate the
rejection of the cult of the Old World after the Revolution, and uses
the novel as an example of early fiction which contained "solid
centers of local detail in manners and familiar objects."

1958.1   LOSHE, LILLIE DEMING. The Early American Novel 1789-1830.
         New York: Frederick Ungar, pp. 7-9.
             Reprint of 1907.1.

1959.1   MARTIN, TERENCE. "William Hill Brown's Ira and Isabella."
         NEQ 33 (June):238-42.
             Describes Brown's preface to Ira and Isabella, and sees
Brown facing the problem of artistic creation in a hostile environment. Finds that Brown both questions and employs the conventions of
sentimental fiction.

1960.1   FIEDLER, LESLIE. Love and Death in the American Novel. New
         York: Criterion Books, pp. 96-105.
             In The Power of Sympathy Brown is oppressed by the sense
that sentiment is old-fashioned and the novel is a form not to be

trusted. The novel is "more a psychological, even a metaphysical essay, than a lurid story." In volume one and in the opening of volume two "Nature" is used to describe a realm of peace and pleasure, but later nature is what brings Harriot and Harrington to their impasse and is the handmaiden of God. In the end the book equivocates between the smugness of liberal gentility and the factitious sensationalism of antibourgeous sentimentality.

Ira and Isabella is not a tragedy of incest but a "howling travesty." Still, Brown is a considerable figure.

1960.2   JONES, JOSEPH, E. MARCHAND, H.D. PIPER, J.A. ROBBINS, and H.E. SPIVEY, comps. American Literary Manuscripts: A Checklist of Holdings in Academic, Historical and Public Libraries in the United States. Compiled and published under the auspices of the American Literature group of the Modern Language Association. Austin: University of Texas Press, p. 50.
        Lists libraries containing primary sources.

1961.1   BROWN, HERBERT, ed. Critical Introduction to The Power of Sympathy, by William Hill Brown. Boston: New Frontiers Press, pp. iii–xiii.
        Brown was indebted to Richardson, both for subject matter and for epistolary form, though Brown's limitations prevented his full development of the letter form. His language was stilted and the correspondence artificial. Nor was he successful at imitating the style of Sterne.

1961.2   GERSTENBERGER, DONNA, and GEORGE HENDRICK. The American Novel 1787–1959: A Checklist of Twentieth-Century Criticism. Denver: Alan Swallow, p. 32.
        Lists one secondary work.

1961.3   MARTIN, TERENCE. The Instructed Vision: Scottish Common Sense Philosophy and the Origins of American Fiction. Indiana University Humanities Series, no. 48. Bloomington: Indiana University Press, p. 82.
        Brief mention of The Power of Sympathy.

1962.1   HERZBERG, MAX J., and the staff of the Thomas Y. Crowell Co. The Reader's Encyclopedia of American Literature. New York: Thomas Y. Crowell Co., p. 116.
        Brown's The Power of Sympathy is based on an incident in Sarah Wentworth Morton's family. The family tried to destroy all copies of the novel. In 1895 the novel was reproduced serially in the Bostonian.

1963.1   SINGER, GODFREY FRANK. The Epistolary Novel: Its Origin, Development, Decline, and Residuary Influence. New York: Russell & Russell, pp. 195–96.
        Reprint of 1933.3.

1965.1   SPILLER, ROBERT E.   "New Wine in Old Bottles."   In The
          Third Dimension: Studies in Literary History.   New York:
          Macmillan Co., p. 83.
              In a discussion of the literary movement at the end of
the eighteenth century, cites Brown as an example of a weak imitation
of Richardson.

1966.1   HALL, ERNEST JACKSON.   The Satirical Element in the American
          Novel.   New York: Haskell House, pp. 8-9, 60-61.
              The Power of Sympathy by Sarah Wentworth Morton is a
satire aimed at "a vicious form of hypocrisy, that of the libertine."
It inaccurately portrays Boston at the time.   Reprint of 1922.1.

1966.2   STODDARD, ROGER E.   "Daniel Edward Kennedy, a Forgotten
          Collector of Charles Brockden Brown and Early American Lit-
          erature."   Kent State Serif 3 (December):11-16.
              Brief mention of William Hill Brown.

1968.1   KETTLER, ROBERT RONALD.   "The Eighteenth-Century American
          Novel: The Beginning of a Fictional Tradition."   Ph.D.
          Dissertation, Purdue University, pp. 50, 144.
              The preface to Ira and Isabella rails against public
taste, the printer's pandering, and the writer's timidity.   After the
preface, the novel itself must be read as parody.
              The Power of Sympathy develops the conventional early
American theme of horror in a slightly atypical way.

1968.2   STAFFORD, JOHN.   "The Power of Sympathy."   Midcontinent
          American Studies Journal 9 (Spring):52-57.
              Notes the place of the concept of sympathy during the age
of Jefferson.   Cites and quotes freom The Power of Sympathy by Brown.

1968.3   WAGER, WILLIS.   American Literature: A World View.   New
          York: New York University Press, p. 46.
              Brief mention of Brown.

1969.1   KABLE, WILLIAM S., ed.   Editor's Introduction to The Power
          of Sympathy, by William Hill Brown.   Columbus: Ohio State
          University Press, pp. xi-xxxvi.
              Surveys the contenders for the "first" American novel,
and explains why none of them is an American novel.   Examines the
problems of the authorship of The Power of Sympathy and the stories
of the novel's suppression.   Presents a biography of Brown.   Defines
the literary influences on The Power of Sympathy and criticizes its
style.   See 1971.3.

1970.1   GERSTENBERGER, DONNA, and GEORGE HENDRICK.   The American
          Novel: A Checklist of Twentieth-Century Criticism on Novels
          Written since 1789.   Vol. 2, Criticism Written 1960-1968.
          Chicago: Swallow Press, p. 32.
              Lists one secondary work.

1970.2   OSBORNE, WILLIAM S., ed. Introduction to The Power of
         Sympathy and The Coquette. Masterworks of Literature
         Series. New Haven: College & University Press, pp. 13-18.
              Narrative in The Power of Sympathy is supplemented with
lessons for young ladies. The book succeeded more as a didactic
tract than as a novel, for the book had glaring weaknesses.

1971.1   BYERS, JOHN R., Jr. "Further Verification of the
         Authorship of The Power of Sympathy." AL 43 (November):
         421-27.
              Further evidence that Brown wrote The Power of Sympathy.

1971.2   PETTER, HENRI. The Early American Novel. Columbus: Ohio
         State University Press, passim.
              Describes The Power of Sympathy and explains its success.
Compares it to Ira and Isabella. Criticizes Brown's inability to
treat adequately the conflict he created.

1971.3   TANSELLE, G. THOMAS. "Two Editions of Eighteenth-Century
         Fiction." EAL 6 (Winter):274-83.
              Criticizes Kable's edition of The Power of Sympathy
(1969.1). Asks why it does not collate all possible editions, and
questions various matters of style, design, and form.

1972.1   TEBBEL, JOHN. A History of Book Publishing in the United
         States. Vol. 1, The Creation of an Industry 1630-1865. New
         York and London: R.R. Bowker, pp. 67, 150.
              Brief mention of the publication of The Power of
Sympathy.

1972.2   WINANS, ROBERT. "The Reading of English Novels in
         Eighteenth-Century America, 1750-1800." Ph.D. Dissertation,
         New York University, p. 152.
              In a discussion of Sterne in America, notes that The
Power of Sympathy contains a reference to Sterne's A Sentimental
Journey.

1973.1   ARNER, ROBERT D. "Sentiment and Sensibility: The Role of
         Emotion and William Hill Brown's The Power of Sympathy."
         SAF 1 (Autumn):121-32.
              Brown tried to unite the strains of Richardsonian senti-
ment and Sternian sentiment. He sought to express a moral purpose.
He encountered difficulties because as a New Englander he "inherited
a literary tradition in which emotion plays a major role and a cast
of thought that distrusts all emotions as the breeding ground of
vice." As a result, the reader finishes the novel without being
impressed with any particular idea.
              A frequent theme in the novel is that no one can tell
what the last issue of sin will be. The novel deserves to be linked
with Hawthorne's novels as testifying to the power of blackness.

1974.1   STEIN, ROGER B.   "Pulled Out of the Bay: American Fiction
         in the Eighteenth Century."   SAF 2 (Spring):19-20.
         Ira and Isabella contains sea imagery which functions
throughout "in emblematic ways to illuminate the psychological and
moral situation."

1974.2   TILLINGHAST, CHARLES ALLEN.   "The Early American Novel: A
         Critical Revaluation."   Ph.D. Dissertation, Syracuse Univer-
         sity, pp. 75-78.
         The Power of Sympathy raises questions it does not solve,
for it undermines both "reason" and "nature."

1974.3   WILSON, JAMES D.   "Incest and American Romantic Fiction."
         SLitI 7 (Spring):31-50.
         "Adopting sibling incest as a symbol of solipsism, the
American 'dark' Romantics, William Hill Brown, Charles Brockden
Brown, Hawthorne, Melville, and Poe portray self-absorption as the
avenue to dementia and eventual destruction."
         The similarities between The Power of Sympathy and
Richardson are superficial.   The novel is antisentimental.

1975.1   DAVIDSON, CATHY.   "The Power of Sympathy Reconsidered:
         William Hill Brown as Literary Craftsman."   EAL 10
         (Spring):14-29.
         "Discusses the craft of The Power of Sympathy, especially
the ironic treatment of the moral spokesmen; the juxtaposition of
significant letters and the use of the epistolary form for psychological purposes; and the progression of the interior stories and sub-
plots which suggest a much wider theme than the prefatory 'dangerous
consequences of seduction.'"   [Annotation by Cathy N. Davidson.]

1975.2   DAY, MARTIN STEELE.   A Handbook on American Literature: A
         Comprehensive Study from Colonial Times to the Present Day.
         New York: Crane, Russak & Co., p. 35.
         A survey written for an international audience.   Brief
mention of Brown.

1975.3   KIRBY, DAVID K., comp.   American Fiction to 1960:   A Guide
         to Information Sources.   Detroit: Gale Research Co.,
         pp. 43-44.
         Annotated bibliography of primary and secondary works.

1975.4   McALEXANDER, PATRICIA JEWELL.   "The Creation of the American
         Eve: The Cultural Dialogue on the Nature and Role of Women
         in Late Eighteenth-Century America."   EAL 9 (Winter):260-61.
         The Power of Sympathy was one of several novels of the
period in which the hero imitated Werther.

1976.1   CALLOW, JAMES T., and ROBERT J. REILLY.   Guide to American
         Literature from its Beginnings through World War II.   New
         York: Harper & Row.
         Brief mention of Brown.

1976.2   SILVERMAN, KENNETH. A Cultural History of the American
          Revolution: Painting, Music, Literature, and the Theatre in
          the Colonies and the United States from the Treaty of Paris
          to the Inauguration of George Washington, 1763-1789. New
          York: Crowell, pp. 589-91.
          Rates the publication of The Power of Sympathy as one of
four major cultural events which occurred during the first presiden-
tial election. This publication marks the beginning of "a huge vogue
of novel-reading in America." The novel connected extreme sensibility with the social and moral principles underlying Republican virtue, but its claim to attention lies mainly in its distraught style
and shadow of incest and suicide.

1977.1   BRUCCOLI, MATTHEW J., E. FRAZER CLARK, Jr., RICHARD LAYMAN,
          and BENJAMIN FRANKLIN V, eds. First Printings of American
          Authors: Contributions Toward Descriptive Checklists.
          Vol. 1. Detroit: Gale Reserach Co., p. 51.
          Lists the first publication of The Power of Sympathy, The
Better Sort, and Ira and Isabella.

1977.2   ROBBINS, J. ALBERT et al. American Literary Manuscripts: A
          Checklist of Holdings In Academic, Historical, and Public
          Libraries, Museums, and Authors' Homes in the United States.
          Athens: University of Georgia Press, p. 44.
          Lists six items in two locations.

1977.3   STANFORD, ANN. "Images of Women in Early American Litera-
          ture." In What Manner of Women: Essays on English and
          American Life and Literature. Edited by Marlene Springer.
          New York: New York University Press, p. 203.
          In a survey of early American literature, describes
Brown's epistolary romance. Finds it "less an entertainment than a
grim case history."

1978.1   BAYM, NINA. Women's Fiction: A Guide to Novels by and
          about Women in America, 1820-1870. Ithaca and London:
          Cornell University Press, p. 51.
          From a woman's point of view, The Power of Sympathy is "a
demoralized literature."

1978.2   BYERS, JOHN R. "A Letter of William Hill Brown's." AL 49
          (January):606-11.
          Traces the history of the controversy over the authorship
of The Power of Sympathy. Notes the dearth of papers on Brown. Has
been able to find only three examples of his handwriting, one a verse
letter and prose postscript located in the Massachusetts Historical
Society. Prints the letter recording a debilitating illness and
containing a self-description.

1978.3   LISCHER, TRACY KINYON. "The Passive Voice in American Lit-
          erature: Vehicle for Tragedy in Brown, Hawthorne, O'Neill,
          and Frost." DAI 39:1573A.

Defines the American literary dilemma as the problem of
passivity in the crucial moment when the nourishing female principle
is essential. Examines Brown's Power of Sympathy in this context as
an illustration of this dilemma at its inception: "the womanly force
isolated, unable to save the woman or the man; the view of reality
distorted in the reputed seduction episodes; and underlying issues of
the power of woman, the presence of evil, and the duality of human
nature evaded."

1978.4   WHITE, ISABELLE. "The American Heroine, 1789-1899: Noncon-
          formity and Death." Ph.D. Dissertation, University of
          Kentucky, pp. 11-26.
          A study of eight dying heroines, including heroines in
The Power of Sympathy. Traces the fall of the various women in the
novel and finds a confusing message conveyed. Maria's comforting
death contradicts the book's message about seduction: she is both
ruined and glorified at the same time. If they are not completely
guilty, heroines can die beautifully. The most severely punished are
those who sinned most actively. The stated moral, a warning against
seduction, is itself confusing.

1982.1   DAVIDSON, CATHY. "Flirting with Destiny: Ambivalence and
          Form in the Early American Sentimental Novel." SAF 10
          (Spring):17-39.
          An examination of the ways early American novels used the
sentimental form to question the very propositions they extolled.
Cites The Power of Sympathy as an example of the way authors pretended to advocate virtue while indulging in rumor-mongering and as
an example of the way proponents of standard ideals were portrayed as
too shallow and priggish to be taken seriously. The main character's
suicide shows him to be quite fallibly human.

1982.2   WALSER, RICHARD. "Boston's Reception of the First American
          Novel." EAL 17 (Spring):65-74.
          Describes the publication of The Power of Sympathy and
the affair between Perez Morton and Fanny Apthorp. Shows that the
reports of the suppression of the novel were unfounded and that the
novel "caused but little stir."

VIII. James Butler (c. 1755-1842)

1806.1 ANON. Review of Fortune's Football. London Monthly Mirror; Reflecting Men and Manners, with Strictures on their Epitome, the Stage 22 (August):119.
  "To be the sport of Fortune, and to have almost every bone in one's skin broken for her amusement, is really a deplorable case. Such, however, has been the unhappy fate of the subject of this memoir. Yet, after all these calamities, he is able to relieve both his mind and body by the exertions of his pencil, and will, we hope, as he deserves, derive some advantage from this publication."

1907.1 LOSHE, LILLIE DEMING. The Early American Novel. New York: Columbia University Press, pp. 24-25.
  Describes the story. Reprinted: 1958.1.

1927.1 McDOWELL, TREMAINE. "Sensibility in the Eighteenth-Century American Novel." SP 24 (July):382-402.
  Cites examples of the physical manifestations of sensibility and diction in Fortune's Football.

1932.1 FULLERTON, BRADFORD M. Selective Bibliography of American Literature 1775-1900: A Brief Survey of the More Important Authors and a Description of Their Works. New York: William Farquhar Payson, pp. 40-41.
  Fortune's Football was "probably the first original tale of foreign adventure written in America." It is more romantic in its handling of the topic of the Algerian slave trade than was Tyler's treatment.

1936.1 QUINN, ARTHUR HOBSON. American Fiction: An Historical and Critical Survey. New York: D. Appleton-Century, p. 13.
  Fortune's Football is inferior to The Algerian Captive by Tyler. Butler's novel uses the conventions of the earlier British romance of adventure and reflects nothing of the United States.

1956.1 HART, JAMES D. The Oxford Companion to American Literature. 3d ed. New York: Oxford University Press, p. 122.
  Brief mention of Butler.

1957.1. STIMSON, FREDERICK. "Spanish Inspiration in the First American Adventure Stories." Hispania 40 (March):66.
  Fortune's Football includes brief Spanish episodes.

1958.1 LOSHE, LILLIE DEMING. The Early American Novel 1789-1830. New York: Frederick Ungar Publishing Co., pp. 24-25.
  Reprint of 1907.1.

1968.1 KETTLER, ROBERT RONALD. "The Eighteenth-Century American Novel: The Beginnings of a Fictional Form." Ph.D. Dissertation, Purdue University, pp. 168, 179.

Fortune's Football is a picaresque novel, which, in its attempt to emulate European masters, alienates itself from the American fictional tradition. The book extends the traditional picaresque form because it is didactic.

1969.1   WRIGHT, LYLE H. American Fiction, 1774-1850: A Contribution toward a Bibliography. Rev. ed. San Marino: Huntington Library, p. 53.
          Lists eight libraries having copies of Fortune's Football.

1971.1   PETTER, HENRI. The Early American Novel. Columbus: Ohio State University Press, p. 287.
          Criticizes the too-rapid succession of events, repetitive material, and uniformity of tone and speed. Describes the novel as an account of a contest between "fortune" and "providence."

IX. John Davis (1774-1853)

1801.1   ANON. Review of The Farmer of New Jersey. New York American Review and Literary Journal 1 (January):83.
      Finds the book simple and lacking in authenticity. Criticizes the language as unrealistic.

1801.2   ANON. Review of The Wanderings of William; or the Inconstancy of Youth. American Review and Literary Journal 1 (October–December):427–30.
      Summarizes the plot of the novel and criticizes its improbabilities and evil characters.

*1801.3   ANON. Review of The Farmer of New Jersey. New York Review 1.
      Cited in 1924.1.

*1801.4   ANON. Review of The Wanderings of William. Philadelphia Port Folio: A Monthly Magazine, Devoted to Useful Science, the Liberal Arts, Legitimate Criticism, and Polite Literature, 19 September.
      Cited in 1924.1.

1854.1   ALLIBONE, S. AUSTIN. A Critical Dictionary of English Literature and British and American Authors Living and Deceased from the Earliest Accounts to the Latter Half of the Nineteenth Century. Vol. 1. Philadelphia: Childs & Peterson, p. 483.
      Brief mention of Davis.

1898.1   HERRINGSHAW, THOMAS WILLIAM. Herringshaw's Encyclopedia of American Biography of the Nineteenth Century. Chicago: American Publishers Association, p. 286.
      Brief mention of Davis.

1907.1   LOSHE, LILLIE DEMING. The Early American Novel. New York: Columbia University Press, pp. 74–77.
      Finds Davis's first fictions silly and offensive. Davis has "no ability as a novelist," but he is an observant and interested traveler. Reprinted: 1958.1.

1909.1   STANTON, THEODORE, in collaboration with members of the faculty of Cornell University. A Manual of American Literature. New York and London: G. P. Putnam's Sons, Knickerbocker Press, p. 12.
      A textbook which notes that Davis is an Englishman whose Ferdinand and Elizabeth was a conventional story of seduction and suicide. The most that can be said of his works is "that their author was shrewd and observant, and had some journalistic skill."

1915.1   ELLIS, HAROLD MILTON. "Joseph Dennie and His Circle: A
         Study in American Literature from 1792 to 1812." Bulletin
         of the University of Texas, no. 40, pp. 153–54.
              Brief description of Davis's life and mention of his
works.

1918.1   BRADSHER, EARL L. "Some Aspects of the Early American
         Novel." Texas Review 3 (April):246.
              The First Settlers of Virginia illustrates writers' un-
willingness to differentiate between the novel and the historical
narrative.

1924.1   KELLOGG, T.L.   The Life and Work of John Davis, 1774–1853.
         University of Maine Studies, 2d ser., no. 1. Orono: Uni-
         versity of Maine Press, 121 pp.
              Biography; summary of the plots of the fictional works
and descriptions of the poetry.

1927.1   McDOWELL, TREMAINE. "Sensibility in the Eighteenth-Century
         American Novel." SP 24 (July):382–402.
              Cites an example of the physical manifestations of sen-
sibility in Ferdinand and Elizabeth. This novel is one of only two
instances when "the resources of romantic attachment are fully exploited in the stimulation of exquisite agony."

1928.1   CLARK, DAVID LEE, ed. Introduction to Edgar Huntley, by
         Charles Brockden Brown. New York: Macmillan Co., p. xiv.
              Brief mention of and quotation from The Original Letters
of Ferdinand and Elizabeth, which expresses "the temper of American
novels of that day."

1932.1   FULLERTON, BRADFORD M. Selective Bibliography of American
         Literature 1775–1900: A Brief Survey of the More Important
         Authors and a Description of Their Works. New York:
         William Farquhar Payson, p. 79.
              Davis is a "literary tramp." Though English, he is
claimed by America. His place in American fiction rests primarily of
The First Settlers of Virginia.

1933.1   SINGER, GODFREY FRANK. The Epistolary Novel: Its Origin,
         Development, Decline, and Residuary Influence. Philadelphia:
         University of Pennsylvania Press, p. 197.
              Brief mention of The Original Letters of Ferdinand and
Isabella. Reprinted: 1963.1.

1940.1   BLACK, FRANK GEES. The Epistolary Novel in the Late Eight-
         eenth Century. University of Oregon Publications,
         no. 2. Eugene: University of Oregon Press,
         pp. 70, 80, 132.
              Cites Davis as an example of American sentimental fiction
and as an example of the imitation of Goethe's Werther.

1940.2   BROWN, HERBERT ROSS. The Sentimental Novel in America 1789–
             1860. Durham: Duke University Press, passim.
             Ferdinand and Elizabeth expresses a qualified admiration
for Sterne. Fortune's Football exploits the suicide motif. The
Wanderings of William addresses female novel addicts.

1948.1   COWIE, ALEXANDER. The Rise of the American Novel. New
             York: American Book Co., pp. 33–36.
             Describes The First Settlers of Virginia and praises his
"fresh and intimate" descriptions, especially of Indians.

1952.1   WAGENKNECHT, EDWARD. Cavalcade of the American Novel:
             From the Birth of the Nation to the Middle of the Twentieth
             Century. New York: Holt, Rinehart, & Winston, p. 7.
             Brief mention of The First Settlers of Virginia as the
first full-fledged Indian story.

1954.1   HUBBELL, JAY B. The South in American literature 1607–1900.
             Durham: Duke University Press, pp. 196–97.
             Brief biography. Davis is of no importance compared to
English writers but of considerable importance in the United States.
His best claim is as a novelist.
             Summarizes the three versions of the Pocahontas story.

1956.1   HART, JAMES D. The Oxford Companion to American Literature.
             3d ed. New York: Oxford University Press, p. 180.
             Brief mention of Davis's works.

1958.1   LOSHE, LILLIE DEMING. The Early American Novel 1789–1830.
             New York: Frederick Ungar Publishing Co., pp. 74–77.
             Reprint of 1907.1.

1960.1   JONES, JOSEPH, E. MARCHAND, H.D. PIPER, J.A. ROBBINS, and
             H.E. SPIVEY, comps. American Literary Manuscripts: A
             Checklist of Holdings in Academic, Historical and Public
             Libraries in the United States. Compiled and published
             under the auspices of the American Literature group of the
             Modern Language Association. Austin: University of Texas
             Press, p. 60.
             Lists locations of primary sources.

1962.1   BURKE, WILLIAM J., and WILL D. HOWE. American Authors
             and Books, 1640 to the Present Day. Augmented and
             revised by Irving R. Weiss. New York: Crown Publishing,
             p. 181.
             Bibliography of primary and secondary works.

1963.1   SINGER, GODFREY FRANK. The Epistolary Novel: Its Origin,
             Development, Decline, and Residuary Influence. New York:
             Russell & Russell, p. 197.
             Reprint of 1933.1.

1964.1   DAVIS, RICHARD B. <u>Intellectual</u> <u>Life</u> <u>in</u> <u>Jefferson's</u>
          <u>Virginia,</u> <u>1790-1830</u>. Chapel Hill: University of North
          Carolina Press, passim.
              Brief biography and brief references to various writings,
mostly nonfiction.

1971.1   PETTER, HENRI. <u>The</u> <u>Early</u> <u>American</u> <u>Novel</u>. Columbus:
          Ohio State University Press, pp. x, 56 n. 8, 58 n. 16, 159,
          174, 369 n. 82, 389 n. 6.
              Calls Davis English and does not include him in the list
of American fiction writers.

1974.1   KRIBBS, JAYNE K. "Setting the Record Straight on the Real
          John Davis." <u>PBSA</u> 68:329-30.
              Distinguishes the novelist from contemporaries of the
same name. Notes that none of the five libraries listed in <u>American</u>
<u>Literary</u> <u>Manuscripts</u> as holding Davis's papers actually possesses any
manuscripts belonging to the novelist.

1974.2   TILLINGHAST, CHARLES ALLEN. "The Early American Novel: A
          Critical Revaluation." Ph.D. Dissertation, Syracuse Univer-
          sity, p. 91.
              <u>Ferdinand</u> <u>and</u> <u>Elizabeth</u> implies the superiority of Amer-
icans by citing European characteristics not congenial to Americans.

X. Thomas Atwood Digges (c. 1741- c. 1821)

1775.1   ANON. "Catalogue of New Publications." <u>Gentleman's</u>
        <u>Magazine</u> <u>and</u> <u>Historical</u> <u>Chronicle</u> (London) 45 (August):393.
        The novel contains some striking anecdotes of the present
prime minister of Portugal.

1775.2   ANON. Review of <u>Adventures</u> <u>of</u> <u>Alonso</u>. <u>Critical</u> <u>Review;</u> <u>or,</u>
        <u>Annals</u> <u>of</u> <u>Literature</u> (London) 15 (August):163-64.
        "The writer of this work amuses himself with too much
political matter, (especially as it relates chiefly to a foreign
kingdom), to render his book a favourite with the readers of novels."
The adventures are extravagant if sometimes amusing, and the style is
"tolerable" with a few peculiar phrases.

1775.3   ANON. Review of <u>Adventures</u> <u>of</u> <u>Alonso</u>. <u>Monthly</u> <u>Review</u>
        (London) 53 (September):274.
        "The author of this novel has contrived to mix just so
much political anecdote and reflection with his love-tale, as to make
it dull and tedious. It is one of those performances, which though
it may not shock the reader with glaring faults, will be read without
emotion, and forgotten as soon as it is laid aside."

1775.4   ANON. Review of <u>Adventures</u> <u>of</u> <u>Alonso</u>. <u>Town</u> <u>and</u> <u>Country</u>
        <u>Magazine;</u> <u>or,</u> <u>Universal</u> <u>Repository</u> <u>of</u> <u>Knowledge,</u> <u>Instruc-</u>
        <u>tion,</u> <u>and</u> <u>Entertainment</u> (London) 8 (September):492.
        Brief mention, calling the novel "truly romantic."

1776.1   ANON. Review of <u>Adventures</u> <u>of</u> <u>Alonso</u>. <u>London</u> <u>Magazine</u>
        45 (January-February):16, 46, 86-88.
        " . . . the adventures contain some pleasing particulars,
and extraordinary events; some of them too extraordinary to be
true. . . ." Quotes at length from the novel.

1787.1   ANON. Review of <u>Adventures</u> <u>of</u> <u>Alonso</u>. <u>Allegemeine</u>
        <u>Literatur-Zeitung</u> 298 (December):686-87.
        In German. This novel is an English product which did
not deserve German translation. The political discussions are simple-
minded and the hero is a good-for-nothing. The translation is worthy
of the original. Quotes briefly from the novel.

1937.1   HEILMAN, ROBERT BECHTOLD. <u>America</u> <u>in</u> <u>English</u> <u>Fiction</u> <u>1760-</u>
        <u>1800:</u> <u>The</u> <u>Influences</u> <u>of</u> <u>the</u> <u>American</u> <u>Revolution</u>. Baton
        Rouge: Louisiana State University Press, pp. 70, 84, 201-2,
        220, 307, 322, 388.
        Cites references in <u>Adventures</u> <u>of</u> <u>Alonso</u> to the American
colonies and trade with Spanish settlements.

1940.1   WASHINGTON, GEORGE. Writings. Edited by John C.
         Fitzpatrick. Vol. 33. Washington: Government Printing
         Office, pp. 340-41.
              In a letter to John Fitzgerald, 27 April 1794, states
that Digges's conduct toward the United States has been "zealous."
Quotes John Trumbull's statement that Digges was always "well
attached to the rights and interests of the United States."

1941.1   BROOKS, PHILIP. "Notes on Rare Books." New York Times
         Review, 14 September, p. 21.
              If The Adventures of Alonso was written by Digges, it has
some value as the earliest known novel by a United States citizen.
Evidence exists both for and against Digges as author.

1941.2   ELIAS, ROBERT H. "The First American Novel." AL 12
         (January):419-34.
              Offers evidence of Digges's authorship of Adventures of
Alonso. Defends Digges against charges of disloyalty during the
Revolution. Notes the autobiographical qualities of the book but
still finds it a novel. Reprinted: 1943.1, 1966.1.

1943.1   ELIAS, ROBERT H. "The First American Novel." In The
         Adventures of Alonso. Edited by Rev. Thomas J. McMahon.
         New York: United States Catholic Historical Society,
         pp. x-xxviii.
              Reprint of 1941.2. Reprinted: 1966.1.

1951.1   COWIE, ALEXANDER. The Rise of the American Novel. New
         York: American Book Co., pp. 9-10.
              Names no author for Adventures of Alonso, and calls the
novel "only in limited degree American."

1953.1   CLARK, WILLIAM BELL. "In Defense of Thomas Digges." PMHB
         77 (October):381-438.
              Summarizes criticism of Digges made during his lifetime
and during the nineteenth century. "Despite the odium heaped upon
him, Thomas Digges was not as bad as he has been portrayed." Details
Digges's life during and after the Revolution.

1956.1   HART, JAMES D. The Oxford Companion to American Literature.
         3d ed. New York: Oxford University Press, p. 196.
              Brief mention of Digges as possible author of The Adven-
tures of Alonzo.

1957.1   STIMSON, FREDERICK S. "Spanish Inspiration in the First
         American Adventure Stories." Hispania 40 (March):66.
              Digges was one of a few authors who used authentic
Spanish backdrops.

1962.1   KELLOCK, KATHARINE A. Colonial Piscataway in Maryland.
         Accokeek, Md.: Alice Ferguson Foundation, pp. 15-20.

Biography, tracing the influential Digges family, and viewing with sympathy Digges's activities in England during the Revolution.

1964.1　PURSELL, CARROLL W.　"Thomas Digges and William Pearce:　An Example of the Transit of Technology."　WMQ, 3d ser. 21 (October):551-60.
Biography, focusing on Digges's efforts to bring to the United States skilled mechanics from England and Ireland.

1965.1　PARSONS, LYNN HUDSON.　"The Mysterious Mr. Digges."　WMQ, 3d ser. 22 (July):486-92.
Biography, documenting the meeting and friendship of Digges and the Irish patriot Theobald Wolfe Tone.　Cites evidence to show that Digges was a kleptomaniac and that he betrayed the organization of United Irishmen in 1793.

1966.1　ELIAS, ROBERT H.　"The First American Novel."　In Evidence for Authorship:　Essays on Problems of Attribution.　Edited by David V. Erdman and Ephim G. Fogel.　New York:　Cornell University Press, pp. 311-20.
Reprint of 1943.1.

1966.2　PRICE, L.M.　The Reception of United States Literature in Germany.　Chapel Hill:　University of North Carolina Press, p. 81.
The Adventures of Alonzo was translated into German in 1787.

1969.1　LEMAY, LEO.　"Appendix Containing Sixty-Eight Additional Writers of the Colonial South."　In A Bibliographical Guide to the Study of Southern Literature.　Edited by Louis B. Rubin, Jr.　Baton Rouge:　Louisiana State University Press, p. 342.
Bibliography.

1971.1　PETTER, HENRI.　The Early American Novel.　Columbus: Ohio State University Press, pp. 285-87, 304 n. 34, 404-5.
Compares the character of Alonso to Mrs. Wood's Ferdinand in Ferdinand and Elmira.

1972.1　ELIAS, ROBERT H., and MICHAEL M. STANTON.　"T.A. Digges and the Adventures of Alonso:　Evidence from Robert Southey."　AL 44:118-22.
Describes the history of criticism of Digges's novel since 1941 when Elias first identified Digges as author.　Now offers conclusive proof of Digges's authorship, discovered by Stanton while editing Robert Southey's letters at the University of Rochester. Notes the biographical interest of Digges's reputation among Southey's relatives and points out new areas for investigation of Digges and the Southey family.

1977.1   ROBBINS, J. ALBERT et al. American Literary Manuscripts: A
Checklist of Holdings In Academic, Historical, and Public
Libraries, Museums, and Authors' Homes in the United States.
Athens: University of Georgia Press, p. 90.
Lists holdings in four locations.

XI. Hannah Webster Foster (1759-1840)

1788.1   ANON. "Extract of a Letter from Boston." Boston
         Independent Chronicle and Universal Advertiser,
         11 September, p. 2.
              Recounts the death of a lady in Danvers which may serve
    "as a good moral lecture to young ladies."

1788.2   CURIOSOS. "Miscellany. For the Centinel." Massachusetts
         Centinel, 20 September, n.p.
              Relates the story of a young woman named Whitman who died
    in childbirth at the Bell Tavern, Danvers. Attributes her downfall
    to her habit of reading romances. Includes a poem and a letter by
    her.

1800.1   ANON. Review of The Boarding School. Columbian Phoenix and
         Boston Review 1 (May):275-78.
              Describes the book as "a plan of female education," and
    recommends it for young ladies, especially its sample "epistolary
    correspondence."

1801.1   ANON. Review of The Boarding School. New York American
         Review and Literary Journal 1 (January-March):85-86.
              Criticizs the book as merely a compilation of ideas from
    English educators. Criticizes the style as affected.

1806.1   ANON. "Literature of North Carolina." Monthly Anthology
         and Boston Review 3 (July):356.
              Brief mention of The Coquette.

1808.1   ANON. Review of Modern Chivalry, by Hugh Henry
         Brackenridge. Monthly Anthology and Boston Review 5:498.
              Briefly mentions The Coquette as one of several books
    which causes "fair misses" to weep.

1835.1   ANON. Review of The Coquette. Knickerbocker; or New York
         Monthly Magazine 5 (March):254.
              Praises The Coquette for its natural and exciting inci-
    dents, for its cheerful and didactic episodes, and for its "judicious
    reflection, and keen knowledge of life."

1854.1   ALLIBONE, S. AUSTIN. A Critical Dictionary of English
         Literature and British and American Authors Living and
         Deceased from the Earliest Accounts to the Latter Half of
         the Nineteenth Century. Vol. 1. Philadelphia: Childs &
         Peterson, p. 620.
              Brief mention of The Coquette "founded on fact."

1855.1   LOCKE, JANE E. Historical Preface to The Coquette; or, The
         History of Eliza Wharton. Boston: William P. Fetridge &
         Co., pp. 3-30.

Critical praise from a nineteenth-century Boston poet.
Includes a genealogy of Elizabeth Whitman and her biography. Includes three poems by Elizabeth Whitman.

1875.1   DALL, CAROLINE. The Romance of the Association; or, One
          Last Glimpse of Charlotte Temple and Eliza Wharton, a
          Curiosity of Life. Cambridge, Mass.: John Wilson & Son,
          102 pp.
          Recounts the discovery of previously unknown letters of
Eliza Wharton. Defends Wharton's reputation, and describes her
romantic correspondence with Joel Barlow. Defends the authenticity
of both Charlotte Temple and The Coquette, explaining the
blood relation between Charlotte Temple and Eliza Wharton. Contrasts
Wharton's actual letters with the plot of the novel to present
Wharton as a cultivated woman, not a coquette.

1887.1   ANON. "Hannah Foster." In Appleton's Cyclopaedia of Amer-
          ican Biography. Edited by James Grant Wilson and John
          Fiske. Vol. 2. New York: D. Appleton & Co., p. 510.
          Brief biography and mention of the novels.

1898.1   HERRINGSHAW, THOMAS WILLIAM. Herringshaw's Encyclopedia of
          American Biography of the Nineteenth Century. Chicago:
          American Publishers Association, p. 375.
          Brief biographical mention.

1901.1   BRONSON, WALTER COCHRANE. A Short History of American
          Literature. Boston: D.C. Heath & Co., p. 94.
          The style of The Coquette is old-fashioned and formal,
and it is modelled on Richardson, but it has "considerable animation
and pathos."

1903.3   THOMPSON, ADELE E. "Woman's Place in Early American
          Fiction." Era 12 (November):473.
          Brief mention of The Coquette.

1904.1   CRAWFORD, MARY C. Romance of Old New England Churches.
          Boston: L.C. Page & Co., pp. 12-43.
          Recounts the biography of Eliza Wharton because The
Coquette distorted the facts. The novel might "have been written by
a Boccaccio without genius." Hawthorne may have found his heroine
for The Scarlet Letter in Elizabeth Whitman.

1907.1   LOSHE, LILLIE DEMING. The Early American Novel. New York:
          Columbia University Press, p. 14.
          Although The Coquette lacks Morton's (sic) sentimentality
and Rowson's sensationalism, it remains the most readable of all
early fiction by women. Its popularity in the early nineteenth
century rivalled Charlotte Temple. Reprinted: 1958.1.

1909.1   SIMONDS, WILLIAM EDWARD. A Student's History of American
         Literature. Boston: Houghton Mifflin, p. 86.
              In The Coquette "the theme of indiscretion and desertion
is treated in the sentimental, didactic style." The popularity of
the novel outlasted its generation.

1909.2   STANTON, THEODORE, in collaboration with members of the
         faculty of Cornell University. A Manual of American
         Literature. New York and London: G. P. Putnam's Sons,
         Knickerbocker Press, p. 117.
              Brief mention of The Coquette, "a story of desertion,
showing the marked influence of Richardson."

1911.1   BATES, KATHARINE LEE. American Literature. New York:
         Macmillan Co., pp. 85-86.
              Brief mention of Foster.

1912.1   BOLTON, CHARLES KNOWLES. The Elizabeth Whitman Mystery.
         Peabody, Mass.: Peabody Historical Society, 145 pp.
              Tells the story of Elizabeth Whitman at the Bell Tavern,
Danvers. Suspects Mrs. Foster of having written the lines that
appeared on Whitman's gravestone. Lists sources for the story and
accuses Foster of concocting all adverse description of Elizabeth
Whitman.
              Identifies Whitman's family. Speculates about why she
chose Danvers and about the identity of her lover.

1912.2   CAIRNS, WILLIAM B. A History of American Literature. New
         York: Oxford University Press, p. 138.
              Brief mention of The Coquette.

1912.3   VAN DOREN, CARL. The American Novel. New York: Macmillan
         Co., p. 7.
              The Coquette is one of two of the most important novels
of the early period. It was very popular. Revised edition: 1940.3.

1915.1   ELLIS, HAROLD MILTON. "Joseph Dennie and his Circle. A
         Study in American Literature from 1792 to 1812." Bulletin
         of the University of Texas, no. 40 (July), p. 77.
              Brief mention of Foster.

1917.1   VAN DOREN, CARL. "Fiction I: Brown, Cooper." Cambridge
         History of American Literature. Edited by William
         Peterfield Trent et al. Vol. 1, Colonial and Revolutionary
         Literature. Early National Literature. New York: G.P.
         Putnam's Sons, pp. 285-86.
              The Coquette is better than The Power of Sympathy by
William Hill Brown. The Coquette and Charlotte Temple "stole upon a
community which winced at fiction."

1920.1   TRENT, WILLIAM PETERFIELD. A History of American Literature
         1607-1865. New York and London: D. Appleton & Co.,
         p. 196n.
              Brief mention of The Coquette, which ranks above
Charlotte Temple.

1926.1   WILLIAMS, STANLEY THOMAS. "The Era of Washington and
         Jefferson." In The American Spirit in Letters. Pageant
         of America Series, edited by Ralph Henry Gabriel. New Haven:
         Yale University Press, p. 92.
              Notes the popularity of Foster's "tales." Notes that The
Coquette is "deeply in debt to the novels of Richardson." Includes a
picture of Eliza Wharton from the 1831 edition of The Coquette.

1927.1   McDOWELL, TREMAINE. "Sensibility in the Eighteenth-Century
         American Novel." SP 24 (July), pp. 387, 396.
              Eliza Wharton is a notable example of a young heroine
brought to an untimely grave. The author's moralizing resembles
Richardson's.

1928.1   CLARK, DAVID LEE, ed. Introduction to Edgar Huntley, by
         Charles Brockden Brown. New York: Macmillan Co., p. xiv.
              Brief mention of Foster.

1929.1   BROWN, HERBERT ROSS. "Elements of Sensibility in the
         Massachusetts Magazine." AL 1 (1929):289.
              Quotes from The Boarding School to illustrate the seduc-
tion theme in literature.

1929.2   LEISY, ERNEST E. American Literature: An Interpretive
         Survey. New York: Thomas Y. Crowell Co, p. 50.
              Brief mention of Foster.

1930.1   FOSTER, RICHARD ALLEN. The School in American Literature.
         Baltimore: Warwick & York, pp. 57-58.
              Cites The Boarding School as an example of fiction about
the education of girls. Finds that it smacks of Maria Edgeworth and
belongs to "the class of educational fiction." Assumes this work was
written to offset the effect of The Coquette, but this purpose of
instruction kept Foster from making her second book a creditable
work.

1931.1   ANGOFF, CHARLES. A Literary History of the American People.
         Vol. 2. New York: Alfred A. Knopf, p. 218.
              Brief mention of The Coquette by a "second-rate
Mrs. Rowson."

1931.2   BOWERMAN, SARAH G. "Hannah Webster Foster." In Dictionary
         of American Biography. Edited by Allen Johnson and Dumas
         Malone. Vol. 6. New York: Charles Scribner's Sons,
         pp. 548-49.

Biography. Notes a family connection between Elizabeth Whitman and Hannah Foster's husband. Finds that The Coquette follows Samuel Richardson and Susanna Rowson.

1932.1   BROWN, HERBERT R. "Richardson and Sterne in the Massachu-
          setts Magazine." NEQ 5 (January):69.
              Cites Hannah Foster as an example of one who was offended
by Sterne. Reprinted: 1932.2.

1932.2   _____. Richardson and Sterne in the "Massachusetts Maga-
          zine." [Boston?]: Southworth Press, 1 p.
              Reprint of 1932.1.

1932.3   FULLERTON, BRADFORD M. A Selective Bibliography of American
          Literature 1775-1900: A Brief Survey of the More Important
          Authors and a Description of Their Works. New York:
          William Farquhar Payson, pp. 105.
              The Coquette, despite serious shortcomings, remains the
most readable of early American novels by women.

1932.4   SHURTER, ROBERT L. "Mrs. Hannah Foster and the Early Amer-
          ican Novel." AL 4 (November):306-8.
              Biography. Finds her life and work characteristic of
women novelists after the Revolution. In addition to her novels, her
other claim to remembrance is her connection with Phineas Adams who
founded the Monthly Anthology or Magazine of Polite Literature.

1933.1   SINGER, GODFREY FRANK. The Epistolary Novel: Its Origin,
          Development, Decline, and Residuary Influence. Philadelphia:
          University of Pennsylvania Press, passim.
              Brief mention of the popularity of The Coquette.
Reprinted: 1963.1.

1934.1   BROWN, HERBERT ROSS, ed. Introduction to The Coquette, or
          The History of Eliza Wharton, by Hannah Webster Foster. New
          York: Columbia University Press, Facsimile Text Society,
          pp. v-xix.
              Quotes from advertisements for the novel and documents
its publishing history. Locates copies of various editions. Identifies the plot with the Whitman case and notes its derivation from
Richardson. Praises Foster's use of the letter form as better than
that of her contemporaries. Credits the character of the heroine
with being more than a stock figure.

1935.1   BENSON, MARY SUMNER. Women in Eighteenth-Century America:
          A Study of Opinion and Social Usage. New York: Columbia
          University Press, pp. 178, 181, 189-92, 201.
              Describes the plot of The Coquette as one of several
examples of women in early American literature.

1935.2   PATTEE, FRED LEWIS. The First Century of American Litera-
         ture 1770–1870. New York and London: D. Appleton–Century
         Co., pp. 90–91.
            Attributes the popularity of The Coquette to its authen-
ticity and finds in the novel "unexpected excellence."

1935.3   WINTERICH, JOHN TRACEY. Early American Books and Printing.
         Boston: Houghton Mifflin Co., p. 151.
            Brief mention of The Coquette.

1936.1   BOYNTON, PERCY H. Literature and American Life. Boston:
         Ginn & Co., pp. 191–93.
            Brief mention of Foster.

1936.2   LEISY, ERNEST E. "The Novel in America: Notes for a
         Survey." SWR 22 (Autumn):89.
            Brief mention of The Coquette as one of a host of seduc-
tion stories.

1936.3   QUINN, ARTHUR HBSON. American Fiction: An Historical and
         Critical Survey. New York: Appleton–Century Crofts, p. 20.
            The Coquette was a popular novel containing a character
as real as any of Mrs. Rowson's progeny.

1938.1   KUNITZ, STANLEY J., and HOWARD HAYCRAFT. American Authors
         1600–1900. New York: H.W. Wilson Co., p. 284.
            Biography and brief criticism. The Coquette was real-
istic but The Boarding School was a dull homily.
            Includes a bibliography of primary and secondary works.

1939.1   BROWN, HERBERT R., ed. Introduction to The Coquette, or,
         The History of Eliza Wharton. New York: Columbia Univer-
         sity Press, for the Facsimile Text Society, pp. v–xix.
            Cites and describes editions of The Coquette. Traces the
effects of Richardson on The Coquette. Finds the appeal to modern
readers in Eliza's rebellion against stifling decorums of her time.

1940.1   _____. The Sentimental Novel in America 1789–1860. Durham:
         Duke University Press, passim.
            Quotes Foster to show that her works were characteristic
in their didacticism, their use of seduction, and their imitation of
Richardson. Describes The Coquette as the most memorable seduction
story of eighteenth-century American fiction.

1940.2   RADDIN, GEORGE GATES. An Early New York Library of Fiction
         with a Checklist of the Fiction on H. Caritat's Circulating
         Library, No. 1 City Hotel, Broadway, New York. New York:
         H.W. Wilson Co., p. 30.
            Includes Foster's works in the checklist.

1940.3   VAN DOREN, CARL. The American Novel 1789-1939. Rev. and
         enl. ed. New York: Macmillan Co.
           Slight changes in wording from 1912.1.

1943.1   BURKE, WILLIAM J., and WILL D. HOWE. American Authors
         and Books, 1640-1940. New York: Gramercy Publishing Co.,
         p. 254.
           Bibliography of primary works.

1944.1   BROOKS, VAN WYCK. The World of Washington Irving. New
         York: E.P. Dutton & Co., pp. 49-50.
           In a chapter on New England, mentions The Coquette as a
popular seduction tale. Describes the plot.

1946.1   COWIE, ALEXANDER. "The Beginnings of Fiction and Drama."
         In Literary History of the United States. Edited by Robert
         E. Spiller et al. Vol. 1. New York: Macmillan Co.,
         p. 178.
           The Coquette closely followed the case of Elizabeth
Whitman. The book is part of the stream of Richardsonian fiction and
is "more finished as a novel" than its contemporaries.

1947.1   MOTT, FRANK LUTHER. Golden Multitudes: The Story of Best
         Sellers in the United States. New York: Macmillan Co.,
         p. 305.
           Lists The Coquette as an "over-all best seller." Cites
the book's sales record.

1948.1   SPILLER, ROBERT E., WILLARD THORP, THOMAS H. JOHNSON,
         HENRY SEIDEL CANBY, HOWARD MUMFORD JONES, DIXON WECTER, and
         STANLEY T. WILLIAMS, eds. "The Beginnings of Fiction and
         Drama." In The Literary History of the United States.
         Vol. 1. New York: Macmillan Co., p. 178.
           The Coquette closely followed the case of Elizabeth
Whitman. The book presented an inescapable moral.

1950.1   HART, JAMES D. The Popular Book: A History of America's
         Literary Taste. New York: Oxford University Press, pp. 54,
         58, 63.
           Briefly notes that The Coquette was based on fact and was
set in the United States.

1951.1   COWIE, ALEXANDER. The Rise of the American Novel. New
         York: American Book Co., pp. 15-16.
           Summarizes the plot of The Coquette. Finds its use of
letter form skillful but compares it unfavorably to Charlotte Temple.

1951.2   QUINN, ARTHUR HOBSON. The Literature of the American
         People: An Historical and Critical Survey. New York:
         Appleton-Century Crofts, p. 192.

Brief mention of the story of Elizabeth Whitman as the basis for The Coquette.

1952.1 WAGENKNECHT, EDWARD. Cavalcade of the American Novel:
        From the Birth of the Nation to the Middle of the Twentieth
        Century. New York: Holt, Rinehart & Winston, pp. 5-6.
            The Coquette is better literature than Charlotte Temple.
The main character is complicated, and the book approaches its climax
skillfully.

1956.1 HART, JAMES D. The Oxford Companion to American Literature.
        3d ed. New York: Oxford University Press, p. 252.
            Brief mention of Foster.

1956.2 PAPASHVILY, HELEN WAITE. All the Happy Endings: A Study of
        the Domestic Novel in America, the Women Who Wrote It, the
        Women Who Read It, in the Nineteenth Century. New York:
        Harper & Brothers Publishers, pp. 30-31.
            Brief biography of Foster and description of the plot of
The Coquette and the scandal on which it was based. The Coquette is
cited as an example of the seduction novel.

1956.3 TAYLOR, WALTER F. The Story of American Letters. Chicago:
        Henry Regnery Co., p. 93.
            Brief mention of The Coquette.

1958.1 LOSHE, LILLIE DEMING. The Early American Novel 1789-1830.
        New York: Frederick Ungar Publishing Co., p. 14.
            Reprint of 1907.1.

1959.1 BLANCK, JACOB. "Hannah Webster Foster." In Bibliography of
        American Literature. Vol. 3. New Haven: Yale University
        Press, p. 211.
            Bibliography of primary works and selected bibliography
of secondary works.

1961.1 MARTIN, TERENCE. The Instructed Vision: Scottish Common
        Sense Philosophy and the Origins of American Fiction.
        Indiana Humanities Series, no. 48. Bloomington:
        Indiana University Press, p. 82.
            Brief mention of The Coquette.

1962.1 HERZBERG, MAX J., and the staff of the Thomas Crowell Co.
        The Reader's Encyclopedia of American Literature. New York:
        Thomas Y. Crowell Co., p. 211.
            The Coquette recounts the seduction of the author's
cousin, Elizabeth Whitman. The seducer was supposedly either the son
of Jonathan Edwards or Aaron Burr.

1963.1 SINGER, GODFREY FRANK. The Epistolary Novel: Its Origin,
        Development, Decline, and Residuary Influence. New York:
        Russell & Russell.
            Reprint of 1933.1.

1964.1   DAVIS, RICHARD BEALE. Intellectual Life in Jefferson's
         Virginia 1790-1830. Chapel Hill: University of North
         Carolina Press, pp. 78, 349.
             Brief mention of The Coquette.

1965.1   SPILLER, ROBERT E. "New Wine in Old Bottles." In The
         Third Dimension: Studies in Literary History. New York:
         Macmillan Co., p. 83.
             In a discussion of the literary movement following the
Revolution, cites The Coquette as an example of one of the imitations
of Richardson.

1968.1   FREE, WILLIAM. The Columbian Magazine and American Literary
         Nationalism. Studies in American Literature, vol. 15. The
         Hague and Paris: Mouton, pp. 62, 94.
             Brief reference to Foster as one of the sentimental women
novelists, more skilled than their predecessors in the Columbian
Magazine.

1968.2   KETTLER, ROBERT RONALD. "The Eighteenth-Century American
         Novel: The Beginning of a Fictional tradition." Ph.D.
         Dissertation, Purdue University, pp. 121-28.
             Eliza Wharton is the most impressive of the youthful
protagonists in early American fiction. As is typical in early
novels, she succeeds not in changing anything but only in destroying
herself.

1969.1   WRIGHT, LYLE H. American Fiction, 1774-1850: A Contri-
         bution toward a Bibliography. 2d rev. ed. San Marino:
         Huntington Library, pp. 103-104.
             Lists editions of The Boarding School and The Coquette
and their locations.

1970.1   OSBORNE, WILLIAM S., ed. Introduction to The Power of
         Sympathy and The Coquette. New Haven: College & University
         Press, pp. 18-23.
             The Coquette appeals to modern readers. The main char-
acter is one of few in early fiction to emerge as a real person and
whose plight is convincing. The character of Sanford is equally
believable. The lessons rise naturally and effectively from the
plot, and though the book has weaknesses, it holds its dignity.

1971.1   BROWN, HERBERT ROSS. "Foster, Hannah Webster." In Notable
         American Women 1607-1950: A Biographical Dictionary.
         Edited by Edward T. James, Janet Wilson James, and Paul S.
         Boyer. Cambridge, Mass.: Harvard University Press, Belknap
Press, pp. 650-51.
             The Coquette is the most readable of early American
sentimental novels. Foster based her narrative on the case of
Elizabeth Whitman and drew her moral and epistolary pattern from
Samuel Richardson. The heroine transcends the stock figure of the

seduced female. The book enjoyed a modest success, greatest between 1824 and 1828.

1971.2   PETTER, HENRI. The Early American Novel. Columbus: Ohio
         State University Press, pp. 258-64 and passim.
         Contrasts Sanford to Brown in Manvill's Lucinda and con-
trasts Eliza to Richardson's Clarissa and other heroines. Examines
the characters in some detail. Praises Foster's handling of the
epistolary form.

1972.1   WINANS, ROBERT. "The Reading of English Novels in
         Eighteenth-Century America 1750-1800." Ph.D. Dissertation,
         New York University, pp. 163, 181, 190-91, 193, 198.
         In a discussion of Sterne in America, notes that Foster's
Boarding School displays concern with Sterne's "indelicacy" and compares Sterne with Jonathan Swift on the issue of obscenity, or indelicacy. In a discussion of Richardson in America, quotes Foster's
praise of Richardson in The Boarding School.

1974.1   EARNEST, ERNEST. The American Eve in Fact and Fiction 1775-
         1914. Urbana: University of Illinois Press, p. 30.
         Brief mention of Foster.

1975.1   McALEXANDER, PATRICIA JEWELL. "The Creation of the American
         Eve: The Cultural Dialogue on the Nature and Role of Women
         in Late Eighteenth-Century America." EAL 9 (Winter):261.
         Brief mention of The Coquette as a novel which focuses on
the evil results of passion while also portraying its attractions.

1977.1   WENSKA, WALTER P. "The Coquette and the American Dream of
         Freedom." EAL 7 (Winter):243-55.
         Foster anticipates most of our major writers in her
complex treatment of the theme of freedom. Eliza Wharton's quest for
freedom prefigures many self-reliant American heroines; like them she
flees in a last effort to achieve her dream.

1978.1   BAYM, NINA. Women's Fiction: A Guide to Novels by and
         about Women in America, 1820-1870. Ithaca and London:
         Cornell University Press, pp. 50-51.
         From a woman's point of view, The Coquette is a "demor-
alized literature."

1978.2   WHITE, ISABELLE. "The American Heroine, 1789-1899: Non-
         conformity and Death." Ph.D. Dissertation, University of
         Kentucky, pp. 43-59.
         In an examination of eight dying American heroines, in-
cludes the heroine of The Coquette. Eliza Wharton differs from the
heroines in The Power of Sympathy and Charlotte Temple, because
she does not conform to social expectation. Unlike them, she brings on
her own ruin.

1979.1   HORNSTEIN, JACQUELINE. "Literary History of New England
         Women Writers, 1630–1800." DAI 39:7347A.
         In this study of the influences on and characteristics of
New England women writers, chapter five includes Hannah Foster.

1982.1   DAVIDSON, CATHY N. "Flirting with Destiny: Ambivalence and
         Form in the Early American Sentimental Novel." SAF 10
         (Spring):17–39.
         An examination of the ways early American novels went
beyond the conventional pieties while avoiding moral censure by
advocating virtue. Examines The Coquette in detail as an example of
a representative work. Finds that the trappings of sentimentalism are
subsumed into a story that questions social roles of women and argues
against docile acceptance of those roles.

XII. Philip Freneau (1752-1832)

1854.1   ALLIBONE, S. AUSTIN. A Critical Dictionary of English
          Literature and British and American Authors Living and
          Deceased from the Earliest Accounts to the Latter Half of
          the Nineteenth Century. Vol. 1. Philadelphia: Childs &
          Peterson, p. 638.
              Biography of Freneau as a "patriotic pest."

1941.1   LEARY, LEWIS. That Rascal Freneau: A Study in Literary
          Failure. New Brunswick: Rutgers University Press,
pp. 25-26.
              Describes Freneau's contributions to part 3 of "Father
Bombo's Pilgrimage," parts 1 and 2 having been lost.

1942.2   _____. "Father Bombo's Pilgrimage." PMHB 66 (October):
          459-78.
              Though "exaggerated, ridiculous, and full of youthful
bombast," "Father Bombo's Pilgrimage" deserves preservation because
it is the earliest known writing of two of our earliest men of
letters. Prints the full surviving manuscript.

1967.1   AXELROD, JACOB. Philip Freneau. Austin and London:
          University of Texas Press, p. 27.
              Brief description of "Father Bombo's Pilgrimage."

1971.1   PETTER, HENRI. The Early American Novel. Columbus: Ohio
          State University Press, p. 104.
              Brief mention of Freneau.

1977.1   ROBBINS, J. ALBERT et al., comps.   American Literary Manu-
          scripts: A Checklist of Holdings In Academic, Historical,
          and Public Libraries, Museums, and Authors' Homes in the
          United States.   2d ed. Athens: University of Georgia
          Press, p. 119.
              Lists holdings in fifteen locations.

XIII. Michel-René Hilliard d'Auberteuil (1751-1789?)

1907.1   LOSHE, LILLIE DEMING. <u>The</u> <u>Early</u> <u>American</u> <u>Novel</u>. New York:
Columbia University Press, pp. 61-63.
     Includes <u>Miss</u> <u>McRae</u> because it is the first novel both
written and published in America. Notes that the author contrasted
the ferocity of savages with the virtues of their chiefs and American
innocence with European vices. Summarizes the plot. Reprinted:
1958.2.

1943.1   HOWARD, LEON. <u>The</u> <u>Connecticut</u> <u>Wits</u>. Chicago: University
of Chicago Press, p. 195.
     Brief mention of Hilliard d'Auberteuil.

1948.1   COWIE, ALEXANDER. <u>The</u> <u>Rise</u> <u>of</u> <u>the</u> <u>American</u> <u>Novel</u>. New
York: American Book Co., p. 29.
     Brief mention of Hilliard d'Auberteuil.

1952.1   WAGENKNECHT, EDWARD. <u>Cavalcade</u> <u>of</u> <u>the</u> <u>American</u> <u>Novel:</u>
<u>From</u> <u>the</u> <u>Birth</u> <u>of</u> <u>the</u> <u>Nation</u> <u>to</u> <u>the</u> <u>Middle</u> <u>of</u> <u>the</u> <u>Twentieth</u>
<u>Century</u>. New York: Holt, Rinehart & Winston, p. 1.
     <u>Miss</u> <u>McRae</u>'s claim to the title "first American novel" is
weakened by its having been written in French by a Frenchman.

1958.1   LEARY, LEWIS. Introduction to <u>Miss</u> <u>McCrea:</u> <u>A</u> <u>Novel</u> <u>of</u> <u>the</u>
<u>American</u> <u>Revolution</u>. A Facsimile Reproduction Together with
a Translation from the French by Eric LaGuardia. Gainesville:
Scholars' Facsimiles & Reprints, 64 pp.
     Biography of Hilliard and description of his writings.
Relates the story of Jane McCrea and documents several versions of
the story in prose and poetry. Notes distinctions in Hilliard's
version.

1958.2   LOSHE, LILLIE DEMING. <u>The</u> <u>Early</u> <u>American</u> <u>Novel</u> <u>1789-1830</u>.
New York: Frederick Ungar Publishing Co., pp. 61-63.
     Reprint of 1907.1.

1971.1   PETTER, HENRI. <u>The</u> <u>Early</u> <u>American</u> <u>Novel</u>. Columbus: Ohio
State University Press, p. 390n.
     Brief mention of Hilliard d'Auberteuil.

XIV. Enos Hitchcock (1744-1803)

1790.1   ANON. Review of Memoirs of The Bloomsgrove Family.
          Columbian Magazine and Universal Asylum 5 (July):47-48;
          (August):114-15; (September):177-81.
          Describes the educational principles set forth in the
book and quotes extensively. Recommends the book highly, especially
for mothers. See 1968.1.

1790.2   ANON. Review of Memoirs of The Bloomsgrove Family.
          Massachusetts Magazine 2 (July):433-35.
          Describes the book as an original, valuable, and instruc-
tive work. Finds the language neat and perspicuous, though the
author's characterizations never rise above mediocrity. Includes a
lengthy extract.

1877.1   BELKNAP, JEREMY. Letter to Ebenezer Hazard, 14 September
          1790. Massachusetts Historical Society Collections, 5th
          ser. 3:232.
          "I have read Bloomsgrove. It is a piece of patchwork, as
all the productions of that genius are. He is indebted much to Lord
Kaimes, and much to other writers. It is, however, as good as can be
expected from a man who never had any children to try his theory
upon."

1887.1   ANON. "Enos Hitchcock." In Appleton's Cyclopaedia of Amer-
          ican Biography. Edited by James Grant Wilson and John
          Fiske. Vol. 3. New York: D. Appleton & Co., p. 217.
          Brief biography and mention of Hitchcock's works.

1898.1   HERRINGSHAW, THOMAS WILLIAM. Herringshaw's Encyclopedia of
          American Biography of the Nineteenth Century. Chicago:
          American Publishers Association, p. 484.
          Brief biography.

1907.1   LOSHE, LILLIE DEMING. The Early American Novel. New York:
          Columbia University Press, pp. 20-21.
          Hitchcock's purposes were both didactic and patriotic.
Reprinted: 1958.1.

1918.1   BRADSHER, EARL L. "Some Aspects of the Early American
          Novel." Texas Review 3 (April):243.
          The full title of The Farmer's Friend demonstrates
that Hitchcock is but a type, teaching worldly wisdom through
sentimentality.

1927.1   McDOWELL, TREMAINE. "Sensibility in the Eighteenth-Century
          American Novel." SP 24 (July):283-402.
          Quotes from The Bloomsgrove Family to indicate
Hitchcock's position on the use of sensibility for social ends.

Quotes Mrs. Bloomsgrove's warning against the dangers of novels for young girls.

1932.1   BROWN, HERBERT R.   "Richardson and Sterne in the <u>Massachu-setts Magazine</u>." <u>NEQ</u> 5 (January):67, 68, 71.
            Brief mention, quoting Hitchcock's praise of Richardson in <u>The Bloomsgrove Family</u>.

1932.2   FULLERTON, BRADFORD M.   <u>Selective Bibliography of American Literature 1775-1900</u>: <u>A Brief Survey of the More Important Authors and a Description of Their Works</u>. New York: William Farquhar Payson, p. 140.
            Calls Hitchcock's novels sermons in fiction form and finds them representative of the "cultural outlook" of America at the time.

1936.1   QUINN, ARTHUR HOBSON.   <u>American Fiction</u>: <u>An Historical and Critical Survey</u>. New York: Appleton-Century Crofts, pp. 7-8.
            <u>Memoirs of The Bloomsgrove Family</u> is too artificial, its characters too perfect, though it does have some delightful features.

1937.1   CURTI, MERLE.   "The Great Mr. Locke, America's Philosopher 1765-1865." <u>Huntington Library Bulletin</u> 9 (April):107-51.
            Hitchcock's <u>Bloomsgrove Family</u> treated readers to "a generous feast of Locke." The book was one of several parental guides that reflected Locke's influence.

1940.1   BLACK, FRANK GEES.   <u>The Epistolary Novel in the Late Eight-eenth Century</u>: <u>A Descriptive and Bibliographical Study</u>. University of Oregon Monograph Studies in Literature and Philology, no. 2. Eugene: University of Oregon Press, p. 38.
            In <u>The Bloomsgrove Family</u> the story interest is small. "What narrative there is consists in large measure in tales and anecdotes which illustrate the educational theories." The letters are impersonal and essaylike.

1940.2   BROWN, HERBERT ROSS.   <u>The Sentimental Novel in America 1789-1860</u>. Durham: Duke University Press, passim.
            Hitchcock's novels warn against novelists but approve of stories "founded on fact" and sentimental tales. They praise female letter-writers but qualify praise of Richardson. They emphasize the importance of education and decrie the evils of slavery. Reprinted: 1959.1.

1948.1   COWIE, ALEXANDER.   <u>The Rise of the American Novel</u>. New York: American Book Co., pp. 17-19.
            The Bloomsgrove family is "the very cambric tea of American fiction." Only the observations on education have pertinence.

1952.1   WAGENKNECHT, EDWARD. Cavalcade of the American Novel:
          From the Birth of the Nation to the Middle of the Twentieth
          Century. New York: Henry Holt & Co., p. 6.
                Brief mention of Hitchcock.

1956.1   HART, JAMES D. The Oxford Companion to American Literature.
          3d ed. New York: Oxford University Press, p. 326.
                Brief mention of Hitchcock.

1957.1   SPENCER, BENJAMIN. The Quest for Nationality. Syracuse:
          Syracuse University Press, pp. 31, 36.
                Briefly cites Hitchcock and others who portrayed for
          American women readers "manners and sentiments and codes consonant
          with the national milieu."

1958.1   LOSHE, LILLIE DEMING. The Early American Novel 1789-1830.
          New York: Frederick Ungar Publishing Co., pp. 20-21.
                Reprint of 1907.1.

1959.1   BROWN, HERBERT ROSS. The Sentimental Novel in America 1789-
          1860. Durham: Duke University Press, passim.
                Reprint of 1940.2.

1962.1   BURKE, WILLIAM J., and WILL D. HOWE. American Authors
          and Books, 1640 to the Present Day. Augmented and revised
          by Irving R. Weiss. New York: Crown Publishing, p. 345.
                Bibliography of primary works.

1968.1   FREE, WILLIAM. The Columbian Magazine and American Literary
          Nationalism. Studies in American Literature, vol. 15. The
          Hague and Paris: Mouton, pp. 62-63.
                Brief reference to a review of The Bloomsgrove Family in
          the Columbian Magazine. See 1790.1.

1968.2   KETTLER, ROBERT RONALD. "The Eighteenth Century American
          Novel: The Beginning of a Fictional Tradition." Ph.D.
          Dissertation, Purdue University, pp. 93-94, 115.
                Discusses The Bloomsgrove Family as an example of the
          theme of the contrast between America and Europe. Notes that The
          Farmer's Friend contains the characterization of the conventional
          "new man," Mr. Worthy.

1969.1   WRIGHT, LYLE H. American Fiction, 1774-1850: A Contri-
          bution toward a Bibliography. 2d rev. ed. San Marino:
          Huntington Library, p. 190.
                Lists editions and locations of The Farmer's Friend and
          The Bloomsgrove Family.

1971.1   PETTER, HENRI. The Early American Novel. Columbus: Ohio
          State University Press, passim.

The Farmer's Friend is "the relation of a Franklinesque
career from rags to riches." Hitchcock's style is heavily sentimental. The Bloomsgrove Family displays characteristics of fiction
of its time. It uses affected diction and conventional cliches.

1972.1   SHIPTON, CLIFFORD K. Biographical Sketches of Those Who
         Attended Harvard College in the Classes 1764-1767. Sibley's
         Harvard Graduates, vol. 16. Boston: Massachusetts Histor-
         ical Society, pp. 475-84.
             Biography of Hitchcock that briefly mentions The
Bloomsgrove Family. Describes The Farmer's Friend as a "thin thread
of fictitious biography on which were strung moral anecdotes." Notes
that the book was quickly forgotten.

1972.2   WINANS, ROBERT B. "The Reading of English Novels in
         Eighteenth Century America, 1750-1800." Ph.D. Dissertation,
         New York University, pp. 182, 187, 192.
             In a discussion of Richardson in America, quotes the
reference to Richardson in The Bloomsgrove Family. Notes that Mrs.
Bloomsgrove praises Richardson's writings for uniting "sentiment with
character, and present images of life," but then condemns his effect
on readers' moral behavior. Notes that Hitchcock criticized Fielding
for exciting the passions.

1977.1   ROBBINS, J. ALBERT et al., comps. American Literary Manu-
         scripts: A Checklist of Holdings In Academic, Historical,
         and Public Libraries, Museums, and Authors' Homes in the
         United States. 2d ed. Athens: University of Georgia
         Press, p. 150.
             Lists holdings in fourteen locations.

XV. Francis Hopkinson (1737-1791)

1791.1 RUSH, BENJAMIN. "Account of the Late Francis Hopkinson
Esq." Philadelphia <u>Columbian</u> <u>Magazine</u> <u>and</u> <u>Universal</u> <u>Asylum</u>
1 (May):291-93.
Calls "A Pretty Story" "a most beautiful allegory" and
praises Hopkinson's satirical talents.

1848.1 LOSSING, BENSON J. <u>Biographial</u> <u>Sketches</u> <u>of</u> <u>the</u> <u>Signers</u>
<u>of</u> <u>the</u> <u>Declaration</u> <u>of</u> <u>American</u> <u>Independence.</u> New York:
George F. Cooledge & Brother, pp. 85-87.
Biography, including portrait.

1855.1 DUYCKINCK, EVERT A., and GEORGE L. DUYCKINCK. <u>Cyclopaedia</u>
<u>of</u> <u>American</u> <u>Literature:</u> <u>Embracing</u> <u>Personal</u> <u>and</u> <u>Critical</u>
<u>Notices</u> <u>of</u> <u>Authors,</u> <u>and</u> <u>Selections</u> <u>from</u> <u>Their</u> <u>Writings.</u>
<u>From</u> <u>the</u> <u>Earliest</u> <u>Period</u> <u>to</u> <u>the</u> <u>Present</u> <u>Day.</u> New York:
Charles Scribner, pp. 219-229.
Biography and comment on writings, including a brief
mention of "A Pretty Story." Reprinted: 1975.1.

1862.1 DUYCKINCK, EVERT L. <u>A</u> <u>National</u> <u>Portrait</u> <u>Gallery</u> <u>of</u> <u>Eminent</u>
<u>Americans:</u> <u>Including</u> <u>Orators,</u> <u>Statesmen,</u> <u>Naval</u> <u>and</u> <u>Military</u>
<u>Heroes,</u> <u>Jurists,</u> <u>Authors,</u> <u>Etc.</u> <u>From</u> <u>Original</u> <u>Full</u> <u>Length</u>
<u>Paintings</u> <u>by</u> <u>Alonzo</u> <u>Chappell.</u> Vol. 2. New York: Johnson,
Fry & Co., pp. 338-44.
In a laudatory biography, praises "A Pretty Story" as an
ingenious allegory with "excellent humor."

1878.1 HART, JOHN S. <u>A</u> <u>Manual</u> <u>of</u> <u>American</u> <u>Literature.</u> Philadelphia: Eldredge & Brother, pp. 75-76.
Biography and bibliography of primary works.

1878.2 HILDEBURN, CHARLES R. "Francis Hopkinson." <u>Pennsylvania</u>
<u>Magazine</u> 2:314-24.
Biography, including letters from Hopkinson.

1880.1 JENKINS, Rev. O.L. <u>The</u> <u>Student's</u> <u>Handbook</u> <u>of</u> <u>British</u> <u>and</u>
<u>American</u> <u>Literature,</u> <u>with</u> <u>Selections</u> <u>from</u> <u>the</u> <u>Writings</u> <u>of</u>
<u>the</u> <u>Most</u> <u>Distinguished</u> <u>Authors.</u> Baltimore: John Murphy &
Co., pp. 405-6.
Brief mention of "A Pretty Story."

1888.1 ANON. "Hopkinson, Thomas" [<u>sic</u>]. In <u>Appleton's</u> <u>Cyclopaedia</u>
<u>of</u> <u>American</u> <u>Biography.</u> Edited by James Grant Wilson and
John Fisk. Vol. 3. New York: D. Appleton & Co., p. 260.
"A Pretty Story" is one of Hopkinson's most important
political writings.

1897.1   TYLER, MOSES COIT. The Literary History of the American
           Revolution 1763-1783. Vol. 1. New York: G.P. Putnam's
           Sons, pp. 279-91.
                In a discussion of a "new method" of writing the history
           of ideas, moods, motives, and passions which allows writers to speak
           for themselves, includes "A Pretty Story" as the only work of fic-
           tion. Quotes extensively and summarizes the story. Notes that it
           resembles Arbuthnot only in one particular. It "is an example of
           the use of allegory in the facetious treatment of national or inter-
           national politics." Concludes that this work marked Hopkinson as one
           of three leading Whig satirists, the others being John Trumbull and
           Philip Freneau. Reprinted: 1970.2.

1898.1   HERRINGSHAW, THOMAS WILLIAM. Herringshaw's Encyclopedia of
           American Biography of the Nineteenth Century. Chicago:
           American Publishers Association, p. 496.
                Brief biography.

1901.1   BRONSON, WALTER COCHRANE. A Short History of American Lit-
           erature. Boston: D.C. Heath & Co., p. 54n.
                Brief mention of "A Pretty Story."

1902.1   MARBLE, ANNIE RUSSELL. "Francis Hopkinson: Man of Affairs
           and Letters." New England Magazine, n.s. 27 (November):
           289-302.
                Biography, including portrait. Includes a description of
           "A Pretty Story."

1906.1   OBERHOLTZER, ELLIS PAXTON. The Literary History of Phila-
           delphia. Philadelphia: George W. Jacobs & Co., p. 114.
                Finds Hopkinson's work "a very thin note." Quotes from
           the preface to "A Pretty Story."

1907.1   MARBLE, ANNIE RUSSELL. Heralds of American Literature.
           Chicago: University of Chicago Press, pp. 28-29.
                "A Pretty Story" was an early and popular satire which
           ridiculed the king and Parliament and used irony to demonstrate the
           results of the Stamp Act, the taxes, and war-vessels in Boston
           Harbor. Describes two other fictional satires by Hopkinson.

1909.1   STANTON, THEODORE, in collaboration with members of the
           faculty of Cornell University. A Manual of American
           Literature. New York and London: G. P. Putnam's Sons,
           Knickerbocker Press, pp. 67-68.
                Praises "A Pretty Story" for its aptness, delicacy and
           humor and notes that Hopkinson satirizes "without malice or heat."

1912.1   CAIRNS, WILLIAM B. A History of American Literature. New
           York: Oxford University Press, pp. 145-46.
                Brief biography and bibliography of primary works.

1912.2   HOLLIDAY, CARL. The Wit and Humor of Colonial Days (1607–
         1800). Philadelphia: J.B. Lippincott, pp. 155–60.
              Describes "A Pretty Story" as an allegory telling of the
disturbance between the mother country and the colonies. Finds it a
genial narrative, "full of bright surprises," having "a flavor of
French vivacity and French simplicity about it. Quotes extensively
from the story. Reprinted: 1970.1.

1912.3   VAN DOREN, CARL. The American Novel. New York: Macmillan
         Co., p. 4.
              "A Pretty Story" is an allegory "which lies nearly as
close to fiction as to history." It is effective satire. Revised
edition: 1940.1.

1915.1   ELLIS, HAROLD MILTON. "Joseph Dennie and his Circle: A
         Study in American Literature from 1792 to 1812." Bulletin
         of the University of Texas, no. 40 (July), pp. 136, 160,
         184.
              Brief mention of Hopkinson.

*1918.1   HASTINGS, GEORGE EVERETT. "The Life and Works of Francis
         Hopkinson." Ph.D. Dissertation, Harvard University, 136 pp.
              See 1926.1.

1925.1   PRESCOTT, FREDERICK, and JOHN H. NELSON, eds. Prose and
         Poetry of the Revolution: The Establishment of the Nation,
         1765–1789. New York: Thomas Y. Crowell, pp. 114–123.
              Includes selections from "A Pretty Story," "perhaps our
first example of American prose fiction.

1926.1   HASTINGS, GEORGE E. The Life and Works of Francis
         Hopkinson. Chicago: University of Chicago Press,
         pp. 193–99.
              Summarizes "A Pretty Story." Notes that the preface is
"cheery and debonair in tone." Cites Moses Coit Tyler's objection
that it is not original. Defends Hopkinson, noting the difference
between Arbuthnot's John Bull and this work. Quotes Tyler's evaluation of the literary value of the story and the reputation it brought
its author. Derived from 1918.1.

1929.1   _____. "John Bull and His American Descendants." AL 1
         (1929):40–68.
              Traces the relationship between "A Pretty Story" and
Arbuthnot's History of John Bull. Compares "A Pretty Story" to The
Foresters. Examines Irving's "John Bull" essay for its influence on
Arbuthnot. Examines Paulding's "The Diverting History of John Bull
and Brother Jonathan" and compares it to "A Pretty Story." Concludes
that Belknap's The Foresters decidedly imitates The History of John
Bull but does not heavily imitate "A Pretty Story."

1930.1   PARMA, V. VALTA. "The Rare Book Collection of the Library
          of Congress." Colophon, pt. 7, n.p.
              "A Pretty Story" is the earliest extant example of Amer-
ican fiction.

1931.1   MARBLE, ANNIE RUSSELL. Builders and Books: The Romance of
          American History and Literature. New York and London:
          D. Appleton & Co., p. 68.
              Brief biography of Hopkinson and mention of his use of
irony in "A Pretty Story."

1931.2   RICHARDSON, LYON N. A History of Early American Magazines
          1741-1789. New York: Thomas Nelson & Sons, pp. 183-88.
              Lists unsigned prose pieces by Hopkinson in The Penn-
sylvania Magazine, some hitherto not recognized as belonging to
Hopkinson. Evaluates Hopkinson's writings and finds him "on the
verge" of breaking out of the bounds of the essay.

1932.1   FULLERTON, BRADFORD M. A Selective Bibliography of American
          Literature 1775-1900: A Brief Survey of the More Important
          Authors and a Description of Their Works. New York:
          William Farquhar Payson, p. 147.
              Hopkinson is the author of the "first bit of original
fiction" written and published in the United States, but he is better
known for his poetry.

1932.2   HASTINGS, GEORGE E. "Francis Hopkinson." In Dictionary of
          American Biography. Edited by Dumas Malone. Vol. 9. New
          York: Charles Scribner's Sons, pp. 220-22.
              Biography and description of Hopkinson's works. Notes
that "A Pretty Story" recalls Swift and Arbuthnot but has original
qualities. It has a vigorous style.

1935.1   PATTEE, FRED LEWIS. The First Century of American Lit-
          erature 1770-1870. New York: D. Appleton-Century Co.,
          pp. 18-20.
              Brief mention of "A Pretty Story" in a discussion of
Hopkinson as the author of literary propaganda, prose satires, and
lyrics.

1935.2   WINTERICH, JOHN TRACEY. Early American Books and Printing.
          Boston: Houghton Mifflin Co., pp. 150, 233.
              Brief mention of "A Pretty Story."

1936.1   QUINN, ARTHUR HOBSON. American Fiction: An Historical and
          Critical Survey. New York: Appleton-Century Crofts, p. 4.
              "A Pretty Story" is not the first American novel but it
does have real characters and a clear and vigorous style.

1940.1   VAN DOREN, CARL. The American Novel 1789-1939. Rev. and
          enl. ed. New York: Macmillan Co., p. 4.
              See 1912.3.

1940.2   WECTER, DIXON. "Francis Hopkinson and Benjamin Franklin."
         AL 12 (May):201.
            Brief mention of "A Pretty Story."

1948.1   COWIE, ALEXANDER. The Rise of the American Novel. New
         York: American Book Co., p. 9.
            Brief mention of "A Pretty Story" as political satire,
not a novel.

1948.2   SPILLER, ROBERT E., WILLARD THORP, THOMAS H. JOHNSON,
         HENRY SEIDEL CANBY, HOWARD MUMFORD JONES, DIXON WECTER, and
         STANLEY T. WILLIAMS, eds. "Fiction." In Literary History
         of the United States. Vol. 3. New York: Macmillan Co.,
         p. 98.
            Brief mention of "A Pretty Story," "sometimes alleged to
be the first novel written and printed in Ameria."

1956.1   HART, JAMES D. The Oxford Companion to American Literature.
         3d ed. New York: Oxford University Press, p. 334.
            Biography and description of Hopkinson's writings.

1961.2   LOOMIS, EMERSON ROBERT. "The Title of America's First Work
         of Fiction." N&Q 8 (July):264.
            Hopkinson borrowed the idea for his title "A Pretty
Story, Written in the Year of Our Lord 2774" from Louis Sebastien
Mercier's futuristic L'An 2440 (1770).

1962.1   HERZBERG, MAX J., and the staff of the Thomas Crowell Co.
         The Reader's Encyclopedia of American Literature. New York:
         Thomas Y. Crowell Co., p. 84–85.
            Brief biography and brief mention of "A Pretty Story."

1968.1   CHRISTADLER, MARTIN. Der amerikanische Essay 1720–1820.
         Heidelberg: Carl Winter, pp. 154–55.
            In German. In "A Pretty Story" the epic elements are
subordinated to the propaganda and political theme.

1968.2   FREE, WILLIAM J. The Columbian Magazine and American Lit-
         erary Nationalism. Studies in American Literature, vol. 15.
         The Hague and Paris: Mouton, pp. 28–30.
            Describes Hopkinson as editor and magazine contributor
and briefly mentions "A Pretty Story."

1969.1   WRIGHT, LYLE H. American Fiction, 1774–1850: A Contri-
         bution toward a Bibliography. 2d rev. ed. San Marino:
         Huntington Library, p. 131.
            Lists locations of three editions of "A Pretty Story."

1970.1   HOLLIDAY, CARL. The Wit and Humor of Colonial Days (1607–
         1800). Detroit: Gale Research Co., pp. 155–60.
            Reprint of 1912.2.

1970.2   TYLER, MOSES COIT. The Literary History of the American
         Revolution 1763–1783. New York: Burt Franklin,
         pp. 279–91.
              Reprint of 1897.1.

1971.1   PETTER, HENRI. The Early American Novel. Columbus: Ohio
         State University Press, pp. 88–90.
              Describes the satire and its political purposes. "The
         combination of the general with the precise and topical, a feature of
         all allegorical presentation, is ingeniously and thoroughly realized
         in A Pretty Story." Its irony is sensed in shifts from the general
         to the particular.

1975.1   DUYCKINCK, EVERT A., and GEORGE L. DUYCKINCK. Cyclopaedia
         of American Literature: Embracing Personal and Critical
         Notices of Authors, and Selections from Their Writings.
         From the Earliest Period to the Present Day. Detroit: Gale
         Research Co., pp. 219–229.
              Reprint of 1855.1.

1976.1   ZALL, PAUL M. Introduction to The Comical Spirit of
         Seventy-Six: The Humor of Francis Hopkinson. San Marino:
         Huntington Library, pp. 1–24, 33–35.
              Analyzes revisions of "A Pretty Story" and other works to
         discuss Hopkinson's comic style. Describes the publication and popu-
         larity of "A Pretty Story" and the political situation surrounding it.

1977.1   ROBBINS, J. ALBERT et al., comps. American Literary Manu-
         scripts: A Checklist of Holdings In Academic, Historical,
         and Public Libraries, Museums, and Authors' Homes in the
         United States. 2d ed. Athens: University of Georgia
         Press, p. 154.
              Lists forty-one libraries with Hopkinson holdings.

XVI. Gilbert Imlay (c. 1754-1828?)

1793.1   ANON. Review of The Emigrants. Monthly Review; or Literary
          Journal (London) 9 (August):468-69.
          Finds in this book more than what is commonly found in
the sentimental tale, for this author can appeal both to the lover
and to the philosopher. Praises the lively descriptions of American
scenes, the characterization, and the philosophical speculation.
Disagrees with Imlay's view on marriage.

1887.1   ANON. "Gilbert Imlay." In Appleton's Cyclopaedia of Amer-
          ican Biography. Edited by James Grant Wilson and John
          Fiske. New York: D. Appleton & Co., p. 345.
          Biography with brief mention of Imlay's writings.

1907.1   LOSHE, LILLIE DEMING. The Early American Novel. New York:
          Columbia University Press, pp. 68-69.
          Imlay's name is remembered only for its association with
Mary Wollstonecraft. The aim of The Emigrants is "to call attention
to the political questions then occupying Europe, and particularly to
the effects of laws concerning marriage and divorce." The novel
holds interest today only because of its frontier American setting.
The descriptions of pioneer life "are too much in the idyllic
spirit." Reprinted: 1958.1.

1907.2   TOWNSEND, JOHN WILSON. Kentuckians in History and Litera-
          ture. New York and Washington: Neale Publishing Co.,
          pp. 13-25.
          A discussion of Imlay as "the first Kentucky novelist."
Includes biography and description of his writings. Knows of only
four extant copies of The Emigrants.

1908.1   GARNETT, RICHARD. "Imlay, Gilbert." In Dictionary of
          National Biography. Edited by Sidney Lee. Vol. 10. New
          York: Macmillan Co., pp. 417-18.
          Biography and description of Imlay's writings. Notes
that The Emigrants is set in America; "the conduct of the story is
artless, the style matter of fact."

1911.1   TAYLOR, GEORGE ROBERT STIRLING. Mary Wollstonecraft: A
          Study in Economics and Romance. New York: John Lane Co.,
          p. 137.
          Imlay published The Emigrants, but we do not know whether
its ideas came from Wollstonecraft or Imlay. "But they were both of
one mind." Reprinted: 1969.1.

1917.1   COOPER, LANE. "Travellers and Observers, 1763-1846." In
          The Cambridge History of American Literature. Edited by
          William Peterfield Trent et al. Vol. 1, Colonial and

Revolutionary Literature. Early National Literature.
New York: G.P. Putnam's Sons, p. 151.
Brief mention of Imlay.

1923.1 RUSK, RALPH LESLIE. "The Adventures of Gilbert Imlay."
Indiana University Studies 10 (March):26 pp.
Biography. Offers evidence that The Emigrants was
written in Europe, but believes Mary Wollstonecraft's influence on
the book was slight.

1924.1 EMERSON, OLIVER FARRAR. "Notes on Gilbert Imlay, Early
American Writer." PMLA 39:406-39.
Discusses the relationship between de Crevocoeur and
Imlay and Imlay's relations with Girondists and the mutual friends
through whom he met Wollstonecraft. Discusses the "wider influences"
on Imlay's works. Includes a bibliography of primary works.

1927.1 McDOWELL, TREMAINE. "Sensibility in the Eighteenth-Century
American Novel." SP 24 (July):382-402.
Cites examples of the physical manifestations of the
novel of sensibility in The Emigrants. Finds the novel one of only
two instances when the "resources of romantic attachment [are] fully
exploited in the stimulation of exquisite agony."

1929.1 WYATT, EDITH FRANKLIN. "The First American Novel."
Atlantic Monthly 144 (October):466-75.
Imlay's The Emigrants was the first American novel. The
book has historical interest and is distinct as the first fiction
concerned with a social problem. Despite its silliness it expresses
a love of freedom and fascination with virgin country.
Summarizes the plot and includes a biography of Imlay.

1932.1 RUSK, RALPH L. "Imlay, Gilbert." In Dictionary of American
Biography. Edited by Dumas Malone. Vol. 9. New York:
Charles Scribner's Sons, pp. 461-62.
Biography of Imlay as author and political adventurer.
Believes The Emigrants was written after Imlay's arrival in Europe.

1936.1 QUINN, ARTHUR HOBSON. American Fiction: An Historical and
Critical Survey. New York: D. Appleton-Century.
Imlay's chief claim to our notice lies in the fact that
he knew about the country he describes first hand. The Emigrants has
several purposes: to show the superior social organization of the
United States over that of Great Britain, to advocate divorce, and to
champion the rights of women. The book has historical interest as a
combination novel of adventure, sentimental novel of intrigue, and
the fiction of social reform.

1940.1 BLACK, FRANK GEES. The Epistolary Novel in the Late Eighteenth Century. University of Oregon Publications, no. 2.
Eugene: University of Oregon Press, pp. 70, 83, 88, 137.

Cites The Emigrants as an example of fiction as propaganda, because it justified divorce. Cites the novel as an example of the travel writer's communicated impressions.

1948.1   COWIE, ALEXANDER. "Gilbert Imlay." In The Rise of the
          American Novel. New York: American Book Co., pp. 38-43.
          Describes Imlay's life as "romantic" and suggests The
Emigrants was written before his association with Wollstonecraft.
Summarizes the novel, and sees its larger theme as the contrast
between the Old World and the New. States Imlay's position regarding
divorce laws and notes Imlay's praise of the New World.

1952.1   WAGENKNECHT, EDWARD. Cavalcade of the American Novel:
          From the Birth of the Nation to the Middle of the Twentieth
          Century. New York: Holt, Rinehart & Winston, p. 8.
          Imlay is a novelist who realized that America did not
stop short at the Alleghenies. The Emigrants argues both for and
against divorce.

*1957.1   HARE, ROBERT R. "The Base Indian: A Vindication of the
          Rights of Mary Wollstonecraft." M.A. Thesis, University of
          Delaware.

1958.1   LOSHE, LILLIE DEMING. The Early American Novel 1789-1830.
          New York: Frederick Ungar Publishing Co., pp. 68-69.
          Reprint of 1907.1.

1964.1   HARE, ROBERT R., ed. Introduction to The Emigrants. Tra-
          ditionally Ascribed to Gilbert Imlay But, More Probably,
          by Mary Wollstonecraft. A Facsimile Reproduction of the
          Dublin Edition (1794). Gainesville: Scholars' Facsimiles &
          Reprints; pp. v-xv.
          The Emigrants is an example of "the novel of purpose."
It was written in London for the purpose of pleading for reform in
divorce laws.
          Describes extant copies. Includes a biography of Imlay
and evidence why Imlay did not write the book. Attributes the book
to Mary Wollstonecraft.

1968.1   FREE, WILLIAM J. The Columbian Magazine and American Lit-
          erary Nationalism. Studies in American Literature, vol. 15.
          The Hague and Paris: Mouton, pp. 51, 111, 120-22.
          Brief references to Imlay's comments on western terri-
tories in the Columbian Magazine.

1969.1   TAYLOR, GEORGE ROBERT STIRLING. Mary Wollstonecraft: A
          Study in Economics and Romance. New York: Haskell House
          Publishers, p. 137.
          Reprint of 1911.1.

1971.1   PETTER, HENRI. The Early American Novel. Columbus: Ohio
          State University Press, pp. 216-19.
                 Summarizes the plot of The Emigrants. Notes the serious-
ness of the author's interest in the divorce question but finds the
main emphasis on the story of Caroline and Captain Arl___ton. Names
the other ingredients that deflect from Imlay's stated purpose:
the feminist discussion of education, the predictable indictment of
seducers, and the propaganda for the backwoods settlement of America.
Concludes that the novel needs more detailed localized description.

1974.1   TOMALIN, CLAIRE. The Life and Death of Mary Wollstonecraft.
          New York: Harcourt Brace Jovanovitch, pp. 145-46.
                 Imlay's Emigrants was about to be published when Mary
Wollstonecraft met Imlay. The book "was a wholly atrocious piece of
work."

1975.1   SUNSTEIN, EMILY W. A Different Face: The Life of Mary
          Wollstonecraft. New York: Harper & Row, p. 238.
                 The Emigrants "reads as if it were aimed at convincing
Mary Wollstonecraft to accept a love and go to America with" Imlay.
Clearly Wollstonecraft had a hand in sections of the book.

XVII. Herman Mann (1772-1833)

1850.1   ELLET, ELIZABETH F. <u>Women</u> <u>of</u> <u>the</u> <u>American</u> <u>Revolution</u>.
         Vol. 2. New York: Baker & Scribner, pp. 122-35.
              Biography of Sampson. Reports her inability to locate
<u>The</u> <u>Female</u> <u>Review</u> but has been told it was unreliable and that
Deborah Sampson felt displeased with it. Reprinted: 1969.1.

1866.1   VINTON, JOHN ADAMS, ed. Introduction and Notes to <u>Life</u> <u>of</u>
         <u>Deborah</u> <u>Sampson,</u> <u>the</u> <u>Female</u> <u>Soldier</u> <u>in</u> <u>the</u> <u>War</u> <u>of</u> <u>the</u> <u>Revo-</u>
         <u>lution</u>. Boston: J.K. Wiggin & Parsons Lunt, pp. ix-xxxii.
              Attests to the authenticity of the story. Notes the
rarity of Mann's 1797 publication and criticizes it for its pompous
style and its straining after effect. Calls the work "a kind of
novel." Claims to tell the true story in this edition. Relates the
history of the original Mann version and its revision by both Mann
and his son. Reprints the original version with the new one.

1895.1   WELLS, KATE GANNETT. "Deborah Sampson: A Heroine of the
         American Revolution." <u>New</u> <u>England</u> <u>Magazine</u>, n.s. 13
         (September):156-58.
              Biography of Deborah Sampson. Refers to Mann's publica-
tion, with which both Sampson and Mann felt dissatisfaction. Notes
that after Mann died, his son remodeled and published the book in
1850. Vinton added information from other sources.

1907.1   LOSHE, LILLIE DEMING. <u>The</u> <u>Early</u> <u>American</u> <u>Novel</u>. New York:
         Columbia University Press, pp. 65-66.
              Describes <u>The</u> <u>Female</u> <u>Review</u>. Reprinted: 1958.1.

1927.1   McDOWELL, TREMAINE. "Sensibility in the Eighteenth-Century
         American Novel." <u>SP</u> 24 (July):385-86.
              Describes the physical manifestations of sensibility in
<u>The</u> <u>Female</u> <u>Review</u> and the author's application of humanity for human-
ity's sake.

1951.1   COWIE, ALEXANDER. <u>The</u> <u>Rise</u> <u>of</u> <u>the</u> <u>American</u> <u>Novel</u>. New
         York: American Book Co., p. 30.
              Calls <u>The</u> <u>Female</u> <u>Review</u> an anonymous tale full of incred-
ible adventures.

1958.1   LOSHE, LILLIE DEMING. <u>The</u> <u>Early</u> <u>American</u> <u>Novel</u> <u>1789-1830</u>.
         New York: Frederick Ungar Publishing Co., pp. 65-66.
              Reprint of 1907.1.

1969.1   ELLET, ELIZABETH F. <u>Women</u> <u>of</u> <u>the</u> <u>Revolution</u>. Vol. 2. New
         York: Haskell House, pp. 122-35.
              Reprint of 1850.1.

1971.1   PETTER, HENRI. The Early American Novel. Columbus: Ohio
         State University Press, pp. 381-83.
              The Female Review is "an ill-ordered account . . . of a
    disguised girl's anxieties over the possible discovery of her sex."
    Several episodes are inconsistent with Mann's professed desire to
    make the novel beneficial.

1982.1   DAVIDSON, CATHY N.   "Flirting with Destiny: Ambivalence and
         Form in the Early American Novel."   SAF 10 (Spring):17-39.
              An examination of the way early American novels used the
    sentimental form to question the very propositions they pretended to
    extoll.   Cites The Female Review as an example of the way some novels
    demonstrated the success of women who defied conventional roles.

XVIII. Peter Markoe (c. 1752-1792)

1854.1   ALLIBONE, S. AUSTIN. A Critical Dictionary of English
          Literature and British and American Authors Living and
          Deceased from the Earliest Accounts to the Latter Half of
          the Nineteenth Century. Vol. 2. Philadelphia: Childs &
          Peterson, p. 1220.
              Brief biography. "Mr. Markoe was supposed to be the
author of The Algerine Spy."

1898.1   HERRINGSHAW, THOMAS WILLIAM. Herringshaw's Encyclopedia of
          American Biography of the Nineteenth Century. Chicago:
          American Publishers Association, p. 616.
              Brief mention, biographical only.

1906.1   OBERHOLTZER, ELLIS PAXTON. The Literary History of Phila-
          delphia. Philadelphia: George W. Jacobs & Co., p. 153.
              Brief mention of Markoe.

1912.1   CAIRNS, WILLIAM BRADFORD. A History of American Literature.
          New York: Oxford University Press, 1912, p. 148.
              Brief mention of Markoe.

1931.1   ANGOFF, CHARLES. A Literary History of the American People.
          New York: Alfred A. Knopf, p. 338.
              Brief mention of Markoe.

1933.1   BAUGH, ALBERT C. "Markoe, Peter." In Dictionary of Amer-
          ican Biography. Edited by Dumas Malone. Vol. 12. New
          York: Charles Scribner's Sons, pp. 287-88.
              Biography. Notes that although it is usually said Markoe
was in England during the revolution, he is listed in 1775 as a
captain in a Philadelphia militia. Describes The Algerine Spy as
being attributed to him by Evans. Includes bibliography of secondary
works.

1938.1   KUNITZ, STANLEY J., and HOWARD HAYCRAFT. American Authors
          1600-1900: A Biographical Dictionary of American Litera-
          ture. New York: H.W. Wilson, p. 508.
              Biography and description of writings. "Markoe had, for
his day, considerable literary versatility, but his writings retain
only an historical significance."

1939.1   JACKSON, JOSEPH. Literary Landmarks of Philadelphia.
          Philadelphia: David McKay Co., pp. 227-28.
              Markoe has been called "the city poet" of Philadelphia.
Brief biography and listing of his writings.

1941.1   HART, JAMES D. The Oxford Companion to American Literature.
          1st ed. New York: Oxford University Press, p. 460.

Brief biography and listing of Markoe's works. Lists The
Algerine Spy as an attribution.

1943.1   BURKE, WILLIAM J., and WILL D. HOWE. American Authors and
          Books, 1640-1940. New York: Gramercy Publishing Co.,
          p. 459.
          Bibliography of primary works.

1944.1   DIEBELS, Sister MARY CHRYSOSTOM. Peter Markoe (1752?-1792):
          A Philadelphia Writer. Washington, D.C.: Catholic Univer-
          sity Press, 116 pp.
          Biography. Describes Markoe's plays and his prose
satire, The Algerine Spy in Pennsylvania. Includes a bibliography
of primary and secondary works.

1957.1   SPENCER, BENJAMIN. The Quest for Nationality. Syracuse:
          Syracuse University Press, p. 65.
          Quotes from Markoe as an example of the way writers
accused the American public of an excessive "love of gain."

1960.1   JONES, JOSEPH, E. MARCHAND, H.D. PIPER, J.A. ROBBINS, and
          H.E. SPIVEY, comps. American Literary Manuscripts: A
          Checklist of Holdings in Academic, Historical and Public
          Libraries in the United States. Compiled and published
          under the auspices of the American Literature group of the
          Modern Language Association. Austin: University of Texas
          Press, p. 246.
          Lists holdings in two locations.

1968.1   FREE, WILLIAM J. The Columbian Magazine and American Lit-
          erary Nationalism. The Hague and Paris: Mouton, p. 44.
          Notes Markoe's poetic contributions to the Columbian
Magazine.

1969.1   WRIGHT, LYLE H. American Fiction, 1774-1850: A Contri-
          bution toward a Bibliography. 2d rev. ed. San Marino:
          Huntington Library, p. 193.
          Lists eleven libraries holding copies of The Algerine Spy.

1971.1   PETTER, HENRI. The Early American Novel. Columbus: Ohio
          State University Press, pp. 107-8.
          In a chapter on "Satirical and Polemical Fiction" de-
scribes Markoe's aim in The Algerine Spy as underscoring the "neces-
sity of radical change in the system of government in America."
Finds the book "slight yet entertaining."

1977.1   ROBBINS, J. ALBERT et al., comps. American Literary Manu-
          scripts: A Checklist of Holdings In Academic, Historical,
          and Public Libraries, Museums, and Authors' Homes in the
          United States. 2d ed. Athens: University of Georgia
          Press, p. 213.
          Lists holdings in three locations.

XIX. Isaac Mitchell (1759-1812)

*1775.1   ANON. Review of Adventures of Alonso. Westminster Magazine
           or The Pantheon of Taste 3 (September):502.
               Cited in 1941.2.

1904.1   JACKSON, H. BRADLEY. "Alonzo and Melissa." New York Times
           Book Review, 3 September, p. 594.
               Asserts that the novel was written from fact by Jackson's
grandfather, Daniel Jackson, Jr. Relates the circumstances under
which Jackson came to write the book.

1904.2   REED, EDWARD B. "A Neglected American Author." Nation 79
           (December):458.
               Takes issue with Jackson (see 1904.1). Shows that
Mitchell published his version first. Can find no biographical
information about Mitchell. Documents the popularity of Alonzo
and Melissa and documents the publication of Jackson's revision.

1905.1   RIDER, SIDNEY S. "Mitchell's Alonzo and Melissa. A Huge
           Literary Fraud Unique in American Literature." Providence
           (R.I.) Book Notes 22 (14 January):1-6.
               Alonzo and Melissa was written by Jackson in 1809-10. No
other novel has had such a duration of life. Mitchell's book was a
fraud, and the January and October 1811 newspaper notices were merely
advertisements he inserted. A comparison of various lines from the
Mitchell and Jackson versions shows their similarities. Mitchell's
book was a swindle, now for the first time disclosed.

1905.2   "L., M.C." "Alonzo and Melissa." New York Times Book
           Review, 20 January, p. 48.
               Rider has his dates wrong (see 1905.1). Mitchell's pub-
lication came first.

1905.3   RIDER, SYDNEY S. "Alonzo and Melissa Again." New York
           Times Book Review, 21 January, p. 44.
               Alonzo and Melissa was written by Daniel Jackson, and
Isaac Mitchell's 1811 publication of The Asylum copies Jackson's
work. No other novel has had such a long duration of life.

1905.4   REED, EDWARD B. "Alonzo and Melissa." Nation 80
           (2 February):91.
               Has discovered a copy of Jackson's version dated 1811.
Takes issue with Rider (see 1905.1), citing as proof of Mitchell's
authorship the advertisements of the Mitchell publication, 2 December
1810. Notes that Jackson's version was never copyrighted.

1905.5   RIDER, SIDNEY S. Untitled. Providence (R.I.) Book Notes 22
           (11 February): 17.

Acknowledges his blunder in computing dates but maintains Mitchell is still a fraud.

1905.6   PLATT, EDMUND. The Eagle's History of Poughkeepsie: From the Earliest Settlements 1683 to 1905. Poughkeepsie: Platt & Platt, 91.
Alonzo and Melissa was originally published by Joseph Nelson in 1811.

1905.7   REED, EDWARD W. "A Neglected American Author." Nation 88 (25 February):192-93.
Summarizes the Jackson-Mitchell controversy. Refers to Platt's discovery of an 1804 serial publication of Alonzo and Melissa by Mitchell and concludes Jackson cribbed from it (see 1905.6). Notes the Gothic character of the novel and calls for a modern edition.

1905.8   "S., E.S." "Alonzo and Melissa." New York Times Book Review, 4 March, p. 138.
The real author is Isaac Mitchell's daughter, who was too young and modest to publish the book under her own name.

1905.9   RIDER, SIDNEY S. "Mitchell's Alonzo and Melissa A Hug[e] Fraud in American Literature Exposed and Now Demonstrated." Providence (R.I.) Book Notes 22 (25 March):41-48.
Refers to the various assaults on his conclusions, and refutes them. Denies that Jackson's was a revision. Offers internal evidence for Jackson's as the original version. Calls Reed's arguments absurdities.

1907.1   LOSHE, LILLIE DEMING. The Early American Novel. New York: Columbia University Press, p. 53-56.
Notes the controversy over the true authorship of The Asylum and believes Mitchell's was the earlier version. Summarizes the plot of the 1824 version and finds the effect naive and the tale an inadequate representative of Mrs. Radcliffe's school. Reprinted: 1958.1.

1917.1   VAN DOREN, CARL. "Fiction I: Brown, Cooper." In The Cambridge History of American Literature. Edited by William Peterfield Trent et al. Vol 1, Colonial and Revolutionary Literature. Early National Literature. New York: G.P. Putnam's Sons, p. 292.
Brief mention of The Asylum as "an absurd" but popular romance.

1918.1   BRADSHER, EARL L. "Some Aspects of the Early American Novel." Texas Review 3 (April):245, 247-48.
Quotes a critical theory of the early novel from the preface to The Asylum. Notes that Mitchell shared with his readers confusion as to what a novel really is.

1925.1   COAD, ORAL SUMNER.   "The Gothic Element in American Litera-
         ture before 1835."   JEGP 24:83.
             The Asylum illustrates the dangers to which American
novelists' method of treating terrors exposed them.   The Gothic
elements are injected incongruously with insufficient
rationalization.

1928.1   PEARSON, EDMUND.   "Alonzo and Melissa."   In Queer Books.
         New York: Doubleday, Doran & Co., pp. 41-68.
             Claims that the novel lost favor fifty years ago but
prior to that it was immensely popular.   Credits Mitchell with the
original.   Recounts the plot of the Daniel Jackson version.

1933.1   RANKIN, DANIEL S.   "Mitchell, Isaac."   In Dictionary of
         American Biography.   Edited by Dumas Malone.   Vol. 13.   New
         York: Charles Scribner's Sons, pp. 48-49.
             Biography of Mitchell as newspaper editor and novelist.
Details the story of the plagiarism of Alonzo and Melissa by Joseph
Nelson and Daniel Jackson.   Notes that Jackson's book enjoyed "phenom-
enal popularity."

1940.1   BROWN, HERBERT ROSS.   The Sentimental Novel in America,
         1789-1860.   Durham: Duke University Press, pp. 97, 127,
         141-42, 175.
             The Asylum shows the way writers catered to morbid taste.
The landscape descriptions commit the pathetic fallacy.   The book is
further weakened by Mitchell's "shameless trickery" in playing with a
reader's expectations, which then requires explanation.

1941.1   HART, JAMES D.   The Oxford Companion to American Literature.
         1st ed.   New York: Oxford University Press, p. 487.
             A plagiarized version of The Asylum was published in 1811
by Daniel Jackson and achieved great popularity.

1952.1   WAGENKNECHT, EDWARD.   Cavalcade of the American Novel:
         From the Birth of the Nation to the Middle of the Twentieth
         Century.   New York: Holt, Rinehart & Winston, p. 7.
             Alonzo and Melissa is an example of the Gothic element in
early fiction.   For two generations the novel was read with rapture.

1958.1   LOSHE, LILLIE DEMING.   The Early American Novel 1789-1830.
         New York: Frederick Ungar Publishing Co., pp. 53-56.
             Reprint of 1907.1.

1972.1   TUTTLETON, JAMES W.   The Novel of Manners in America.
         Chapel Hill: University of North Carolina Press, p. 18.
             The medieval castle on Long Island in Alonzo and Melissa
is an example of American writers' excessive need for "romantic
settings."

*1982.1   DAVIDSON, CATHY N. "Isaac Mitchell's The Asylum; or, Gothic
          Castles in the New Republic." Prospects: An Annual of
          American Cultural Studies 7 (Fall):280-299.
          The gothic novel marked a new stage in the development of
American fiction by building upon the sentimental formula but also
revising it to allow for more independent female characters and
multidimensional hero/villains. The structural differences in the
two forms are especially evident in Mitchell's The Asylum where we
have, essentially, a gothic novel grafted onto a more conventional
sentimental plot. Significantly, it was the second half of the novel
(the gothic portion) that was reprinted throughout the nineteenth
century. [Annotation by Cathy N. Davidson.]

XX. Joseph Morgan (1671- post 1745)

1946.1   SLATTER, RICHARD, ed. Introduction to The History of the
          Kingdom of Basaruah, and Three Unpublished Letters, by
          Joseph Morgan. Cambridge, Mass.: Harvard University Press,
          pp. 3-21.
              The Kingdom of Basaruah may be called the first American
novel. It can be read as allegory and can be read with interest by
the literary historian, but it is best read as a historical document.
With a few additions, the doctrine it contains is identical with the
doctrine of The Day of Doom, traditional covenant theology.
              Gives biographical information and evidence for Morgan as
author. Includes a bibliography of primary and secondary works.

1951.1   BELL, WHITFIELD J., Jr. "The Reverend Mr. Joseph Morgan, an
          American Correspondent of the Royal Society, 1732-1739."
          Proceedings of the American Philosophical Society 95
          (June):254-64.
              Biography. Notes the significance of a rural New Jersey
minister whose mind speculated on questions of science, technology,
and politics.

1971.1   PETTER, HENRI. The Early American Novel. Columbus: Ohio
          State University Press, pp. 65-66.
              Finds The Kingdom of Basaruah more demanding than
Pilgrim's Progress. Compares it to Botsford's The Spiritual Voyage
(1819).

XXI. Judith Sargent Murray (1751-1820)

1854.1   ALLIBONE, S. AUSTIN. A Critical Dictionary of English
         Literature and British and American Authors Living and
         Deceased from the Earliest Accounts to the Latter Half of
         the Nineteenth Century. Vol. 2. Philadelphia: Childs &
         Peterson, p. 1393.
             Brief mention of Murray.

1881.1   EDDY, Rev. RICHARD. "Mrs. Judith Murray." Universalist
         Quarterly and General Review, n.s. 18 (April):194-202.
             Biography. The attack on Judith Murray in 1793-94 may
have been caused by one of the Gleaner essays which advocated Uni-
versalism. People now alive who knew Mrs. Murray remember her with
esteem.

1882.1   _____. "Mrs. Judith Murray." Universalist Quarterly and
         General Review, n.s. 19 (April):140-51.
             Biography. Prints extracts from Murray's letters to her
parents describing visits to Washington and Philadelphia.

*1903.1 CORBETT, A. "Famous Women in New England History." In
         Original Studies in Local History.
             Cited in 1931.1.

1915.1   ELLIS, HAROLD MILTON. "Joseph Dennie and his Circle: A
         Study in American Literature from 1792 to 1812." Bulletin
         of the University of Texas, no. 40 (July), p. 76.
             Brief mention of Murray.

1927.1   McDOWELL, TREMAINE. "Sensibility in the Eighteenth-Century
         American Novel." SP 24 (July):382-402.
             Brief mention of The Story of Margaretta as one of the
novels of sensibility.

1931.1   FIELD, VERA BERNADETTE. "Constantia: A Study of the Life
         and Works of Judith Sargent Murray 1751-1820." Maine
         Bulletin 33 (February):6-118.
             Biography. In a detailed discussion of The Gleaner,
describes the Margaretta episode as a "loosely constructed novel."
Summarizes the story. Attributes the artificiality of speech and
actions to the influence of English romantic novels. Describes the
minor characters as representatives of types. Describes the rest of
the Gleaner essays as well as Murray's dramatic works, poems, and
editorial work.

1932.1   BROWN, HERBERT ROSS. "Richard and Sterne in the Massachu-
         setts Magazine." NEQ 5 (January):66.
             Brief mention of Murray.

1934.1   ELLIS, MILTON. "Murray, Judith Sargent." In Dictionary of
         American Biography. Edited by Dumas Malone. Vol. 13. New
         York: Charles Scribner's Sons, p. 364.
             Biography including description of her works. Describes
The Gleaner as a series of essays. Although her poetry and drama are
negligible, her essays "rival in firmness of texture and in interest
those of Joseph Dennie, Freneau, and Noah Webster, her best contemporaries." Includes a short bibliography of secondary works.

1940.1   BROWN, HERBERT ROSS. The Sentimental Novel in America,
         1789-1860. Durham: Duke University Press, passim.
             Murray's works indicated a relaxed opposition to novels
and approval of Richardson with qualifications. Murray endowed her
heroine Margaretta with charms of sensibility but warned of false
sensibility. She included a Shandian episode in The Gleaner.

1940.2   JORGENSON, CHESTER E. "Gleanings from Judith Sargent
         Murray." AL 12 (March):73-78.
             Murray combined an exquisite and tender heart with a
masculine mind. Although she never defined an aesthetic, her allusions show that it was consonant with fundamental ideas of neoclassi-
cism. She deserves recognition as the first American woman to write
articulate defenses of the American federal idea.

1957.1   SPENCER, BENJAMIN. Quest for Nationality. Syracuse:
         Syracuse University Press, pp. 30, 44, 46, 216.
             In a discussion of Americans' search for a sense of
nationality after the Revolution, quotes from The Gleaner as an
example of the way Americans sought to reject the culture of the Old
World and as an example of the way women humbly sought to use their
talents to record the less sublime and heroic elements.

1960.1   JONES, JOSEPH, E. MARCHAND, H.D. PIPER, J.A. ROBBINS, and
         H.E. SPIVEY, comps. American Literary Manuscripts: A
         Checklist of Holdings in Academic, Historical and Public
         Libraries in the United States. Compiled and published
         under the auspices of the American Literature group of the
         Modern Language Association. Austin: University of Texas
         Press, p. 268.
             Lists holdings in three locations.

1971.1   JAMES, JANET WILSON. "Murray, Judith Sargent." In Notable
         American Women 1607-1950: A Biographical Dictionary.
         Edited by Edward T. James, Janet Wilson James, and Paul S.
         Boyer. Vol. 2. Cambridge, Mass.: Harvard University
         Press, Belknap Press, pp. 603-6.
             Biography and description of writings. Notes that The
Gleaner expressed the author's opinions on religion, politics, education, manners, and customs. The author strongly believed women
needed education.

1971.2   PETTER, HENRI. The Early American Novel. Columbus: Ohio
         State University Press, pp. 71-73.
             Classifies The Gleaner as didactic fiction. Describes
         Murray's attitude toward fiction. Finds "nothing very original
         either in the conception or the execution of The Gleaner."

1977.1   ROBBINS, J. ALBERT et al., comps. American Literary Manu-
         scripts: A Checklist of Holdings In Academic, Historical,
         and Public Libraries, Museums, and Authors' Homes in the
         United States. 2d ed.   Athens: University of Georgia
         Press, p. 232.
             Lists holdings in four locations.

XXII. Mrs. Patterson

1968.1   KETTLER, ROBERT RONALD. "The Eighteenth-Century American
          Novel: The Beginning of a Fictional Tradition." Ph.D.
          Dissertation, Purdue University, pp. 111-12.
               The Unfortunate Lovers and Cruel Parents is an example of
the new man, a typical character in early American fiction.

1969.1   WRIGHT, LYLE H. American Fiction, 1774-1850: A Contri-
          bution toward a Bibliography. 2d rev. ed. San Marino:
          Huntington Library, p. 213.
               Lists three editions of The Unfortunate Lovers and their
locations.

1971.1   PETTER, HENRI. The Early American Novel. Columbus: Ohio
          State University Press, p. 191.
               The Unfortunate Lovers and Cruel Parents is "an atrocious
performance," yet "another instance of rebellion against parents in
the name of love and honor."

XXIII. Samuel Peters (1735-1826)

*1814.1   ANON.   Review of The General History of Connecticut.
            Atlantic Magazine.
                Cited in 1876.1.

1855.1   DUYCKINCK, EVERT A., and GEORGE L. DUYCKINCK. Cyclopaedia
            of American Literature: Embracing Personal and Critical
            Notices of Authors, and Selections from Their Writings.
            From the Earliest Period to the Present Day. Vol. 1.
            New York: Charles Scribner, pp. 200-205.
                Peters was "deservedly much impugned as an author."   The
        The History of Connecticut is "as good, in its way, as Knicker-
        bocker's New York." Its style is irresistible and the book is "inde-
        pendent of time, place and probability." Quotes extensively and
        includes biography. Reprinted: 1975.1.

1859.1   PETERS, JOHN S. "Samuel Peters." In Annals of the American
            Pulpit; or Commemorative Notices of Distinguished American
            Clergymen of Various Denominations. Edited by William B.
            Sprague. Vol. 5. New York: Robert Carter & Brothers,
            pp. 191-95.
                Biography detailing the story of the mob attack on
        Peters's house, his flight to Boston and then to England, his return,
        and attempts to procure compensation. Calls The General History of
        Connecticut "apocryphal and ludicrous."

1859.2   CHAPIN, A.B. "Samuel Peters." In Annals of the American
            Pulpit; or Commemorative Notices of Distinguished American
            Clergymen of Various Denominations. Edited by William B.
            Sprague. Vol. 5. New York: Robert Carter & Brothers,
            p. 195.
                Describes Peters's ministry at Hebron. Calls false the
        charges that Peters "invented or forged the so-called Blue-Laws of
        Connecticut," because the laws were in effect before Peters was born.
        Reprinted: 1969.1.

1865.1   BEARDSLEY, E. EDWARDS. The History of the Episcopal Church
            in Connecticut from the Settlement of the Colony to the
            Death of Bishop Seabury. Vol. 1. New York: Hurd &
            Houghton, pp. 306-307.
                Samuel Peters was an obnoxious clergyman whose imprudent
        conduct and intense loyalty led to his removal by a mob. " . . . his
        writings would have been received with more respect had he restrained
        his rashness, and never embellished them with ludicrous and apocry-
        phal statements."

1864.1   SABINE, LORENZO. "Peters, Samuel, D.D." In Biographical
            Sketches of Loyalists of the American Revolution. Vol. 2.
            Boston: Little, Brown & Co., p. 181.

Brief mention of The History of Connecticut, which "is embarrassed in its authority by a number of fables and which is ever referred to in amusement or in disgust."

1876.1   TRUMBULL, JAMES HAMMOND. Introduction to The True-Blue-
          Laws of Connecticut and New Haven and the False Blue-Laws
          Invented by the Rev. Samuel Peters. Hartford: American
          Publishing Co., pp. 29-38.
              Calls Peters's History of Connecticut "fabricated," its
lies "gross as a mountain, open, palpable." Recounts the story of
Peters's encounter with a mob. Cites evidence to disprove the blue
laws as cited by Peters. See 1877.1-2.

1877.1   ANON. Review of The True-Blue Laws of Connecticut and New
          Haven and the False Blue Laws Invented by the Rev. Samuel
          Peters. Churchman 36 (11 August):154-55.
              Defends Peters's blue laws and attacks Trumbull. See
1876.1.

1877.2   TRUMBULL, JOHN HAMMOND. The Reverend Samuel Peters: His
          Defenders and Apologists with a Reply to the Churchman's
          Review. Hartford: n.p., 25 pp. Reprinted from the
          Hartford Daily Courant.
              A reply to 1877.1. Argues that The General History was
never taken as true history by intelligent readers. Describes "what
actually did take place at Hebron" between Peters and the Sons of
Liberty. Claims Peters acknowledged his guilt and asked forgiveness
in public meeting. Defends his own publication of The True-Blue Laws
(1876.1).

1887.1   . The Reverend Samuel Peters. His Defenders and
          Apologists. Hartford: n.p., pp. 3-26. Reprinted from the
          Hartford Daily Courant.
              Denies he has any family connection to the man who served
as governor of Connecticut at the time of Peters's flight. Asserts
that many before him have criticized the History of Connecticut.
Defends his True-Blue Laws (see 1876.1).

1896.1   DEXTER, FRANKLIN BOWDITCH. Biographical Sketches of the
          Graduates of Yale College with Annals of the College His-
          tory. Vol. 2. New York: Henry Holt & Co., pp. 482-87.
              Biography. Asserts that Peters's History of Connecticut
was published to avenge himself on his countrymen. Peters was not to
be depended upon as to any matter of fact.

1897.1   TYLER, MOSES COIT. The Literary History of the American
          Revolution 1763-1783. New York: G.P. Putnam's Sons,
          pp. 412-15.
              Asserts that Peters intended his History of Connecticut
as authentic history but produced instead a work of fiction.
Reprinted: 1970.1.

1898.1   PRINCE, WALTER F.   "An Examination of Peters's 'Blue Laws.'"
         In Annual Report of the American Historical Association.
         Washington: Government Printing Office, pp. 97–138.
              Refutes attacks on Peters's blue laws. Maintains that
many such laws did exist all over New England and over half of them
existed in New Haven.

1909.1   STANTON, THEODORE, in collaboration with members of the
         faculty of Cornell University. A Manual of American
         Literature. New York: G. P. Putnam's Sons,
         Knickerbocker Press, pp. 101–2.
              Peters wrote A General History of Connecticut to wreak
vengeance upon his native state. Despite its negative critical
reception, it has held the public's interest.

1912.1   CAIRNS, WILLIAM B.   A History of American literature.
         New York: Oxford University Press, p. 155.
              The General History of Connecticut is famous as the
authority for "blue laws." It is amusing but "worthless as history,"
and readers have not decided whether it is satire.

1931.1   ROURKE, CONSTANCE.   American Humor: A Study of the National
         Character. New York: Harcourt Brace & Co., p. 37.
              Brief reference to Samuel Peters as a precursor of the
western tall tale.

1934.1   CALDER, ISABEL M.   "Peters, Samuel Andrew."   In Dictionary
         of American Biography. Edited by Dumas Malone. Vol. 14.
         New York: Charles Scribner's Sons, pp. 511–12.
              Biography. Describes The History of Connecticut as "not
as false as some of its critics in New England have maintained."
Includes a bibliography of secondary works.

1938.1   KUNITZ, STANLEY J., and HOWARD HAYCRAFT. American Authors
         1600–1900. New York: H.W. Wilson, pp. 613–14.
              Biography, noting that Peters's LL.D. appears question-
able. Describes The History of Connecticut as "a most unflattering
account," though it is his primary literary achievement. Includes a
bibliography of primary and secondary sources.

1941.1   HART, JAMES D.   The Oxford Companion to American Literature.
         1st ed. New York: Oxford University Press, p. 578.
              Peters's misrepresentations about blue laws have been
innocently copied by later historians. Peters's claim that Reverend
Hugh Peter was his great-grand-uncle was false.

1943.1   HOWARD, LEON. The Connecticut Wits. Chicago: University
         of Chicago Press, pp. 195, 243.
              Brief mention of Peters.

1947.1   MIDDLEBROOK, SAMUEL.   "Samuel Peters: A Yankee Munchausen."
          NEQ 20 (March):75-87.
               Biography with reference to The General History of
Connecticut.   Credits Peters with the origin of the term "blue laws."

1960.1   JONES, JOSEPH, E. MARCHAND, H.D. PIPER, J.A. ROBBINS, and
          H.E. SPIVEY, comps.   American Literary Manuscripts: A
          Checklist of Holdings in Academic, Historical and Public
          Libraries in the United States.   Compiled and published
          under the auspices of the American Literature group of the
          Modern Language Association.   Austin: University of Texas
          Press, p. 293.
               Lists holdings in eight locations.

1962.1   BURKE, WILLIAM J., and WILL D. HOWE.   American Authors
          and Books, 1640 to the Present Day.   Rev. ed.   New York: Crown
          Publisher, p. 581.
               Bibliography of primary and secondary works.

1962.2   HERZBERG, MAX J., and the staff of the Thomas Y. Crowell Co.
          The Reader's Encyclopedia of American Literature.
          New York: Thomas Y. Crowell Co., p. 874.
               The General History of Connecticut mixed truth with in-
ventions and exaggeration.   Peters criticized Puritanism and spun
yarns, all with "proper historical garniture and dignity."

1968.1   FREE, WILLIAM.   The Columbian Magazine and American Literary
          Nationalism.   Studies in American Literature, vol. 15.   The
          Hague and Paris: Mouton, p. 161.
               Peters's description of a riot in Windham, Connecticut
anticipated western humor.

1969.1   CHAPIN, A.B.   "Samuel Peters."   In Annals of the American
          Pulpit; or Commemorative Notices of Distinguished American
          Clergymen of Various Denominations.   Edited by William B.
          Sprague.   Vol. 5.   New York: Arno Press & the New York
          Times.
               Reprint of 1859.2.

1970.1   TYLER, MOSES COIT.   The Literary History of the American
          Revolution 1763-1783.   New York: Burt Franklin, pp. 412-15.
               Reprint of 1897.1.

1971.1   PETTER, HENRI.   The Early American Novel.   Columbus: Ohio
          State University Press, pp. 144-45, 154n, 299.
               Compares Peters's History of Connecticut to Irving's
History of New York.   Includes the work in the chapter on "Satirical
and Polemical Fiction."

1975.1   DUYCKINCK, EVERT A., and GEORGE L. DUYCKINCK. Cyclopaedia
         of American Literature: Embracing Personal and Critical
         Notices of Authors, and Selections from Their Writings.
         From the Earliest Period to the Present Day. Vol. 1.
         Detroit: Gale Research Co., pp. 200–205.
             Reprint of 1855.1.

1977.1   ROBBINS, J. ALBERT et al., comps. American Literary Manu-
         scripts: A Checklist of Holdings In Academic, Historical,
         and Public Libraries, Museums, and Authors' Homes in the
         United States. 2d ed. Athens: University of Georgia
         Press, p. 252.
             Lists holdings in twelve locations.

XXIV. Samuel Relf (1776-1823)

1854.1   ALLIBONE, S. AUSTIN. A Critical Dictionary of English
          Literature and British and American Authors Living and
          Deceased from the Earliest Accounts to the Latter Half of
          the Nineteenth Century. Vol. 2. Philadelphia: Childs &
          Peterson, p. 1771.
              Brief entry, noting Relf's connection with the Federal
Gazette.

1940.1   BROWN, HERBERT ROSS. The Sentimental Novel in America 1789-
          1860. Durham: Duke University Press, passim.
              Infidelity reflected the influence of Sterne and Goethe's
Werther. It used the epistolary form for sentimental interest and
emphasized the author's moral concern.

1940.2   BLACK, FRANK GEES. The Epistolary Novel in the Late Eight-
          eenth Century. University of Oregon Publications, no. 2.
          Eugene: University of Oregon Press, pp. 70, 72.
              Cites Relf as an example of an American sentimental
writer.

1968.1   KETTLER, ROBERT RONALD. "The Eighteenth-Century American
          Novel: The Beginning of a Fictional Tradition." Ph.D.
          Dissertation, Purdue University, pp. 148-53.
              Infidelity contains the same moral duplicity as The Power
of Sympathy. Both novels imply that illicit love is above the re-
strictions of the established order.

1969.1   WRIGHT, LYLE H. American Fiction, 1774-1850: A Contri-
          bution toward a Bibliography. 2d rev. ed. San Marino:
          Huntington Library, p. 227.
              Lists Infidelity and its location in four libraries.

1971.1   PETTER, HENRI. The Early American Novel. Columbus: Ohio
          State University Press, pp. 367-71.
              Discusses Infidelity as a seduction novel which depicts
feelings "too indulgently encouraged." The novel presents the theme
of parental interference in love; it is flawed by sensationalism,
moral ambiguities, and at least one implausibility.

1974.1   TILLINGHAST, CHARLES ALLEN. "The Early American Novel: A
          Critical Revaluation." Ph.D. Dissertation, Syracuse Univer-
          sity, pp. 83-86.
              Infidelity adapts gothic elements into an American novel.

XXV. Susanna Haswell Rowson (1762-1824)

1787.1   ANON. Review of <u>Victoria</u>. <u>Critical</u> <u>Review; or</u> <u>Annals</u> <u>of</u>
          <u>Literature</u> (London), January, pp. 76-77.
                Finds no fault with an author who supports "the cause of
piety and virtue."

1787.2   ANON. Review of <u>Victoria</u>. <u>Monthly</u> <u>Review; or, Literary</u>
          <u>Journal</u> (London), January, p. 83.
                Commends the novel for its "striking colours" and encour-
ages the author in her endeavors.

1788.1   ANON. Review of <u>The</u> <u>Inquisitor</u>. <u>Critical</u> <u>Review; or,</u>
          <u>Annals</u> <u>of</u> <u>Literature</u> (London), June, pp. 568-69.
                The novel more closely resembles <u>The</u> <u>Rambles</u> <u>of</u> <u>Frankly</u>
by Bonhote than the works of Sterne. The "trick" of the ring is
objectionable, but the book has "many pathetic traits which speak to
the heart, and are drawn from nature."

1788.2   ANON. Review of <u>The</u> <u>Inquisitor</u>. <u>Monthly</u> <u>Review; or,</u>
          <u>Literary</u> <u>Journal</u> (London), August, p. 171.
                Finds "nothing of novelty in the idea nor any thing
particularly striking in the execution of the work," but approves
of the novel for young readers and commends the author's "feeling
heart."

1789.3   ANON. Review of <u>The</u> <u>Test</u> <u>of</u> <u>Honour</u>. <u>Critical</u> <u>Review; or,</u>
          <u>Annals</u> <u>of</u> <u>Literature</u> (London), November, p. 408.
                Finds little to commend in the plot or characterization
and finds the whole "trifling" and improbable, the work of an inexperienced writer.

1790.1   ANON. Review of <u>The</u> <u>Test</u> <u>of</u> <u>Honour</u>. <u>Monthly</u> <u>Review; or,</u>
          <u>Literary</u> <u>Journal</u> (London), March, p. 331.
                Assumes the author's youth and inexperience and finds
some parts interesting and "prettily told." Approves of the moral.

1791.1   ANON. Review of <u>Charlotte;</u> <u>A</u> <u>Tale</u> <u>of</u> <u>Truth</u>. <u>Critical</u>
          <u>Review; or</u> <u>Annals</u> <u>of</u> <u>Literature</u> (London), 1 (April):
          pp. 468-69.
                Reviews first London edition. "It may be a Tale
of Truth, for it is not unnatural, and it is a tale of real dis-
tress. . . . The situations are artless and affecting; the descriptions natural and pathetic. We should feel for Charlotte, if such
a person ever existed, who for error scarcely perhaps deserved so
severe a punishment. If it is a fiction poetic justice is not, we
think, properly distributed." Reprinted: 1794.1.

1794.1   ANON. "A New Novel." <u>United</u> <u>States</u> <u>Gazette</u>, 20 May, p. 1.
          Reprint of 1791.1.

1795.1   PORCUPINE, PETER, and WILLIAM COBBETT. "A Kick for a Bite;
          or, a Review upon Review; with a Critical Essay, on the
          Works of Mrs. S. Rowson; in a Letter to the Editor, or
          Editors, of the American Monthly Review." Philadelphia:
          Thomas Bradford.
            A review of the "roma-drama-poet-tic" works of Rowson.
Takes issue with Rowson's feminist statements in "Slaves of Algiers"
and with the patriotic language of the play, especially the word
"liberty." Sarcastically praises Rowson's verses and romances.

1795.2   [SWANWICK, JOHN.] "A Rub from Snub; or, a Cursory Analytical
          Epistle: Addressed to Peter Porcupine, Author of the Bone
          to Gnaw, Kick for a Bite, etc." Philadelphia: Printed for
          the purchaser.
            A defense of Rowson in response to Cobbett's attack
(1795.1). Denies Cobbett's qualifications as critic and faults him
for waiting so long to write his review. Thinks Cobbett should not
take Rowson's feminist statements seriously. Believes distinctions
between the sexes are based on "customs and manners" and a male
education would qualify a woman for a man's duties. Recommends that
Rowson ignore Cobbett.

1796.1   _____. "British Honour and Humanity; or, the Wonders
          of American Patience, as Exemplified in the Modest Pub-
          lications, and Universal Applause of Mr. William Cobbett;
          Including a Variety of Anecdotes and remarks, Personal
          and Political, and a Survey of the Modern State of Amer-
          ican Newspapers. By a Friend of Regular Government."
          Philadelphia: Robert Campbell, p. 10.
            Brief reference to Cobbett's attack on Rowson (1795.1).

1800.1   ANON. Review of Reuben and Rachel. Critical Review; or,
          Annals of Literature (London), n.s. 28 (January):116-17.
            This novel is "a strange medley of romance, history and
novel." It is surprising that a novelist of Mrs. Rowson's experience
should have awkwardly thrown together so much material into two
volumes.

1818.1   ANON. "Remarks on Novels." Boston New England Galaxy and
          Masonic Magazine 1 (6 February):n.p.
            A survey of contemporary novelists, English and American.
Finds Rowson "a writer of no ordinary mind." Praises her extrava-
gantly. "To advance knowledge, excite virtue, and cherish philan-
thropy, have been her objects and her aims. With powers to make
herself distinguished, she has been content to be useful."

1824.1   [KNAPP, SAMUEL LORENZO.] "Obituary Notice of Mrs. Rowson."
          Boston Commercial Gazette, 11 March, p. 2.
            Praises Rowson as a "bright ornament in virtue, religion,
and letters." Includes biographical information. Notes her major
works. Attributes her success to her "delineations drawn from

nature," the easy familiarity of her style, and the "uniformly moral
tendency" of her works. Insists she was pure and virtuous as an
actress, in a day when most were not. Praises her industry, charity,
and disposition. Reprinted: 1828.2; 1834.1.

1828.1   ANON. Review of Charlotte's Daughter; or The Three Orphans.
          Boston American Ladies' Magazine 1 (April):190-91.
          Admits a "want of finish" in Rowson's writings, but
attributes that to the fact that women do not "elaborate their
literary productions." Finds women particularly suited to publications for the young. Describes the story as interesting and well
told; it has faults but is a "valuable addition to the library of
the young."

1828.2   KNAPP, SAMUEL LORENZO. "Memoir of Susanna Rowson." In
          Charlotte's Daughter; or, The Three Orphans. Boston:
          Richardson & Lord, pp. 1-17.
          Reprint of 1824.1. Reprinted: 1834.1.

1828.3   [WHITTIER, JOHN GREENLEAF.] Review of Charlotte's Daughter;
          or, The Three Orphans. Essex Gazette, 17 May, n.p.
          Praises the book for its interesting characters, for its
"moral beauty" and for its language of nature, but finds imperfec-
tions in "style and incident." Reprinted: 1950.2.

1834.1   KNAPP, SAMUEL LORENZO. Female Biography; Containing Notices
          of Distinguished Women, in Different Nations and Ages. New
          York: J. Carpenter-Clinton Hall; Baltimore: Phoenix, Wood
          & Co., pp. 397-403.
          Reprint of 1828.2; 1824.1.

1852.1   BUCKINGHAM, JOSEPH T. Personal Memoirs and Recollections of
          Editorial Life. Vol. 1. Boston: Ticknor, Reed, & Fields,
          pp. 83-85.
          Rowson was a highly valued correspondent of the New
England Galaxy. Presents biographical information and praise for
Rowson's writings and career as a teacher.

1854.1   ALLIBONE, S. AUSTIN. A Critical Dictionary of English
          Literature and British and American Authors Living and
          Deceased from the Earliest Accounts to the Latter Half of
          the Nineteenth Century. Vol. 2. Philadelphia: Childs &
          Peterson, p. 1885.
          Brief biography and bibliography of primary and secondary
works.

1855.1   DUYCKINCK, EVERT A., and GEORGE L. DUYCKINCK. Cyclopaedia
          of American Literature: Embracing Personal and Critical
          Notices of Authors, and Selections from Their Writings.
          From the Earliest Period to the Present Day. Vol. 1.
          New York: Charles Scribner, pp. 502-4.

Biography. Contrasts the mild tone of Rowson's feminism
with that of the present day. Includes selections from her poetry.
Reprinted: 1975.1.

1861.1   DAWSON, HENRY B. <u>New York City During the American Revolu-
         tion</u>. New York: Mercantile Library Association, p. 32.
         Describes Charlotte Temple's house in 1767, a "small,
two-story frame building," near the corner of what is now Pell
Street. A portion of this building "still remains, being occupied
as a drinking shop under the sign of the Old Tree House."

1870.2   NASON, ELIAS. <u>A Memoir of Mrs. Susanna Rowson, with Elegant
         and Illustrative Extracts from Her Writings in Prose and
         Poetry</u>. Albany: Joel Munsell, 212 pp.
         The most complete biography to date. Uses prefaces to
her novels and other works, Revolutionary War records, letters, and
newspaper articles. Quotes extensively from her novels and relies
heavily on letters from Rowson's pupils. Describes the plots of all
the novels. Includes a portrait.

1875.1   DALL, CAROLINE. <u>The Romance of the Association; or, One
         Last Glimpse of Charlotte Temple and Eliza Wharton</u>.
         Cambridge, Mass.: John Wilson & Son, pp. 10–13.
         Traces Eliza Wharton and Charlotte Temple (actually
Charlotte Stanley) back to their common ancestry in England.
Briefly recounts the plot of <u>Charlotte's Daughter</u>, a true story.

1876.1   WHIPPLE, EDWIN P. "A Century of American Literature." In
         <u>The First Century of the Republic: A Review of American
         Progress</u>. Edited by Theodore D. Woolsey et al. New York:
         Harper & Brothers, pp. 349–98.
         Brief·mention of <u>Charlotte Temple</u> as based on "a myste-
rious domestic scandal which affected the reputation of a number of
prominent American families."

1878.1   HART, JOHN S. <u>A Manual of American Literature</u>. Phila-
         delphia: Eldredge & Brother, p. 92.
         A textbook with a brief biography and list of primary
works.

1880.1   SMITH, S.F. <u>History of Newton, Massachusetts, Town and
         City: From its Earliest Settlement to the Present Time,
         1630–1800</u>. Boston: American Logotype Co., p. 718.
         Briefly describes Rowson's life and focuses on her school
in Newton.

1887.1   BOWNE, ELIZA SOUTHGATE. <u>A Girl's Life Eighty Years Ago:
         Selections from the Letters of Eliza Southgate Bowne</u>. New
         York: Charles Scribner's Sons, pp. 17–18, 19, 27, 31.
         Praise for Rowson and her school by a pupil at the
Medford school.

1887.2   WHIPPLE, EDWIN PERCY. American Literature and Other Papers.
          Boston: Ticknor & Co., p. 27.
               Brief mention of Rowson as a leading writer of the post-
          revolutionary period. Notes the popularity of Charlotte Temple but
          confuses its plot with Foster's The Coquette. Reprinted: 1968.5.

1881.1   ANON. "Rowson, Susanna." In Appleton's Cyclopaedia of
          American Biography. Edited by James Grant Wilson and John
          Fiske. Vol. 5. New York: D. Appleton & Co., p. 339.
               Biography.

1889.1   SWEETSER, M.F. King's Handbook of Newton, Massachusetts.
          Boston: Moses King, p. 46.
               Locates and describes Rowson's school in Newton.

1893.1   RICHARDSON, CHARLES FRANCIS. American Literature 1607-1885.
          Vol. 2. New York: G.P. Putnam's Sons, pp. 283, 285-86, 391.
               Describes Charlotte Temple as an early American senti-
          mental novel, extremely popular but without any redeeming value.

1898.1   HERRINGSHAW, THOMAS WILLIAM. Herringshaw's Encyclopedia of
          American Biography of the Nineteenth Century. Chicago:
          American Publishers Association, p. 806.
               Brief biography.

1901.1   BRONSON, WALTER COCHRANE. A Short History of American
          Literature. Boston: D.C. Heath & Co., pp. 93-94.
               Charlotte Temple is vivid and "truly pathetic."

1901.2   MAURICE, ARTHUR BARTLETT. New York in Fiction. New York:
          Dodd, Mead & Co., pp. 79-81.
               Describes the house at the corner of Doyer and Pell
          Streets where Charlotte Temple is supposed to have died and Trinity
          Churchyard where she is buried. Reprinted: 1969.2.

1902.1   ABERNATHY, JULIAN WILLIS. American Literature. New York:
          Maynard, Merrill & Co., p. 99.
               Brief mention of Rowson.

1902.2   SEARS, LORENZO. American Literature in the Colonial and
          National Periods. Boston: Little Brown & Co., pp. 165-68.
               Assumes the truth of the story of Charlotte Temple.
          Describes its popularity and sentimentality. Reprinted: 1970.4.

1903.1   HIGGINSON, THOMAS WENTWORTH, and HENRY WOLCOTT BOYNTON. A
          Reader's History of American Literature. Boston: Houghton
          Mifflin & Co., pp. 92-93.
               Quotes from Nason (1870.2). Finds Charlotte Temple full
          of "horrors."

1903.2   THOMPSON, ADELE E. "Woman's Place in Early American Fic-
          tion." Era 12 (November):473.
             In a survey of American women writers, mentions Rowson
"who can hardly be classed as an American writer."

1903.3   TRENT, WILLIAM PETERFIELD. A History of American Literature
          1607-1865. New York: D. Appleton & Co., pp. 195-96.
             Rowson was an Englishwoman whose Charlotte Temple used
"stilted phraseology, but with exemplary motives."

1904.1   SARGENT, MARY E. "Susanna Rowson." Medford Historical
          Register 7 (April):25-40.
             Biography focusing on Rowson's school at Medford. Only
brief allusions to some of Rowson's publications.

1905.1   HALSEY, FRANCIS W. Historical and biographical introduction
          to Charlotte Temple, a Tale of Truth, by Susanna Rowson.
          New York: Funk & Wagnalls, pp. xvii-cix.
             Biography. Describes the popularity of Charlotte Temple
and describes pirated editions. Describes New York at the time of
the story and establishes the location of the heroine's house.
Accepts the truth of the story and details the life of Charlotte
Stanley on which the character Charlotte Temple was said to have been
based. Identifies Montraville as John Montresor and gives his biography. Includes a bibliography of editions of Charlotte Temple.

1905.2   TAFT, MARY A. "Charlotte Temple in Fiction and in Fact."
          New York Times, 9 July, pt. 4, 2d Magazine sec., n.p.
             Notes the popularity of Charlotte Temple's grave, despite
scholarly doubt of its authenticity. Quotes Rowson's 1815 preface
attesting to the authenticity of the story. Notes the difficulty of
locating the novel today. Traces the life of John Montrésor and
parallels it to the character of Montraville. Locates the house
where Charlotte Temple is said to have died.

1906.1   OBERHOLTZER, ELLIS PAXTON. The Literary History of Phila-
          delphia. Philadelphia: George W. Jacobs & Co., p. 157.
             Rowson wrote The Trials of the Human Heart in
Philadelphia.

1907.1   LOSHE, LILLIE DEMING. The Early American Novel.
          New York: Columbia University Press, pp. 9-13.
             Biography and critical comment on the novels. The
Inquisitor professes to imitate Sterne but lacks sentiment and humor.
Charlotte Temple has an extreme sensationalism which, together with
its simplicity and directness, accounts for the book's longevity.
Rowson's sensationalism is unique in its lack of romance. Trials of
the Human Heart is realistic in its choice of horrors and homely
detail. Reprinted: 1958.1.

1907.2   MARBLE, ANNIE. <u>Heralds</u> <u>of</u> <u>American</u> <u>Literature:</u> <u>A</u> <u>Group</u> <u>of</u>
           <u>Patriot</u> <u>Writers</u> <u>of</u> <u>the</u> <u>Revolutionary</u> <u>and</u> <u>National</u> <u>Periods.</u>
           Chicago: University of Chicago Press, p. 281.
               The brass buttons, American war scenes, and feminine
           tragedy and sensibility make <u>Charlotte</u> <u>Temple</u> more popular than
           Rowson's other works.

1909.1   STANTON, THEODORE, in collaboration with members of the
           faculty of Cornell University. <u>A</u> <u>Manual</u> <u>of</u> <u>American</u>
           <u>Literature.</u> New York and London: G. P. Putnam's Sons,
           Knickerbocker Press, p. 116-17.
               Brief mention of <u>Charlotte</u> <u>Temple</u>, which "despite its
           absurdly stilted phrases and its long-drawn melancholy, has ever been
           popular with a certain class of readers."

1911.1   BATES, KATHARINE LEE. <u>American</u> <u>Literature.</u> New York:
           Macmillan Co., pp. 86-87.
               Brief biography and mention of <u>Charlotte</u> <u>Temple</u>.

1912.1   BRADSHER, EARL L. <u>Matthew</u> <u>Carey,</u> <u>Editor,</u> <u>Author,</u> <u>and</u>
           <u>Publisher.</u> New York: Columbia University Press, p. 50.
               Quotes a letter from Cary to Rowson about the popularity
           of her novels.

1912.2   CAIRNS, WILLIAM B. <u>A</u> <u>History</u> <u>of</u> <u>American</u> <u>literature.</u>
           New York: Oxford University Press, pp. 136-37.
               Brief mention of three novels. Reprinted: 1969.1.

1912.3   TRENT, WILLIAM PETERFIELD, and JOHN ERSKINE. <u>Great</u> <u>American</u>
           <u>Writers.</u> New York: Henry Holt & co., p. 12.
               Brief mention of Rowson as a writer "still read in un-
           sophisticated circles."

1912.4   VAN DOREN, CARL. <u>The</u> <u>American</u> <u>Novel.</u> New York: Macmillan
           Co., pp. 7-8.
               <u>Charlotte</u> <u>Temple</u> has always been popular among "house-
           maids and shopgirls," though it has not received approval of literary
           critics. Rowson used "every device known to the romancer."

1913.1   ADAMS, OSCAR FAY. "Susanna Haswell Rowson." Boston
           <u>Christian</u> <u>Register</u>, 27 March, pp. 296-99; 3 April,
           pp. 321-22.
               Biography of Rowson.

1915.1   ELLIS, HAROLD MILTON. "Joseph Dennie and his Circle: A
           Study in American Literature from 1792 to 1812. <u>Bulletin</u> <u>of</u>
           <u>the</u> <u>University</u> <u>of</u> <u>Texas</u>, no. 40 (July), p. 77.
               Brief mention of Rowson.

1917.1   LONG, WILLIAM J. <u>Outlines</u> <u>of</u> <u>English</u> <u>and</u> <u>American</u> <u>Litera-</u>
           <u>ture.</u> New York: Ginn & Co., pp. 365-66.

The popularity of <u>Charlotte</u> <u>Temple</u> indicates the wide-spread interest in fiction in the late eighteenth century.

1917.2   VAN DOREN, CARL. "Fiction I: Brown, Cooper." In <u>The</u>
          <u>Cambridge</u> <u>History</u> <u>of</u> <u>American</u> <u>Literature</u>. Edited by
          William Peterfield Trent et al. Vol. 1, <u>Colonial</u>
          <u>and</u> <u>Revolutionary</u> <u>Literature</u>. <u>Early</u> <u>National</u> <u>Literature</u>.
          New York: G.P. Putnam's Sons, p. 286.
              Though an American "only by immigration," Rowson wrote a
          "thoroughly naturalized" novel that became quite popular.

1918.1   BRADSHER, EARL L. "Some Aspects of the Early American
          Novel." <u>Texas</u> <u>Review</u> 3 (April):252, 254, 257.
              Cites <u>Reuben</u> <u>and</u> <u>Rachel</u> as an example of the struggle for
          variety, so noticeable in the early American novel. <u>Charlotte</u> <u>Temple</u>
          contained too many short didactic passages.

1919.1   BOYNTON, PERCY H. <u>A</u> <u>History</u> <u>of</u> <u>American</u> <u>Literature</u>.
          Boston: Ginn & Co., p. 103.
              Brief mention of Rowson.

1919.2   WATKINS, WALTER KENDALL. "The Great Street to Roxbury Gate:
          1630–1830." <u>Bostonian</u> <u>Society</u> <u>Publications</u>, 2d. ser. 3:
          103–7.
              Brief biography of Rowson followed by a detailed history
          of the large house in which she held her academy in Boston.

1921.1   LEE, ELIZABETH. "Rowson, Susanna." In <u>Dictionary</u> <u>of</u>
          <u>National</u> <u>Biography</u>. Edited by Sidney Lee. Vol. 17.
          Oxford: Oxford University Press, pp. 367–68.
              Biography and brief bibliography of secondary sources.

*1922.1   HALL, ERNEST JACKSON. "The Satirical Element in the
          American Novel." Ph.D. Dissertation, University of
          Pennsylvania.
              Cited and published in 1966.2.

1926.1   WILLIAMS, STANLEY THOMAS. "The Era of Washington and
          Jefferson." In <u>The</u> <u>American</u> <u>Spirit</u> <u>in</u> <u>Letters</u>. Pageant
          of America Series, edited by Ralph Henry Gabriel. New Haven:
          Yale University Press, pp. 77, 91.
              Cites Rowson as an example of an early American senti-
          mental writer. Includes brief biography and mention of her novels.

1927.1   McDOWELL, TREMAINE. "Sensibility in the Eighteenth-Century
          American Novel." <u>SP</u> 24 (July):382–402.
              Cites various examples of sensibility in <u>The</u> <u>Inquisitor</u>,
          <u>Charlotte</u> <u>Temple</u>, and <u>Trials</u> <u>of</u> <u>the</u> <u>Human</u> <u>Heart</u>.

1928.1   CLARK, DAVID LEE, ed. Introduction to <u>Edgar</u> <u>Huntley</u>, by
          Charles Brockden Brown. New York: Macmillan Co., p. xiv.
              Brief mention of <u>Charlotte</u> <u>Temple</u>.

1929.1   LEISY, ERNEST E. <u>American</u> <u>Literature</u>: <u>An</u> <u>Interpretive</u>
         <u>Survey</u>. New York: Thomas Y. Crowell Co., p. 50.
            Brief mention of Rowson.

1929.2   WOODY, THOMAS. <u>A</u> <u>History</u> <u>of</u> <u>Women's</u> <u>Education</u> <u>in</u> <u>the</u> <u>United</u>
         <u>States</u>. New York: Science Press, pp. 154-58.
            Biography. Quotes from Eliza Southgate's letters.
See 1887.1.

1931.1   ANGOFF, CHARLES. <u>A</u> <u>Literary</u> <u>History</u> <u>of</u> <u>the</u> <u>American</u> <u>People</u>.
         Vol. 2. New York: A.A. Knopf, pp. 199-206.
            Biography. Describes Rowson's poetry, lyrics, and other
works. Describes <u>Charlotte</u> <u>Temple</u>, its plot, and its popularity,
and calls for a more extensive biographical study of Rowson.

1932.1   FULLERTON, BRADFORD M. <u>A</u> <u>Selective</u> <u>Bibliography</u> <u>of</u> <u>American</u>
         <u>Literature</u> <u>1775-1900</u>: <u>A</u> <u>Brief</u> <u>Survey</u> <u>of</u> <u>the</u> <u>More</u> <u>Important</u>
         <u>Authors</u> <u>and</u> <u>a</u> <u>Description</u> <u>of</u> <u>Their</u> <u>Works</u>. New York:
         William Farquhar Payson, P. 234.
            Biography. Only two of Rowson's novels, <u>Charlotte</u> <u>Temple</u>
and <u>Reuben</u> <u>and</u> <u>Rachel</u>, are significant. Both are stilted but simple
and direct. <u>Charlotte</u> <u>Temple</u> can justly be called the first best
seller.

1932.2   JOHNSON, MERLE. <u>American</u> <u>First</u> <u>Editions</u>: <u>Bibliographic</u>
         <u>Check</u> <u>Lists</u> <u>of</u> <u>the</u> <u>Works</u> <u>of</u> <u>146</u> <u>American</u> <u>Authors</u>. Rev. and
         enl. ed. New York: R.R. Bowker Co., p. 313.
            Bibliography of primary works.

1932.3   KNIGHT, GRANT COCHRAN. <u>American</u> <u>Literature</u> <u>and</u> <u>Culture</u>.
         New York: Ray Long & Richard R. Smith, pp. 97-99.
            Summarizes the plot of <u>Charlotte</u> <u>Temple</u> to show the
kind of literature "our novel-readers then preferred." Asserts that
Rowson's claim to truth was valid.

1933.1   SINGER, GODFREY FRANK. <u>The</u> <u>Epistolary</u> <u>Novel</u>: <u>Its</u> <u>Origin</u>,
         <u>Development</u>, <u>Decline</u>, <u>and</u> <u>Residuary</u> <u>Influence</u>. Philadelphia:
         University of Pennsylvania Press, p. 197.
            Brief mention of <u>Trials</u> <u>of</u> <u>the</u> <u>Human</u> <u>Heart</u>.
Reprinted: 1963.1.

1933.2   VAIL, ROBERT W.G. "Susanna Haswell Rowson, the Author of
         Charlotte Temple: A Bibliographical Study." <u>American</u> <u>Anti-</u>
         <u>quarian</u> <u>Society</u> <u>Proceedings</u>, n.s. 42:47-160.
            The most comprehensive biography to date, including a
description of Rowson's musical and theatrical careers. Includes an
annotated bibliography of all editions of her works and secondary
sources. Includes locations of all editions of her writings. Includes a hitherto unpublished portrait. Notes that Rowson became a
"successful writer of realistic fiction some years before 'realism'

had been invented" and that realism and sentiment made her one of the
most popular novelists of the day. Reprinted: 1933.3.

1933.3   VAIL, ROBERT W.G. Susanna Haswell Rowson, the Author of
          Charlotte Temple: A Bibliographical Study. Worcester,
          Mass.: American Antiquarian Society, 116 pp.
             Reprint of 1933.2.

1935.1   BENSON, MARY SUMNER. Women in Eighteenth-Century America:
          A Study of Opinion and Social Usage. New York: Columbia
          University Press, pp. 184-91.
             Examines Charlotte Temple as an example of a heroine in
early American literature and presents some biographical information
about Rowson.

1935.2   ELLIS, HAROLD MILTON. "Susanna Rowson." In Dictionary of
          American Biography. Edited by Dumas Malone. Vol. 16. New
          York: Charles Scribner's Sons, pp. 203-4.
             Biography of Rowson and very brief description of her
main works. Includes a short bibliography.

1935.3   PATTEE, FRED LEWIS. The First Century of American Litera-
          ture 1770-1870. New York and London: D. Appleton-Century
          Co., pp. 79, 86-90, 351.
             Biography and description of the fame of Charlotte
Temple. The popularity of the novel speaks badly for our reading
public. Most of Rowson's other writings are "worthless stuff," but
Rowson was a pioneer in using the American Revolution as a literary
background and in the use of the American Indian in fiction. Rowson
was a realistic writer.

1935.4   WINTERICH, JOHN T. Early American Books and Printing.
          Boston: Houghton Mifflin Co., pp. 151-52.
             Brief biography and mention of Charlotte Temple and
Charlotte's Daughter.

1936.1   BOYNTON, PERCY. Literature and American life: For Students
          of American Literature. Boston: Ginn & Co., p. 193.
             Cites Charlotte Temple as an example of the seduction
novel popular in the 1790s.

1936.2   LEISY, ERNEST E. "The Novel in America: Notes for a
          Survey." SWR 22 (Autumn):89.
             Brief mention of Rowson.

1936.3   QUINN, ARTHUR HOBSON. American Fiction: An Historical
          and Critical Survey. New York: Appleton-Century Crofts,
          pp. 14-19.
             Finds that the most important aspect of Rowson's fiction
is their reflection of current standards of morality. Surveys her
American novels. Concludes they are "of real significance in the

history of English and American fiction. . . . She had a knack of
compelling interest and a power of description. More importantly,
she was, if not the creator, a vivid portrayer of the virtuous woman
adventuress. . . . She passed on to several of her heroines her own
courage and resourcefulness."

1936.4   TAYLOR, WALTER FULLER. A History of American Letters.
          Boston: American Book Co., p. 67.
          Brief mention of Charlotte Temple.

1937.1   HEILMAN, ROBERT BECHTOLD. America in English Fiction, 1760-
          1800: The Influences of the American Revolution. Louisiana
          State University Studies, no. 33. Baton Rouge: Louisiana
          State University Press, pp. 124-25, 155-56.
                Refers to Rebecca, or The Fille de Chambre as an example
of a narrative treatment of the Revolution, as an example of criticism of the Revolution, as an example of treatment of economic problems during the war, and as an example of an author's contentment
with New England. Notes that Charlotte Temple is placed in America,
though it has no reason for being there. The war serves only to
"transfer an old sentimental tragedy to America." Notes that The
Inquisitor and Mentoria also contain references to the war.

1937.2   LEWISOHN, LUDWIG. The Story of American Literature. New
          York: Harper & Brothers, p. 54.
                Brief mention of Charlotte Temple which dropped the level
at which American literature had begun.

1938.1   KUNITZ, STANLEY J., and HOWARD HAYCRAFT. American Authors
          1600-1900. New York: H.W. Wilson Co., p. 663.
                Biography and bibliography of primary and secondary
works.

1939.1   BLAKEY, DOROTHY. The Minerva Press, 1790-1820. London:
          Printed for the Bibliographic Society at the University
          Press, Oxford, pp. 153, 155, 158, 190.
                Lists Rowson's four novels published by Minerva:
Charlotte Temple, Mentoria, The Fille de Chambre, and Reuben and
Rachel.

1939.2   CLARK, MARY ELIZABETH. Peter Porcupine in America: The
          Career of William Cobbett, 1792-1800. Ph.D. Dissertation,
          University of Pennsylvania, pp. 29-34.
                Recounts the story of Cobbett's attack on Rowson.

1939.3   JACKSON, JOSEPH. Literary Landmarks of Philadelphia.
          Philadelphia: David McKay Co., pp. 268-69.
                Brief biography. Notes that one cannot know where Rowson
lived in Philadelphia as she was not listed in any city directory of
the period.

1940.1   BLACK, FRANK GEES. The Epistolary Novel in the Late Eight-
          eenth Century: A Descriptive and Bibliographical Study.
          University of Oregon Monographs, no. 2. Eugene: University
          of Oregon Press, pp. 6, 61, 70, 77-78, 109n, 147.
               Describes Trials of the Human Heart and praises its
          definition of authentic emotion. Places Mentoria and Reuben and
          Rachel among the propaganda fiction of the 1790s.

1940.2   BROWN, HERBERT ROSS. The Sentimental Novel in America,
          1789-1860. Durham: Duke University Press, passim.
               Quotes Rowson's complaints about the disrepute of novel-
          ists. Notes her fondness for the reformed rake theme, and cites her
          as an example of several characteristics of the sentimental novel.
          Reprinted: 1959.1.

1942.1   ROURKE, CONSTANCE. The Roots of American Culture, and Other
          Essays. New York: Harcourt, Brace, pp. 75-87.
               Biography. Notes the feminism of both the novels and the
          plays. Sees patriotism as a primary theme of the plays. Cites
          Rowson's innovations in teaching and finds her praiseworthy, though
          "not truly a poet, . . . not truly a dramatist, an actress, a novel-
          ist, nor in the full sense an educator." Reprinted: 1965.2.

1943.1   BURKE, WILLIAM J., and WILL D. HOWE. American Authors
          and Books, 1640-1940. New York: Gramercy Publishing Co.,
          pp. 632-33.
               Bibliography of primary and secondary works.

1944.1   BROOKS, VAN WYCK. "New England." In The World of
          Washington Irving. New York: E.P. Dutton & Co., p. 49.
               Briefly describes the plot and popularity of Charlotte
          Temple.

1945.1   PAINE, GREGORY. "American Literature a Hundred and Fifty
          Years Ago." SP 42 (April):388.
               Summarizes the plot of Charlotte Temple and notes its
          popularity.

1947.1   MOTT, FRANK LUTHER. Golden Multitudes: The Story of Best
          Sellers in the United States. New York: Macmillan Co.,
          pp. 39-40.
               Relates the success of Charlotte Temple. Notes that
          Rebecca, or The Fille de Chambre narrowly missed becoming a best
          seller.

1947.2   TAFT, KENDALL B. Minor Knickerbockers. New York: American
          Book Co., p. xxxviiin.
               Brief mention of Rowson as an Englishwoman.

1948.1   COWIE, ALEXANDER. The Rise of the American Novel. New
          York: American Book Co., pp. 10, 12-15, 17, 90, 200.

Finds Charlotte Temple "distinctly superior" to The Power
of Sympathy. Notes Rowson's omission of harsh attitudes toward
fallen women and finds the continued popularity of Charlotte Temple
an indication of its merit.

1948.2 _____. "The Beginnings of Fiction and Drama." In Literary
History of the United States. Edited by Robert E. Spiller
et al. New York: Macmillan Co., pp. 177-78.
Brief mention of the popularity of Charlotte Temple, a
book that is "told with a sincerity and power that can be felt today."

1950.1 HART, JAMES D. The Popular Book: A History of America's
Literary Taste. New York: Oxford University Press,
pp. 63-64.
The popularity of Charlotte Temple is based on its
American setting and "the piquancy attached to a plot based on fact."

1950.2 WHITTIER, JOHN GREENLEAF. "Charlotte's Daughter; or, The
Three Orphans." In The Uncollected Critical Writings of
John Greenleaf Whittier. Edited by Edwin Harrison Cady and
Harry Hayden Clark. Syracuse: Syracuse University Press,
pp. 15-18.
Reprint of 1828.3.

1951.1 WYMAN, MARGARET. "The Rise of the Fallen Woman." AQ 3:167.
"Mrs. Rowson stands out from her fellow novelists for
going beyond conventional expressions of piety to indignant criticism
of an unfeeling world."

1952.1 WAGENKNECHT, EDWARD. Cavalcade of the American Novel:
From the Birth of the Nation to the Middle of the Twentieth
Century. New York: Henry Holt & Co., pp. 4-5.
Charlotte Temple is a healthier book than The Power of
Sympathy. Rowson must have known the world better than many moderns
who sneer at her. She was "no Pharisee" and "no weakling either."

1955.1 KNOX, SARAH. "First U.S. Best Seller is Brought from
Britain and Sold for $5,000." New York Times, 11 November,
p. 27.
Recounts the discovery of the first recorded copy of the
first edition of Charlotte Temple (1791). Comments on the novel's
continuing popularity.

1956.1 HART, JAMES D. The Oxford Companion to American Literature.
3d ed. New York: Oxford University Press, p. 656.
Biography and description of Rowson's novels.

1956.2 TAYLOR, WALTER FULLER. The Story of American Letters.
Chicago: Henry Regnery Co., p. 61.
Brief mention of Rowson.

1957.1   FIEDLER, LESLIE A. "From Clarissa to Temple Drake: Women
          in Love in the Classic American Novel." Encounter 8
          (March):14-20.
               Rowson's character of Montraville was the first popular
image of the seducer, and as such he exemplifies the emasculation of
the male in American literature. Expanded: 1966.1.

1957.2   LEWIS, BENJAMIN M. Register of Editors, Printers, and
          Publishers of American Magazines, 1741-1810. New York:
          New York Public Library, pp. 4-6.
               Cites the editor of the Boston Weekly Magazine as an
example of the difficulty in establishing editorship. Doubts that
Rowson was editor of the magazine, her biographers to the contrary.
Cites as evidence the distance she would have had to travel to the
magazine office and textual evidence. Concludes that Rowson contributed substantially to the magazine but did not edit it.

1957.3   SPENCER, BENJAMIN. The Quest for Nationality. Syracuse:
          Syracuse University Press, p. 41.
               In a discussion of the "Search for National Modes and
Principles, 1783-1814," cites Rowson as an example of the way novelists and dramatists "construed the moral bearing of their works in
nationalistic terms."

1957.4   STIMSON, FREDERICK S. "Spanish Inspiration in the First
          American Adventure Stories." Hispania 40 (March):66-69.
               Brief mention of the use of a Spanish background in
Reuben and Rachel.

1958.1   LOSHE, LILLIE DEMING. The Early American Novel 1789-1830.
          New York: Frederick Ungar Publishing Co., pp. 9-13.
               Reprint of 1907.1.

1959.1   BROWN, HERBERT ROSS. The Sentimental Novel in America,
          1789-1860. New York: Pageant Books.
               Reprint of 1940.2.

1959.2   CHARVAT, WILLIAM. Literary Publishing in America, 1790-
          1850. Philadelphia: University of Pennsylvania Press,
          p. 24.
               Suggests that Carey's publishing the "misery novel of the
Charlotte Temple type" prepared a market that responded to Scott and
later to Cooper.

1960.1   JONES, JOSEPH, E. MARCHAND, H.D. PIPER, J.A. ROBBINS, and
          H.E. SPIVEY, comps. American Literary Manuscripts: A
          Checklist of Holdings in Academic, Historical and Public
          Libraries in the United States. Compiled and published
          under the auspices of the American Literature group of the
          Modern Language Association. Austin: University of Texas
          Press.
               Lists holdings in nine locations.

1960.2   FIEDLER, LESLIE A. Love and Death in the American Novel.
         New York: Criterion Books.
             See 1966.1.

1961.1   MARTIN, TERENCE. The Instructed Vision: Scottish Common
         Sense Philosophy and the Origins of American Fiction.
         Indiana Humanities Series, no. 48. Bloomington:
         Indiana University Press, pp. 126–27.
             Rowson is the most "effectively didactic" of the early
         American writers.

1962.1   BLOCK, ANDREW. "Rowson, Susannah Haswell." In The English
         Novel 1740–1850. 2d ed. London: Dawson's p. 202.
             Bibliography of primary works, taken from Vail (1933.2).

1962.2   HERZBERG, MAX J., and the staff of the Thomas Y. Crowell Co.
         The Reader's Encyclopedia of American Literature. New York:
         Thomas Y. Crowell, p. 981.
             Brief biography and bibliography of Rowson's novels.

1963.1   SINGER, GODFREY FRANK. The Epistolary Novel: Its Origin,
         Development, Decline, and Residuary Influence. New York:
         Russell & Russell.
             Reprint of 1933.1.

1964.1   DAVIS, RICHARD BEALE. Intellectual Life in Jefferson's
         Virginia 1790–1830. Chapel Hill: University of North
         Carolina Press, pp. 78, 98.
             Brief mention of Charlotte Temple in southern libraries.

1964.2   KIRK, CLARA M., and RUDOLPH KIRK, eds. Introduction to
         Charlotte Temple: A Tale of Truth, by Susanna Rowson.
         Masterworks of Literature Series. New York: Twayne
         Publishers; New Haven: College & University Press,
         pp. 11–32.
             Details Rowson's claim for the authenticity of Charlotte
         Temple. Attributes the popularity of the novel to the claim to truth
         and Rowson's concern for her female audience and her manipulation of
         them, as well as her ability to tell a dramatic story. Summarizes
         critics' opinions of Charlotte Temple and details its publishing
         history.

1965.1   DOUTY, ESTHER M. Under the Roof: Five Patriots of the
         Young Republic. Chicago: Rand McNally, pp. 235–75.
             A children's book. Biography of Rowson. Relates the story
         of Charlotte Temple as truth.

1965.2   ROURKE, CONSTANCE. The Roots of American Culture, and Other
         Essays. Port Washington, N.Y.: Kennikat Press.
             Reprint of 1942.1.

1965.3   SPILLER, ROBERT E. "New Wine in Old Bottles." In The Third
          Dimension: Studies in Literary History. New York:
          Macmillan Co., p. 83.
                In a discussion of the literary movement of the last
          decade of the eighteenth century, cites Rowson as an example of a
          writer of novels in imitation of Richardson.

1966.1   FIEDLER, LESLIE A. Love and Death in the American Novel.
          Rev. ed. New York: Stein & Day, pp. 68, 83, 90–91, 93–98.
                Views Montraville in Charlotte Temple as an unfairly
          punished male, suffering a lifetime for a single error. Severely
          criticizes the novel for its style, characterization, and plot.
          Attributes its popularity to the plot. Sees the novel as "completely
          a woman's book," projecting the image of woman as "long-suffering
          martyr," victimized by male lust. Lucy Temple in Charlotte's
          Daughter; or, the Three Orphans establishes the prototype of the
          repentant seducer, reduced to desperate straits by guilt. Expansion
          of 1957.1. See also 1960.2.

1966.2   HALL, ERNEST JACKSON. The Satirical Element in the American
          Novel. New York: Haskell House, pp. 8, 62–63.
                Brief mention of Rowson as a satirist of social condi-
          tions which make seduction possible. Summarizes Rowson's life and
          notes that Charlotte Temple marks an advance in English fiction
          because its satire is largely implied in the situation. Publication
          of 1922.1.

1966.3   MADISON, CHARLES A. Book Publishing in America. New York:
          McGraw Hill, p. 9.
                Quotes a letter from Mathew Carey to Rowson concerning
          the sales record of Charlotte Temple.

1968.1   CHARVAT, WILLIAM. The Profession of Authorship in America,
          1800–1870: The Papers of William Charvat. Edited by
          Matthew J. Bruccoli. Columbus: Ohio State University
          Press, pp. 17–24.
                In a discussion of New York and Philadelphia as publish-
          ing centers, describes Rowson's American publications. Considers
          Charlotte Temple "a British book." Compares the publishing history
          of Charlotte Temple to that of Trials of the Human Heart and attrib-
          utes the poor sales of the latter to its publication by subscription.
          Rowson's "readiness to consult the market and adapt it to her liter-
          ary stock-in-trade, which was didacticism, give Mrs. Rowson standing
          as an early American writer of true professional temperament."

1968.2   FREE, WILLIAM. The Columbian magazine and American Literary
          Nationalism. Studies in American Literature, vol. 15. The
          Hague and Paris: Mouton, p. 94.
                Brief reference to Rowson as one of the women sentimental
          novelists more skilled than their predecessors who wrote for the
          Columbian Magazine.

1968.3   KETTLER, ROBERT RONALD. "The Eighteenth-Century American
          Novel: The Beginning of a Fictional Tradition." Ph.D.
          Dissertation, Purdue University, pp. 60-66.
      Rowson's prefaces show her moving away from claims of
authenticity to assertions about the valuable lessons fiction can
teach. But when she actually became a teacher she gave up fiction
altogether. Charlotte Temple follows the same pattern and tells the
same American tale that other novels do. Rebecca, or the Fille de
Chambre contains an example of the youthful protagonist, a typical
character in early American fiction.

1968.4   WAGER, WILLIS. American Literature: A World View. New
          York: New York University Press, p. 46.
          Brief mention of Charlotte Temple.

1968.5   WHIPPLE, EDWIN PERCY. American Literature and Other Papers.
          New York: Johnson Reprint Co., p. 27.
          Reprint of 1887.2.

1969.1   CAIRNS, WILLIAM B. A History of American literature.
          New York: Johnson Reprint Corp., pp. 136-37.
          Reprint of 1912.2.

1969.2   MAURICE, ARTHUR BARTLETT. New York in Fiction. Port
          Washington, N.Y.: Ira J. Friedman.
          Reprint of 1901.2.

1970.1   GIFFEN, JANE C. "Susanna Rowson and her Academy." Antiques
          98 (Summer):436-40.
      Describes Rowson's school. Includes photographs of nee-
dle artwork by her students, and includes a drawing of the Medford
school and a portrait of Rowson.

1970.2   KABLE, WILLIAM S., ed. Introduction to Three Early American
          Novels. Columbus: Charles E. Merrill Publishing Co.,
          pp. 4-8.
      Sees the central critical problem of Charlotte Temple as
accounting for its popularity. Lists various reasons offered by
critics: its reliance on truth, its reliance on the natural, its
easy style, and its simple plot.

1970.3   NYE, RUSSEL B. American Literary History: 1607-1830. New
          York: Alfred A. Knopf, pp. 193, 230, 237-38.
      Rowson was the "queen" of the Richardsonian imitators,
having an inventive mind and narrative skill.

1970.4   SEARS, LORENZO. American literature in the Colonial and
          National Periods. New York: Burt Franklin, pp. 165-68.
          Reprint of 1902.2.

1971.1   BIRDSALL, RICHARD D.   "Rowson, Susanna Haswell."   In Notable
          American Women 1607–1950: A Biographical Dictionary.
          Edited by Edward T. James, Janet Wilson James, and Paul S.
          Boyer. Vol. 3. Cambridge, Mass.: Harvard University
          Press, Belknap Press, pp. 202–4.
              Detailed biography, with mention and brief description of
Rowson's writings.

1971.2   PETTER, HENRI. The Early American Novel. Columbus: Ohio
          State University Press, pp. 22–45.
              Defines Mentoria and The Inquisitor not as novels but as
"didactic collections." Attributes the success of Charlotte Temple
to Rowson's use of material "which to some extent could be called her
own." Examines Rowson's stated views of the novel as a genre. Describes her novels as novels "of victimization" and describes their
structural patterns. Compares the plot of Charlotte Temple to the
plots of Trials of the Human Heart and Sarah, or the Exemplary Wife.
Praises Charlotte Temple but criticizes the others which fall short
of the more popular work.

1972.1   MARTIN, WENDY. "Seduced and Abandoned in the New World:
          The Fallen Woman in American Fiction." In American Sister-
          hood: Writings of the Feminist Movement from Colonial Times
          to the Present. Edited by Wendy Martin. New York: Harper
          & Row, pp. 258–59.
              A discussion of the archetype of the fallen woman and the
way a myth influences behavior long after the myth itself ceases to
exist. Sees Charlotte Temple as the first of a long line of passive,
dependent heroines doomed to tragedy.

1972.2   TEBBEL, JOHN. A History of Book Publishing in the United
          States. Vol. 1, The Creation of an Industry 1630–1865. New
          York and London: R.R. Bowker, pp. 145–46.
              The seduction theme, the reference to the war, and the
international flavor all contributed to the success of Charlotte
Temple.

1973.1   DAVIDSON, MARSHALL B., and the editors of American Heritage.
          The American Heritage History of the Writers' America. New
          York: American Heritage Publishing Co., McGraw-Hill, p. 76.
              Describes the popularity of Charlotte Temple.

1974.1   BRANDT, ELLEN BARBARA. "Susanna Haswell Rowson: A Critical
          Biography." Ph.D. Dissertation, University of Pennsylvania,
          389 pp.
              Rowson was one of the most "interesting, dynamic, and
accomplished women of the early national period." Her books deal
with women's roles, possibilities, limitations, and education. Her
books present a good picture of social life, behavioral standards,
and morality in various milieus. Since no comprehensive studies of
Rowson exist, presents an extensive monograph of Rowson's works.

1974.2   EARNEST, ERNEST. The American Eve in Fact and Fiction,
         1775-1914. Urbana: University of Illinois Press, pp. 30-
         31, 43.
             Brief mention of Rowson.

1974.3   MARTIN, WENDY. "Profile: Susanna Rowson, Early American
         Novelist." WS 2:1-8.
             A general introduction to Rowson: brief biography and
plot summaries of her major works. Places Rowson's warnings against
seduction in a social and economic context. Finds Charlotte Temple a
role-model for later American heroines.

1974.4   STEIN, ROGER B. "Pulled Out of the Bay: American Fiction
         in the Eighteenth Century." SAF 2 (Spring):13-36.
             The voyage in Charlotte Temple bridges "the pastoral and
family world and the world of tainted experience. . . . The seduction tale transmutes the sea experience into an effective (and affec-
tive) language for inner states of feeling of the mind and the soul."

1974.5   TILLINGHAST, CHARLES ALLEN. "The Early American Novel:
         A Critical Revaluation." Ph.D. Dissertation, Syracuse
         University.
             Calls Rowson an Englishwoman and calls Charlotte Temple
"not an American novel."

1974.6   WEIL, DOROTHY LOUISE. "Susanna Rowson, the Young Lady's
         Friend." DAI 35:3705-6A.
             Rowson's literary task was the complete education of the
young female. In all her variety of works, she attempted to create
models; hence her novels are "tales of truth"; her texts are descriptions of "natural wonders." Rowson's religion is the "controlling
system" for all her teachings and supports her standards for feminine
personality. Her concern for women appears in all her works and she
is especially concerned with their education. Her fiction is made up
of both realistic elements and emblems, symbols, and allegorical
characters. Rowson creates for herself as author a literary persona
embodying the ideals she sets up for women. See 1976.3.

1975.1   DUYCKINCK, EVERT A., and GEORGE L. DUYCKINCK. Cyclopaedia
         of American Literature: Embracing Personal and Critical
         Notices of Authors, and Selections from Their Writings.
         From the Earliest Period to the Present Day. Vol. 1.
         Detroit: Gale Research Co., pp. 502-4.
             Reprint of 1855.1.

1975.2   GINSBERG, ELAINE. "The Female Initiation Theme in American
         Fiction." SAF 3 (Spring):27-37.
             The female initiation story rarely occurs in American
literature because women were to remain pure and innocent and in the
home. When the theme does occur, the initiation experience for the

girl is usually regrettable. Charlotte Temple provides an early
prototype.

1975.3   McALEXANDER, PATRICIA JEWELL. "The Creation of the American
         Eve: The Cultural Dialogue on the Nature and Role of Women
         in Late Eighteenth-Century America." EAL 9 (Winter):261.
              Though Charlotte Temple focuses on the evil results of
passion, the novel also portrays its attractions.

1976.1   PARKER, PATRICIA L. "Charlotte Temple: America's First
         Best Seller." SSF 13 (Fall):518-20.
              Argues that the novel spoke to the hearts of readers
because it was brief and entertaining; it posited a more humanitarian
attitude than was socially conventional and a mild feminism; and it
employed an artlessness that readers enjoyed.

1976.2   _____. "Charlotte Temple by Susanna Rowson." EJ 65
         (January):59-60.
              Recommends Charlotte Temple as readable and teachable in
the high school and college classroom. Notes topics for discussion
and writing.

1976.3   WEIL, DOROTHY. In Defense of Women: Susanna Rowson (1762-
         1824). University Park and London: Pennsylvania State
         University Press, 204 pp.
              Derived from 1974.6.

1977.1   ROBBINS, J. ALBERT et al., comps. American Literary Manu-
         scripts: A Checklist of Holdings In Academic, Historical,
         and Public Libraries, Museums, and Authors' Homes in the
         United States. Compiled and published under the auspices of
         the American Literature group of the Modern Language Asso-
         ciation. 2d ed. Athens: University of Georgia Press,
         p. 27.
              Lists holdings in nine locations.

1977.2   SPENGEMANN, WILLIAM C. The Adventurous Muse: The Poetics
         of American Fiction, 1789-1900. New Haven: Yale University
         Press, pp. 88-93.
              Charlotte Temple owes its popularity to its sentimental-
domestic conventions. All adventures outside the home are hostile,
yet conservative values are compromised by the insistence upon the
truth of the story and by the use of sentiment. Rowson subjugates
her fiction to her moral, yet her authorial asides complicate the
reader's moral apprehension of that meaning. Charlotte Temple may be
the most rigidly programmatic sentimental novel ever written.

1978.1   BAYM, NINA. Woman's Fiction: A Guide to Novels by and
         about Women in America, 1820-1870. Ithaca and London:
         Cornell University Press, pp. 25, 50.
              Rowson is Richardson's American imitator. Charlotte
Temple is, from a woman's point of view, "a demoralized literature."

1978.2   WHITE, ISABELLE. "The American Heroine, 1789-1899: Non-
         conformity and Death." Ph.D. Dissertation, University of
         Kentucky, pp. 27-42.
             A discussion of eight dying American heroines. Like
others, Charlotte Temple is subversive of some of the social patterns
it seeks to reinforce. Rowson does not view Charlotte Temple's death
as an inevitable consequence of seduction. Rather, it is the result
of her unfortunate circumstances and inability to get along in the
world. Rowson suggests that young women need friends and that they
learn to be independent. The moral is inconsistent, as it is in
other novels studied here, because Rowson does not quite believe the
message her inherited motif implies.

1979.1   HORNSTEIN, JACQUELINE. "Literary History of New England
         Women Writers, 1630-1800." DAI 39:7347A.
             A study of the ways in which Puritanism, life in the
American wilderness, and events in eighteenth-century Boston encouraged women to write. Chapters four and five include novelists, of
whom Rowson is one.

1980.1   DAUBER, KENNETH. "American Culture as Genre." Criticism 22
         (Spring):104, 106-9.
             In an examination of the question of which is the first
American novel, looks at Charlotte Temple and finds its claim to
Americanness problematic, because "of its uncertain relation to reading and writing, its failure to define itself as within a rhetorical
field." The rhetorical problems of the novel parallel America's
struggle to define itself after the Revolution. Fiedler's claim that
Charlotte Temple was "the first book by an American to move American
readers" is based on an unconvincing mixture of historical and aesthetic claims (see 1966.1).

1981.1   PARKER, PATRICIA L. "A Critical Biography of Susanna
         Haswell Rowson." Ph.D. Dissertation, New York University,
         263 pp.
             In fiction, Rowson produced women heroes who overcome
trials by virtue of their intelligence and practicality, heroes who
served as models for her readers. In her textbooks, Rowson asserted
women's rights to education and praised women's achievements. Her
stage and musical careers demonstrated her versatility and adapta-
bility and demonstrated her understanding of English and American
popular culture.

1982.1   DAVIDSON, CATHY N. "Flirting with Destiny: Ambivalence and
         Form in the Early American Sentimental Novel." SAF 10
         (Spring):17-39.
             An examination of the ways early American novels used the
sentimental form to question the very propositions they pretended to
extoll. Montraville in Charlotte Temple is a rounded character
instead of a conventional villain, and the standard moral dictum is
compromised by the actions of another villain, Balcour.

XXVI. Henry Sherburne (?)

1907.1   LOSHE, LILLIE DEMING. The Early American Novel.
          New York: Columbia University Press, p. 40n.
             Brief mention. Reprinted: 1958.1.

1958.1   LOSHE, LILLIE DEMING. The Early American Novel 1789-1830.
          New York: Frederick Ungar Publishing Co., p. 40n.
             Reprint of 1907.1.

1971.1   PETTER, HENRI. The Early American Novel. Columbus: Ohio
          State University Press, pp. 151-53.
             Brief description of The Oriental Philanthropist as a
"vague and rhapsodical fantasy, inspired by some tradition of the
Oriental tale."

XXVII. Royall Tyler (1757-1826)

1797.1   M., A. "Literary Miscellany." Boston <u>Columbian</u> <u>Centinel</u>,
         25 October, p. 1.
             Claims Dr. Updike Underhill assists the editor of the
<u>Walpole</u> <u>Paper</u> in writing poetry.

1798.1   ANON. Review of <u>The</u> <u>Algerine</u> <u>Captive</u>. Walpole <u>Farmer's</u>
         <u>Weekly</u> <u>Museum:</u> <u>Newhampshire</u> <u>and</u> <u>Vermont</u> <u>Journal</u> 6
         (24 April):4.
             Attributes the work to "Peter Pencil." Praises the book
but points out a geographical error in the voyage from Gibralter to
Algiers.

1802.1   ANON. "Literature and Polite Arts." <u>New</u> <u>Annual</u> <u>Register</u>
         (London) 23:321.
             Brief mention of <u>The</u> <u>Algerine</u> <u>Captive</u>.

1802.2   ANON. "Novels and Romances." <u>London</u> <u>Monthly</u> <u>Magazine</u> <u>or,</u>
         <u>British</u> <u>Register</u>, 20 July, supplement 13, p. 659.
             Finds this "History of an American Physician" enter-
taining, with some "shrewd remarks on the events of the present day."

1802.3   [DENNIE, JOSEPH.] "Literary Intelligence." Philadelphia
         <u>Port</u> <u>Folio:</u> <u>A</u> <u>Monthly</u> <u>Magazine,</u> <u>Devoted</u> <u>to</u> <u>Useful</u> <u>Science,</u>
         <u>the</u> <u>Liberal</u> <u>Arts,</u> <u>Legitimate</u> <u>Criticism,</u> <u>and</u> <u>Polite</u> <u>Litera-</u>
         <u>ture</u> 12 (16 January):8.
             Quotes from <u>The</u> <u>Farmer's</u> <u>Museum</u> (1798.1) and agrees that
<u>The</u> <u>Algerine</u> <u>Captive</u> is unjustly neglected.

1802.4   ANON. Review of <u>The</u> <u>Algerine</u> <u>Captive</u>. <u>Critical</u> <u>Review;</u> <u>or,</u>
         <u>Annals</u> <u>of</u> <u>Literature</u> (London), n.s. 35 (May):113-14.
             Describes the book as "the real or pretended history of
an American physician." Includes a letter written by the author's
ancestor to Hanserd Knollys.

1803.1   [DENNIE, JOSEPH.] "Literary Intelligence." Philadelphia
         <u>Port</u> <u>Folio:</u> <u>A</u> <u>Monthly</u> <u>Magazine,</u> <u>Devoted</u> <u>to</u> <u>Useful</u> <u>Science,</u>
         <u>the</u> <u>Liberal</u> <u>Arts,</u> <u>Legitimate</u> <u>Criticism,</u> <u>and</u> <u>Polite</u> <u>Litera-</u>
         <u>ture</u> 3 (4 June):8.
             A brief announcement of a new reprint of <u>The</u> <u>Algerine</u>
<u>Captive</u> in England.

1803.2   ANON. Review of <u>The</u> <u>Algerine</u> <u>Captive</u>. <u>Monthly</u> <u>Review;</u> <u>or,</u>
         <u>Literary</u> <u>Journal</u> (London) 42 (September):86-93.
             Summarizes the novel and includes lengthy quotations.
Criticizes its style. Compares it unfavorably with <u>Robinson</u> <u>Crusoe</u>,
<u>Gulliver's</u> <u>Travels</u>, and Montesquieu's <u>Persian</u> <u>Letters</u>, yet finds it
pleasing.

1804.1   [DENNIE, JOSEPH.] "Literary Intelligence for the Port
          Folio." Philadelphia <u>Port</u> <u>Folio</u>: <u>A</u> <u>Monthly</u> <u>Magazine,</u>
          <u>Devoted</u> <u>to</u> <u>Useful</u> <u>Science,</u> <u>the</u> <u>Liberal</u> <u>Arts,</u> <u>Legitimate</u>
          <u>Criticism,</u> <u>and</u> <u>Polite</u> <u>Literature</u> 4 (28 April):134.
              <u>The</u> <u>Algerine</u> <u>Captive</u> is "commended in all the literary
journals of Great Britain," but has not been well received in the
United States. Notes the "uncommon spirit and animation" of the book
and finds it instructive as well as amusing.

1804.2   ANON. Review of the London edition of Dr. Linn's "Powers of
          Genius." Philadelphia <u>Port</u> <u>Folio</u>: <u>A</u> <u>Monthly</u> <u>Magazine,</u>
          <u>Devoted</u> <u>to</u> <u>Useful</u> <u>Science,</u> <u>the</u> <u>Liberal</u> <u>Arts,</u> <u>Legitimate</u>
          <u>Criticism,</u> <u>and</u> <u>Polite</u> <u>Literature</u> 4 (1 September):277.
              Complains that the Robinsons two or three years ago
published the "Life and Adventures of Dr. Underhill" as though its
author were British.

1810.1   ANON. "The Yankee in London." <u>Monthly</u> <u>Anthology</u> <u>and</u> <u>Boston</u>
          <u>Review</u> 8 (January):50–58.
              Calls the book "a very useless addition to the almost
innumerable books of travels, which crowd the shelves of libraries."
Criticizes the way the author has judged the English character and
society. Quotes from Letter 5 and judges "there is a degree of
smartness and some humour in this writer, that would induce us to
think he might do better."

1810.2   ANON. "Retrospective Review. Article 27. <u>The</u> <u>Algerine</u>
          <u>Captive</u>." <u>Monthly</u> <u>Anthology</u> <u>and</u> <u>Boston</u> <u>Review</u> 9
          (November):344–47.
              It is unfortunate that this novel is "hastening to obliv-
ion," for it contains "an admirable picture of the manners of the
interiour of New England," and Yankee shrewdness and simplicity. The
second volume is inferior to the first. It contains a reprehensible
chapter in which the Mollah gets the best of an argument with a
Christian and contains invectives against classical learning.

1822.1   COOPER, JAMES FENIMORE. Review of <u>A</u> <u>New</u> <u>England</u> <u>Tale</u>, by
          Maria Sedgewick. New York <u>Literary</u> <u>and</u> <u>Scientific</u> <u>Reposi-</u>
          <u>tory</u> <u>and</u> <u>Critical</u> <u>Review</u> 4 (May):336.
              <u>The</u> <u>Algerine</u> <u>Captive</u> is a forgotten and perhaps lost
narrative. Tyler should be placed among "the memorials of . . . the
early and authentic historians of the country." Reprinted: 1955.1.

1824.1   ANON. Review of <u>The</u> <u>Algerine</u> <u>Captive</u>. New York <u>Minerva;</u>
          <u>or</u> <u>Literary,</u> <u>Entertaining,</u> <u>and</u> <u>Scientific</u> <u>Journal</u> 1
          (August):331–33.
              Laments that the novel had only one edition. Quotes
extensively from the novel and finds it "admirable writing." Hopes
the book will be revived.

1850.1   BUCKINGHAM, JOSEPH T.   Specimens of Newspaper Literature:
          With Personal Memoirs, Anecdotes, and Reminiscences.
          Vol. 2.   Boston: Charles C. Little & James Brown,
          pp. 202–210.
               The Algerine Captive was popular in its day, "but is now
          entirely out of the market."

1855.1   DUYCKINCK, EVERT A., and GEORGE L. DUYCKINCK.   Cyclopaedia
          of American Literature: Embracing Personal and Critical
          Notices of Authors, and Selections from Their Writings.
          From the Earliest Period to the Present Day.   Vol. 1.
          New York: Charles Scribner, pp. 415–17.
               The Algerine Captive is written with "spirit and neatness
          of style."   The novel is unjustifiably neglected and is, despite two
          editions, now scarce.   Its ingenious thought and descriptions of
          manners deserve a larger audience than it has today.   Includes a
          selection from The Algerine Captive.   Reprinted: 1975.1.

*1859.1   UNDERHILL, JOHN.   "Letters of Captain John Underhill."
          Knickerbocker Magazine 38:426.
               Unlocated.   Cited in Frost, 1932.2.

1876.1   LATHROP, G.P.   "Early American Novelists."   Atlantic Monthly
          37 (April):404–5.
               Criticizes The Algerine Captive as a failed novel; finds
          it merely generalized sketches.

1878.1   HART, JOHN S.   A Manual of American Literature.   Philadel-
          phia: Eldredge & Brother, p. 116.
               Brief mention of Tyler.

1880.1   BURNHAM, HENRY.   Brattleboro, Windham County, Vermont.
          Edited by Abby Maria Hemenway.   Brattleboro: D. Leonard,
          pp. 86–104.
               Biography.

1887.1   BEERS, HENRY.   An Outline Sketch of American Literature.
          New York: Chautauqua Press, p. 79.
               The Algerine Captive is "a rambling tale of adventure,
          constructed somewhat upon the plan of Smollett's novels."

1889.1   ANON.   "Tyler, Royall."   In Appleton's Cyclopaedia of Amer-
          ican Biography.   Edited by James Grant Wilson and John
          Fiske.   Vol. 6.   New York: D. Appleton & Co., p. 201.
               Biography and brief description of Tyler's works.

1890.1   FLETCHER, W.J.   "An Early Call for 'the American Novel.'"
          Critic 16 (February):83.
               Quotes from the preface to The Algerine Captive to show
          the early demand for an American novel.

1896.1   BENT, S. ARTHUR.   "Damon and Pythias Among Our Early Jour-
         nalists." New England Magazine 20 (August):666-75.
             In a description of members of the Literary Club of
Walpole, of which Tyler was a member, briefly describes scenes from
The Algerine Captive.

1898.1   HERRINGSHAW, THOMAS WILLIAM. Herringshaw's Encyclopedia of
         American Biography of the Nineteenth Century. Chicago:
         American Publishers Association, p. 950.
             Brief biography.

1901.1   BRONSON, WALTER COCHRANE. A Short History of American Lit-
         erature. Boston: D.C. Heath, p. 93.
             Brief mention of Tyler.

1903.1   TRENT, WILLIAM PETERFIELD. A History of American Literature
         1607-1865. New York: D. Appleton & Co., pp. 205-6.
             Tyler's wholesome purpose in The Algerine Captive was to
furnish "his countrymen with fiction that should deal with American
rather than with foreign life." But, though clever, Tyler was "not
even artist enough to master a simple form of narrative." He deserves remembrance for his attempt and for his descriptive details.

1906.1   OBERHOLTZER, ELLIS PAXTON. The Literary History of Phila-
         delphia. Philadelphia: George W. Jacobs & Co., p. 177.
             Brief mention of Tyler.

1907.1   LOSHE, LILLIE DEMING. The Early American Novel.
         New York: Columbia University Press, p. 25.
             Tyler satirizes New England customs and realistically
describes a slave-ship in The Algerine Captive. He attacks romantic
ideas about slavery. The novel has a clear and correct style.
Reprinted: 1958.2.

1907.2   MARBLE, ANNIE RUSSELL. Heralds of American Literature: A
         Group of Patriot Writers of the Revolutionary and National
         Periods. Chicago: University of Chicago Press, pp. 281-82.
             Brief mention of Tyler.

1909.1   STANTON, THEODORE, in collaboration with members of the
         faculty of Cornell University. A Manual of American
         Literature. New York and London: G. P. Putnam's Sons,
         Knickerbocker Press, p. 117.
             The Algerine Captive is "a broadly humorous picaresque
tale, of the Smollett type, which introduces rather too many weari-
some details of customs in Algiers." It has, however, a spirited
style and powerful descriptions.

1911.1   BATES, KATHARINE LEE. American Literature. New York:
         Macmillan Co., p. 87.
             The Algerine Captive "smacks of Smollett."

1912.1   CAIRNS, WILLIAM B. A History of American Literature.
         New York: Oxford University Press, pp. 137-38.
              Brief mention of The Algerine Captive as a "story of
piracy and adventure in the form of memoirs interspersed with many
expressions of opinion on political and social topics."

1912.2   VAN DOREN, CARL. The American Novel. New York: Macmillan
         Co., pp. 8-9.
              Finds the value of The Algerine Captive in its fresh,
clear report of facts. Places Tyler's call for a native American
literature in the context of a changing American taste in literature.
Revised edition: 1940.2.

1914.1   METCALF, JOHN CALVIN. American Literature. Atlanta:
         B.F. Johnson Publishing Co., p. 102.
              Brief mention of Tyler.

1915.1   ELLIS, HAROLD MILTON. "Joseph Dennie and his Circle: A
         Study in American Literature from 1792 to 1812." Bulletin
         of the University of Texas, no. 40 (July), p. 125.
              Brief mention of Tyler.

1917.1   VAN DOREN, CARL. "Fiction I: Brown, Cooper." In The
         Cambridge History of American Literature. Edited by
         William Peterfield Trent et al. Vol. 1, Colonial and Revolu-
         tionary Literature. Early National Literature. New York:
         G.P. Putnam's Sons, p. 287.
              The preface to The Algerine Captive has historical impor-
tance. The first volume is entertaining; the second resembles many
contemporary books and pamphlets.

1918.1   BRADSHER, EARL L. "Some Aspects of the Early American
         Novel." Texas Review 3 (April):245.
              The Algerine Captive "furnishes an example of the preach-
ing spirit smothering artistic impulse."

1919.1   BOYNTON, PERCY H. A History of American Literature.
         Boston: Ginn & Co., p. 103.
              Brief mention of Tyler.

1925.2   FREDERICK, TUPPER, and HELEN TYLER BROWN, eds. Grandmother
         Tyler's Book: The Recollections of Mary Palmer Tyler (Mrs.
         Royall Tyler) 1775-1866). New York: G.P. Putnam's Sons,
         326 pp.
              References to Royall Tyler throughout. Includes a
portrait.

1926.1   WILLIAMS, STANLEY THOMAS. "The Era of Washington and
         Jefferson." In The American Spirit in Letters. Pageant
         of America Series, edited by Ralph Henry Gabriel. New Haven:
         Yale University Press, P. 89.

Cites Underhill as an example of the sympathy that exists between the "shin-kicking sailor of Smollett and the rough-and-ready American of 1800."

1927.1 McDOWELL, TREMAINE. "Sensibility in the Eighteenth-Century American Novel." SP 24 (July):395.
Notes that The Algerine Captive quotes "The Seasons" with approval, indicative of British influence on American literature. In a discussion of the application of sensibility to social ends, cites Tyler's demonstration of the inhumanity of slavery.

1928.1 TUPPER, FREDERICK. "Royall Tyler: Man of Law and Man of Letters." Proceedings of the Vermont Historical Society, 7 July, p. 83-89.
Biography and summary of the plot of Tyler's novel.
Notes its review in the Monthly review (1803.2).

1930.1 FOSTER, RICHARD ALLEN. The School in American Literature. Boston: Warwick & York, pp. 81-84.
The Algerine Captive demonstrates sympathy with the hard lot of the school master. Tyler reacts against rural teaching and the curriculum emphatically.

1931.1 ANGOFF, CHARLES. A Literary History of the American People. Vol. 2. New York: Alfred A. Knopf, p. 316.
Quotes from the preface to The Algerine Captive.

1932.1 CHAPMAN, BERTRAND WILLIAM. "The Nativism of Royall Tyler." Master's Thesis, University of Vermont, pp. 19-47.
The Algerine Captive shows the author's interest in American life and his satire. The first part of the novel lacks a defined objective, complications and suspense, but it does have "vitality and ruggedness" indigenous to the period. The book is indebted to Smollett only in a limited way. Tyler borrowed the history of Captain John Underhill from Belknap's History of New Hampshire. There is no link between Tyler and the Underhill family, as some have suggested.
Omits discussion of the second section of the book because it has no bearing on the nativism of Tyler.

1932.2 FROST, JOSEPHINE. Underhill Genealogy: Descendants of Capt. John Underhill. Vol. 2. Boston: Privately printed by Myron C. Taylor in the interests of the Underhill Society of America, pp. 43-50.
Prints a genealogical chart of unknown origin showing Updike Underhill as a descendant of Benoni Underhill, but can authenticate no one on the chart. Quotes letters from members of the real Underhill family telling the unauthenticated history of the ancestors of Updike Underhill, but also quotes a letter from a twentieth-century descendant of Royall Tyler attesting to the fiction of Updike Underhill.

1932.3   FULLERTON, BRADFORD M. Selective Bibliography of American
          Literature 1775–1900: A Brief Survey of the More Important
          Authors and a Description of Their Works. New York:
          William Farquhar Payson, pp. 281–82.
               Calls The Algerine Captive realistic.

1932.4   TUPPER, FREDERICK. "Royall Tyler." In Vermonters: A Book
          of Biographies. Edited by Walter H. Crockett. Brattleboro:
          Stephen Daye Press, pp. 224–27.
               Biography of Tyler and a brief reference to the inter-
          national reputation of The Algerine Captive.

1935.1   BENSON, MARY SUMNER. Women in Eighteenth-Century America:
          A Study of Opinion and Social Usage. New York: Columbia
          University Press, p. 193.
               Brief mention of Tyler.

1935.3   PATTEE, FRED LEWIS. The First Century of American Litera-
          ture 1770–1870. New York and London: D. Appleton-Century,
          pp. 90, 185, 188.
               Quotes from the preface to The Algerine Captive.

1935.4   WINTERICH, JOHN TRACEY. Early American Books and Printing.
          Boston: Houghton Mifflin Co., p. 157.
               Brief mention of Tyler.

1936.1   ANON. "The Royall Tyler Collection." Proceedings of the
          Vermont Historical Society, n.s. 4 (March):3–4.
               Brief description of the Tyler collection.

1936.2   BOYNTON, PERCY H. Literature and American Life. Boston:
          Ginn & Co., pp. 193–94.
               Brief mention of Tyler.

1936.3   FLORY, CLAUDE REHERD. "Economic Criticism in American Fic-
          tion, 1792 to 1900." Ph.D. Dissertation, University of
          Pennsylvania, pp. 41, 105, 200.
               Tyler's Algerine Captive was critical of slavery and
          satirized speculation in land.

1936.4   QUINN, ARTHUR HOBSON. American Fiction: An Historical
          and Critical Survey. New York: Appleton-Century Crofts,
          pp. 12–13.
               Summarizes Algerine Captive and notes Tyler's reference
          to the increase in novel reading.

1936.5   _____. "Royall Tyler." In Dictionary of American
          Biography. Edited by Dumas Malone. Vol. 19. New York:
          Charles Scribner's Sons, pp. 95–97.
               Biography and brief mention of Tyler's Algerine Captive.

1937.1   ROBERTS W.   "The Algerine Captive, 1802."   N&Q 172
         (17 April):282.
              Expresses doubt that the author is the narrator of this
adventure story. Believes the author was American. See 1937.2.

1937.2   MATTHEWS, ALBERT.   "The Algerine Captive, 1802."   N&Q 172
         (22 May):374.
              In reply to 1937.1, states that the author was Royall
Tyler.

1937.3   FORSYTHE, ROBERT S.   "The Algerine Captive, 1802."   N&Q 172
         (29 May):389-90.
              Describes the two parts of the novel. Notes Tyler's
attack on Paine and the patriotic moral. Notes the contemporary
events which probably inspired the book.

1938.1   KUNITZ, STANLEY J., and HOWARD HAYCRAFT. American Authors
         1600-1900. New York: H.W. Wilson Co., pp. 766-67.
              Biography and bibliography of primary and secondary
works.

1940.1   BROWN, HERBERT ROSS. The Sentimental Novel in America 1789-
         1860. Durham: Duke University Press, pp. 15-16, 18-19,
         145, 146, 147, 163.
              Quotes from the preface to Tyler's novel and notes
Tyler's aversion to slavery.

1940.2   VAN DOREN, CARL. The American Novel 1789-1939. Rev. and
         enl. ed. New York: Macmillan Co., pp. 8-9.
              Slight changes in wording from 1912.2.

1943.1   BURKE, WILLIAM J., and WILL D. HOWE. American Authors
         and Books, 1640-1940. New York: Gramercy Publishing Co.,
         p. 771.
              Bibliography of primary and secondary works.

*1943.2 ENGELHART, CARL W. "An Historical and Critical Study of
         Royall Tyler." Master's thesis, University of Minnesota.
              Cited in RT1979.3.

1944.1   BROOKS, VAN WYCK. The World of Washington Irving. New
         York: E.P. Dutton & Co., p. 61.
              Brief mention of Tyler.

1948.1   COWIE, ALEXANDER. The Rise of the American Novel. New
         York: American Book Co., pp. 60-68.
              Describes Tyler's novel in detail. Notes the change from
gaiety to seriousness between the first and second parts, and finds
literary value in the first part. Points out the objects of Tyler's
satire but notes Underhill's patriotism. Concludes that the book has
been unjustifiably neglected, but it is not as significant as others
of the early period.

1948.2   SPILLER, ROBERT E., WILLARD THORP, THOMAS H. JOHNSON,
          HENRY SEIDEL CANBY, HOWARD MUMFORD JONES, DIXON WECTER, and
          STANLEY T. WILLIAMS, eds. "Fiction." In Literary History
          of the United States. Vol. 3. New York: Macmillan Co.,
          p. 49.
             Brief mention of The Algerine Captive as one of the
     earliest works to treat a foreign theme.

1950.1   HART, JAMES D. The Popular Book: A History of America's
          Literary Taste. New York: Oxford University Press, p. 53.
             Brief mention of the preface to The Algerine Captive.

1952.1   WAGENKNECHT, EDWARD. Cavalcade of the American Novel:
          From the Birth of the Nation to the Middle of the Twentieth
          Century. New York: Henry Holt & Co., p. 8.
             Tyler's novel is a readable book full of various kinds of
     satire.

1955.1   COOPER, JAMES FENIMORE. "A New England Tale; or Sketches of
          New-England. Characters and Manners." In Early Critical
          Essays. Edited by James F. Beard, Jr. Gainesville:
          Scholars' Facsimiles & Reprints, pp. 97-132.
             Reprint of 1822.1.

1956.1   HART, JAMES D. The Oxford Companion to American Literature.
          3d ed. New York: Oxford University Press, p. 781-82.
             Biography and mention of Tyler's works.

1957.1   JONES, CLAUDE E., ed. Introduction to "Prefaces to Three
          Eighteenth-Century Novels (1708-1751-1797)." Augustan
          Reprint Society Publication, no. 64. Los Angeles:
          University of California, p. iv.
             In The Algerine Captive Tyler is a crusader for patriot-
     ism and realism. The preface and dedication may well be the most
     significant parts of the book.

1958.1   CHANDLER, FRANK WADLEIGH. The Literature of Roguery.
          Edited by William Allan Neilson. Vol. 2. Types of English
          Literature. New York: Burt Franklin, pp. 405-6.
             The Algerine Captive is the only early American fiction
     which can be said to transplant the rogue tradition.

1958.2   LOSHE, LILLIE DEMING. The Early American Novel 1789-1830.
          New York: Frederick Ungar Publishing Co., p. 25.
             Reprint of 1907.1.

1959.1   CHARVAT, WILLIAM. The Origins of American Critical Thought,
          1810-1835. Philadelphia: University of Pennsylvania Press,
          p. 141.
             Quotes Tyler's preface to The Algerine Captive but finds
     that his portrait of New England manners did not go far, as his scene
     shifted from New England to Algiers.

1960.1   HOWARD, LEON. Literature and the American Tradition.
          Garden City: Doubleday & Co., p. 82.
              Brief mention of Tyler.

1960.2   JONES, JOSEPH, E. MARCHAND, H.D. PIPER, J.A. ROBBINS, and
          H.E. SPIVEY, comps. American Literary Manuscripts: A
          Checklist of Holdings in Academic, Historical and Public
          Libraries in the United States. Compiled and published
          under the auspices of the American Literature group of the
          Modern Language Association. Austin: University of Texas
          Press.
              Lists holdings in twelve locations.

1961.1   GERSTENBERGER, DONNA, and GEORGE HENDRICK. The American
          Novel 1789-1959: A Checklist of Twentieth-Century Criticism.
          Denver: Alan Swallow, p. 342.
              Lists two secondary sources.

1962.1   HERZBERG, MAX J., and the staff of the Thomas Y. Crowell Co.
          The Reader's Encyclopedia of American Literature. New York:
          Thomas Y. Crowell Co., p. 1165.
              Biography and brief mention of The Algerine Captive.

1965.1   TANSELLE, G. THOMAS. "Early American Fiction in New
          England: The Case of The Algerine Captive." PBSA 59
          (October-December):367-84.
              Describes the English publication of The Algerine Captive
and finds its "American traces" were left intact but some changes
were made. Surveys the textual history of the novel.

1966.1   _____. "Some Uncollected Authors XLII: Royall Tyler, 1757-
          1826." BC 15 (Autumn):303-320.
              Notes the neglect of Tyler and the rarity of early edi-
tions of his works. Includes a check list of primary works.

1967.1   MOORE, JACK B., ed. Introduction to The Algerine Captive.
          Gainesville: Scholars' Facsimile & Reprints. Pp. v-xviii.
              Praises the novel for its stylistic purity and clarity.
Finds the only early novel comparable to Tyler in its rational per-
ception is Modern Chivalry by Hugh Henry Brackenridge. Describes the
form of the novel and finds the book highly interesting if partially
flawed.

1967.2   TANSELLE, G. THOMAS. Royall Tyler. Cambridge, Mass.:
          Harvard University Press, pp. 140-80.
              Notes possible sources for The Algerine Captive and
describes the novel's reception and its various editions. Distin-
guishes Tyler's prefaces from others at the time. Evaluates the
social and patriotic purposes and describes the objects of satire.
Evaluates the structure and plot. Praises Tyler's skillful handling

of language, especially his use of irony. Finds the individual
sketches most effective.

1968.1   KETTLER, ROBERT RONALD. "The Eighteenth-Century American
         Novel: The Beginning of a Fictional Tradition." Ph.D.
         Dissertation, Purdue University, pp. 89, 165.
              Discusses The Algerine Captive as a picaresque novel,
though it departs from the traditional picaresque form by being
didactic and by giving its hero a detailed background.

1968.2   WAGER, WILLIS. American Literature: A World View. New
         York: New York University Press, p. 52.
              Brief mention of Tyler.

1969.1   WRIGHT, LYLE H. American Fiction, 1774-1850: A Contri-
         bution toward a Bibliography. 2d rev. ed. San Marino:
         Huntington Library, p. 285.
              Lists editions of The Algerine Captive and their
locations.

1970.1   COOK, DON L., ed. Introduction to The Algerine Captive.
         New Haven: College & University Press, pp. 7-23.
              Tyler's novel should be better known, for it has wit,
vitality, and variety.
              Briefly surveys Tyler's critical reception, noting that
few have observed the satiric element in the preface of the novel.
Places the novel in the context of contemporary travel literature,
literature about Algeria, humorous literature, and biographical
literature.

1970.2   GERSTENBERGER, DONNA, and GEORGE HENDRICK. The American
         Novel: A Checklist of Twentieth-Century Criticism on Novels
         Written since 1789. Vol. 2, Criticism Written 1960-
         1968. Chicago: Swallow Press, p. 349.
              Bibliography of secondary works.

1970.3   NYE, RUSSEL B. American Literary History: 1607-1830. New
         York: Alfred A. Knopf, pp. 179, 239.
              Brief mention of Tyler.

1971.1   PETTER, HENRI. The Early American Novel. Columbus: Ohio
         State University Press, pp. 295-98.
              Compares Updike Underhill to Brackenridge's Captain
Farrago. Finds the satire the strongest element.

1972.1   DENNIS, LARRY ROBERT. "Self-Definition and the Persona:
         The Early American 'Satiric Novel of Adventure.'" DAI
         33:304-5A.
              Tyler is one of several early American authors discussed
in this analysis of the first-person persona as a tactic for American
self-definition. Tyler's pretenses to history and the travel book

illustrate his frustration with the given forms. He eschewed the
stereotyped plots of his contemporaries but had no clear-cut
alternative.

1972.2   GRIFFIN, MARY NELL. "Coming to Manhood in America: A Study
          of Significant Initiation Novels, 1797-1970." DAI 32:3951A.
          An attempt to define and trace the development of the
initiation novel in America. Tyler's The Algerine Captive appeared
at almost the same time as Goethe's Wilhelm Meister and is an example
of the apprentice novel, one of two forms of the initiation novel.

1972.3   PELADEAU, MARIUS B. The Prose of Royall Tyler. Burlington:
          Vermont Historical Society & Charles E. Tuttle Co., pp. 11-
          16, 21-40.
          Biography, placing Tyler's life and works in the context
of the period.
          Explains the relation between The Algerine Captive and
"The Bay Boy." Reviews the contemporary reception of The Algerine
Captive and Tyler's reactions. Describes the surviving manuscript.
Describes sources for the characters and the sociological importance
of Tyler's satire.

1972.4   WARNER, STEPHEN DOUGLAS. "Representative Studies in the
          Picaresque: Investigations of Modern Chivalry, Adventures
          of Huckleberry Finn, and The Adventures of Augie March."
          DAI 32:4582A.
          The final chapter briefly considers the "significant
indebtedness to the picaresque" in The Algerine Captive and other
works.

1974.1   DENNIS, LARRY R. "Legitimizing the Novel: Royall Tyler's
          The Algerine Captive." EAL 9 (Spring):71-80.
          Tyler attempted to legitimize the novel form by replacing
sentimentalism with tough-minded realism, but he undermined that
realism in part with his nationalism and uncritical acceptance of
American public figures.

1974.2   STEIN, ROGER B. "Pulled Out of the Bay: America's Fiction
          in the Eighteenth Century. SAF 2 (Spring):17.
          The sea chapters in The Algerine Captive serve as transi-
tion between the American adventures and the Algerine captivity.
They transform the protagonist into a more complex character.

1974.3   TANSELLE, G. THOMAS. "The Editing of Royall Tyler." EAL 9
          (Spring):83-95.
          A review essay on The Prose of Royall Tyler, edited by
Marius B. Peladeau (1972.3). Objects to Peladeau's procedures and
finds errors and problems with the edition.

1974.4   TILLINGHAST, CHARLES ALLEN. "The Early American Novel: A
          Critical Revalutation." Ph.D. Dissertation, Syracuse Uni-
          versity, pp. 55-62, 93-94, 113-31.

Examines Updike Underhill as an American hero; examines
The Algerine Captive as one of many early novels which promoted
America; and examines the novel as part of the early American "im-
pulse toward realism."

1975.1   DUYCKINCK, EVERT A., and GEORGE L. DUYCKINCK. Cyclopaedia
         of American Literature: Embracing Personal and Critical
         Notices of Authors, and Selections from Their Writings.
         From the Earliest Period to the Present Day. Vol. 1.
         Detroit: Gale Research Co., pp. 415-17.
         Reprint of 1855.1.

1976.1   CARSON, HERBERT L., and ADA LOU CARSON. "The Jews, Royall
         Tyler and America's Divided Mind." American Jewish Archives
         28 (April):79-84.
         The Algerine Captive depicts the first Jewish characters
in American fiction. Tyler's attitude depicts the divided opinion of
his time; Adoneh Ben Benjamin is portrayed with a kindly attitude,
and his son is portrayed as deceptive.

1976.2   DAVIDSON, CATHY N. and ARNOLD E. DAVIDSON. "Royall Tyler's
         The Algerine Captive: A Study in Contrasts." Ariel 7
         (July):53-67.
         "Discusses the satirical method of The Algerine Captive,
especially the periodic bildungsroman and Updike Underhill's development as an American hero, an emblem for the uncertain progress of
the nation after the Revolution." [Annotation by Cathy N. Davidson.]

1976.3   KAY, DONALD, and CAROL McGINNIS KAY. "American Satire in
         the Early National Period, 1791-1830." BB 33 (January):
         19-23.
         A bibliography of primary materials and secondary sources
including biographies, general works, and articles.

1977.1   ROBBINS, J. ALBERT et al., comps. American Literary Manu-
         scripts: A Checklist of Holdings In Academic, Historical,
         and Public Libraries, Museums, and Authors' Homes in the
         United States. 2d ed. Athens: University of Georgia
         Press, p. 326.
         Lists holdings in twenty-three libraries.

1977.2   SPENGEMANN, WILLIAM C. The Adventurous Muse: The Poetics
         of American Fiction. New Haven: Yale University Press,
         pp. 119-38.
         A study of the complex interrelations among New World
travel writing, European literature, and romantic aesthetics and
their effect on American fiction. Finds that Tyler does not fall
within a recognizable tradition. Tyler apparently meant to write
a novel of manners but found his hero's travels more interesting.
Examines Underhill's disapproval of New England society and his

foreign adventures and concludes that in the end the book does become a conventional domestic novel of adventure.

1979.1   CARSON, ADA LOU, and HERBERT L. CARSON. Royall Tyler.
          Twayne United States Authors Series. Boston: Twayne
          Publishers, 172 pp.
              Surveys Tyler's life and works and critically analyzes
the major works. Chapter four compares The Algerine Captive to its
uncompleted revision, "The Bay Boy." Gives background of the novel,
a plot summary, commentary on the novel, and a summary of critical
reactions. Includes a bibliography of primary and secondary sources.

1979.4   WHARTON, DONALD P. In the Trough of the Sea: Selected
          American Sea-Deliverance Narratives, 1610-1766. Contri-
          butions in American Studies, no. 44. Westport, Conn.:
          Greenwood Press, p. 24.
              Brief mention of Tyler.

XXVIII. Helena Wells (fl. 1798-1809)

1798.1   ANON. "Novels and Romances." London Monthly Magazine or
          British Register, supplement 6:517.
          "The Step-Mother is a tale of some merit."

1798.2   ANON. Review of The Step-Mother. Analytical Review; or,
          History of Literature, Domestic and Foreign (London) 28
          (September):298.
               This is "a novel of the second class, possessing consid-
erable merit, which cannot fail, if perused with attention, to interest and improve the reader."

1798.3   ANON. Review of The Step-Mother. British Critic, and
          Quarterly Theological Reivew (London) 12 (July):74.
               The novel may not have fine writing or "ingenious con-
trivance," but at least it is not offensive to good morals or
manners.

1798.4   ANON. Review of The Step-Mother. Critical Review; or
          Annals of Literature (London), n.s. 24 (October):237.
               "There is much merit in these volumes; but it is inju-
dicious to give the history of two generations in the same work.
Each volume now comprehends a different story."

1798.5   ANON. Review of The Step-Mother. Gentleman's Magazine and
          Historical Chronicle (London) 68 (June):516.
               Finds the book bare of incident but diffused with moral
sentiments and safe for "young persons." Regrets that Miss
Williams's disinterested conduct and rigid sense of honor did
not bring greater happiness to herself and her friends.

1798.6   ANON. Review of The Step-Mother. Monthly Review; or
          Literary Journal Enlarged (London) 26 (August):459.
               Finds the incidents natural but not very interesting. At
least the book will not endanger virtue, corrupt the heart or mislead
the imagination.

1799.1   ANON. Review of The Step-Mother. Anti-Jacobin Review and
          Magazine (London) 3 (August):421-22.
               Approves of Wells's aim. Finds the novel "plain and
unaffected in its language, natural in its construction, and moral
in its tendency." Sees a parallel between this novel and Sidney
Biddulph by Mrs. Sheridan.

1800.1   ANON. Review of Constantia Neville. British Critic and
          Quarterly Theological Review (London) 15 (June):676-77.
               Praises the novel's principles and moral but finds
"no extraordinary ingenuity of contrivance, or superior powers of
imagination." Finds "the imputation against the Queen of France . . .

somewhat precipitate, and the work seems spun out to three
volumes. . . ."

1800.2   ANON. Review of Constantia Neville. Critical Review; or,
         Annals of Literature (London) 29 (August):472.
         "The incidents are sufficiently numerous; probability is
rarely violated; the plot is not ill-conducted; and the morality is
unexceptionable. . . . The style is easy and perspicuous, but frequently inaccurate. . . . Upon the whole, the work may be read both
with pleasure and profit."

1800.3   ANON. Review of Constantia Neville. Gentleman's Magazine
         and Historical Chronicle (London) 70 (July):663.
         " . . . the story is natural and interesting, and is
evidently the result of great attention to the modes and customs of
the world, particularly to commercial concerns."

1800.4   ANON. Review of Constantia Neville. Monthly Catalogue
         (London), July, p. 84.
         Approves of the morality, the interest, and the language,
but finds fault with the characterization.

1800.5   ANON. Review of Constantia Neville. Monthly Mirror;
         Reflecting Men and Manners, with Strictures on their Epi-
         tome, the Stage (London) 10 (August):95.
         Finds the characters and incidents "in general, natural
and probable," and the style agreeable.

1800.6   ANON. Review of Constantia Neville. Monthly Review; or,
         Literary Journal (London), n.s. 33 (October):206.
         Reprimands the author for her intolerance toward West
Indians and for expressing unnecessary political opinions. Finds the
incidents real and the language "easy and natural," but neither the
sentiments nor the characters excite admiration.

1800.7   ANON. Review of Constantia Neville. Monthly Visitor and
         Entertaining Pocket Companion (London) 10:193-202.
         "The story is natural, the style pleasing, and the design
perfectly unexceptionable."

1801.1   ANON. Review of Constantia Neville. Anti-Jacobin Review
         and Protestant Advocate; or Monthly Political and Literary
         Censor (London) 8 (January):60.
         Notes the public approval of the book and recommends it
for purity, sound principles, piety, and humility.

*1801.2 ANON. Review of Constantia Neville. Annals of Philosophy,
         Natural History, Chemistry, Literature, Agriculture, and the
         Mechanical and Fine Arts (London) 1:283.
         Cited in 1979.1.

1854.1   ALLIBONE, S. AUSTIN. A Critical Dictionary of English
          Literature and British and American Authors Living and
          Deceased from the Earliest Accounts to the Latter Half of
          the Nineteenth Century. Vol. 3. Philadelphia: Childs &
          Peterson, p. 2642.
              Brief entry, listing Wells's publication.

1907.1   LOSHE, LILLIE DEMING. The Early American Novel.
          New York: Columbia University Press, p. 15.
              Quotes Wells's aim, as stated in the preface to The Step-
Mother and notes that both her novels went into second editions.
Reprinted: 1958.1.

1936.1   QUINN, ARTHUR HOBSON. American Fiction: An Historical
          and Critical Survey. New York and London: Appleton-Century
          Co., p. 22.
              The Step-Mother is "painfully moral" but "not bad
reading."

1940.1   BROWN, HERBERT ROSS. The Sentimental Novel in America 1789-
          1860. Durham: Duke University Press, passim.
              Wells's novels approved of man as "lord and master" and
disapproved of Sterne's affair with Eliza. Wells had a Wordsworthian
view of nature and idealized Indians.

1941.1   HART, JAMES D. The Oxford Companion to American Literature.
          1st ed. New York: Oxford University Press, p. 813.
              Identifies Wells as a Loyalist writer of two sentimental
novels.

1957.1   STIMSON, FREDERICK S. "Spanish Inspiration in the First
          American Adventure Stories." Hispania 40 (March):66.
              Constantia Neville included a brief episode in Puerto
Rico.

1958.1   LOSHE, LILLIE DEMING. The Early American Novel 1789-1830.
          New York: Frederick Ungar Publishing Co., p. 15.
              Reprint of 1907.1

1971.1   PETTER, HENRI. The Early American Novel. Columbus: Ohio
          State University Press, pp. 169, 236-37.
              Describes The Step-Mother as a poor book, with un-
satisfactory characterization, weak structure and a dull style.
Constantia Neville is a didactic novel with an implausible plot
and an independent heroine.

1975.1   PONICK, FRANCES M. "Helena Wells and Her Family: Loyalist
          Writers and Printers of Colonial Charleston." Master's
          Thesis, University of South Carolina, 90 pp.
              Describes the Wells's family and business. Outlines what
is known of Helena Wells's life and describes her works. Quotes from

contemporary reviews. Criticizes the lack of conflict in Wells's
fiction.

1979.1   MOLTKE-HANSEN, DAVID. "A World Introduced: The Writing of
          Helena Wells of Charles Town, South Carolina's First Novel-
          ist." In South Carolina Women Writers. Spartanburg:
          Reprint Co., pp. 61-81.
               The most detailed biography to date. Criticizes Wells's
didacticism, flat characterization, and dullness, but finds the
novels biographically and historically significant. Presents
observations drawn from the novels about roles of women and children,
the world of middle-class gentility, and attitudes toward slavery.
Notes that the novels record Wells's impressions and analyze the
social, economic, and psychological pressures on women.

1982.1   DAVIDSON, CATHY N. "Flirting with Destiny: Ambivalence and
          Form in the Early American Sentimental Novel." SAF 10
          (Spring):17-39.
               Cites Constantia Neville as an example of the way some
American novelists concurred with Dr. Gregory's view of woman as
submissive helpmate.

XXIX. William Williams (1727-1791)

1816.1   ANON. Review of The Journal of Llewellyn Penrose, a Seaman.
         Eclectic Review (London), n.s. 5:396-98.
              Questions the authenticity of the book, and concludes
that internal evidence proves its truth. But external evidence shows
discrepancies about the manuscript and leads one to believe the book
is but a story. Recommends the novel "to every juvenile library."

1855.1   [EAGLES, JOHN.] "The Beggar's Legacy." Blackwood's
         Magazine (Edinburgh) 77 (March):251-72.
              Recounts the story of Williams's begging a place to die.
Includes a description of his self-portrait and the story of the
Penrose manuscript left as a legacy to the artist's benefactor.

1907.1   HUTTON, STANLEY [Albert Edward Tilling]. Bristol and Its
         Famous Associations. Bristol and London: n.p., p. 190.
              An account of the way the manuscript of The Journal of
Llewellyn Penrose came to be in Bristol. Records Byron's reaction to
the book: "I never read so much of a book at one sitting in my life.
He kept me up half the night, and made me dream the other half. It
has all the air of truth, and is most entertaining and interesting in
every point of view."

1969.1   DICKASON, DAVID HOWARD, ed. Introduction to Mr. Penrose.
         The Journal of Penrose, Seaman, by William Williams.
         Bloomington: Indiana University Press, pp. 3-33.
              Biography showing parallels between Williams's life and
that of his hero. Describes the history of the manuscript and indicates Thomas Eagles's revisions. Places Penrose in the genre of
travel narrative. Describes the stylistic devices and discusses
Williams's acceptance of life and his gentle piety. Shows Williams
to have been ahead of his times in themes, attitudes, and use of
speech peculiarities, as well as in his sympathetic views of Indians
and slaves.

*1970.1 MATSUMURA, SHOKA. "Mr. Penrose--America Saisho no
         Shosetsu." Eigo S 116:519.
              Cited in 1971 MLA International Bibliography of Books and
Articles on the Modern Languages and Literatures, comp. Harrison T.
Meserole (New York: Modern Languages Association, 1973), p. 121.

1971.1   PETTER, HENRI. The Early American Novel. Columbus: Ohio
         State University Press, pp. 291-94.
              Praises the simple narrative of Penrose and compares it
to Robinson Crusoe.

1974.1   STEIN, ROGER B. "Pulled Out of the Bay: American Fiction
         in the Eighteenth century." SAF 2 (Spring):13-36.

Williams's hero takes to the sea despite his mother's protestations, wrenching social bonds. This typifies the eighteenth-century view of the sea as disordered. In Penrose the sea images the disorder of the mind and leads to the disorder without, in a series of brutal encounters. In form, the book falls between the religious literature of the seventeenth century and the romantic works of the nineteenth.

1979.1   WHARTON, DONALD P. In the Trough of the Sea: Selected American Sea-Deliverance Narratives, 1610-1766. Contributions in American Studies, no. 44. Wetport, Conn.: Greenwood Press, p. 24.
         Brief mention of Williams.

1980.1   DAUBER, KENNETH. "American Culture as Genre." Criticism 22:104.
         Penrose and Charlotte Temple are similar in that both "have claims to" England and America.

XXX. Sarah Wood (1759-1855)

1854.1   ALLIBONE, S. AUSTIN. A Critical Dictionary of English
          Literature and British and American Authors Living and
          Deceased from the Earliest Accounts to the Latter Half of
          the Nineteenth Century. Vol. 3. Philadelphia: Childs &
          Peterson, p. 2822.
              Brief entry, listing Wood's novels.

1890.1   GOOLD, WILLIAM. "Madam Wood, The First Maine Writer of
          Fiction." Collections and Proceedings of the Maine
          Historical Society, 2d ser. 1:401-8.
              Family history and biography. Brief mention of Ferdinand
and Elmira.

1907.1   LOSHE, LILLIE DEMING. The Early American Novel.
          New York: Columbia University Press, pp. 52-53.
              Wood had a fondness for placing her tales in Europe.
Julia and the Illuminated Baron expresses Wood's dislike of "female
politicians." Dorval has become practically inaccessible. Her later
three books "are of no particular interest." Reprinted: 1958.1.

1909.1   STANTON, THEODORE, in collaboration with members of the
          faculty of Cornell University. A Manual of American
          Literature. New York and London: G. P. Putnam's Sons,
          Knickerbocker Press, p. 121.
              Julia recalls the mysterious evil power and aesthetic
tendencies attributed to the Bavarian order of the Illuminati. Brief
mention of Wood's other novels.

1920.1   DUNNACK, HENRY E. The Maine Book. Augusta: Privately
          printed, p. 140.
              Brief biography of "Madam Wood." Quotes from the preface to
Dorval and summarizes the plot of Ferdinand and Elmira and two
stories in "Tales of the Night."

1925.1   COAD, ORAL SUMNER. "The Gothic Element in American Litera-
          ture Before 1835." JEGP 24:82.
              Wood's Julia is set in France. "Its one scene of horror
is in the Radcliffe manner."

1927.1   McDOWELL, TREMAINE. "Sensibility in the Eighteenth-Century
          American Novel." SP 24 (July):393.
              In a discussion of the sources for Americans' use of
sensibility, notes that The Illuminated Baron described Rousseau's
"pen of fire," but expressed distrust of French republicanism.

1936.1   ELLIS, MILTON. "Sarah Saywood Barrell Keating Wood." In
          Dictionary of American Biography. Edited by Dumas Malone.
          Vol. 20. New York: Charles Scribner's Sons, pp. 472-73.

Biography. Notes that Julia is "perhaps the most thor-
oughgoing example in American literature of the Gothic romance of the
Radcliffe type."

1936.2   QUINN, ARTHUR HOBSON. American Fiction: An Historical
         and Critical Survey. New York: D. Appleton-Century Co.,
         pp. 20-21.
            Of all the feminine imitators of Susanna Rowson, Wood was
the nearest approach to a professional novelist. Julia combines the
Gothic romance, the seduction story, and the moral tale. Dorval
attacks the native desire for quick riches with an interesting description of manners and customs. Amelia "traces the tremendous
effect of an irritating paragon on all who know her."

1939.1   REDDEN, Sister MARY MAURITA. The Gothic Fiction in the
         American Magazines (1765-1800). Washington, D.C.: Catholic
         University Press, pp. 47-57.
            Julia uses almost all the standard English Gothic
devices.

1940.1   BROWN, HERBERT ROSS. The Sentimental Novel in America 1789-
         1860. Durham: Duke University Press, passim.
            Wood recommended poetry and philosophy in female educa-
tion as well as philanthropic activity. Her novels praised uncom-
plaining endurance as a wife's destiny and disapproved of second
marriages. Reprinted: 1959.1.

1941.1   HART, JAMES D. The Oxford Companion to American Literature.
         1st ed. New York: Oxford University Press, p. 846.
            Brief description of the theme of Wood's four Gothic
romances.

1948.1   COWIE, ALEXANDER. The Rise of the American Novel. New
         York: American Book Co., pp. 23-26.
            Examines Julia for "points of reference for a study of
the literary taste of the times." Finds the novel alternates between
adventures and analysis of emotions, which makes it difficult for
modern readers.

1948.2   WRIGHT, LYLE H. American Fiction, 1774-1850: A Contri-
         bution toward a Bibliography. Rev. ed. San Marino:
         Huntington Library, p. 299.
            Lists five novels and their locations.

1952.1   WAGENKNECHT, EDWARD. Cavalcade of the American Novel:
         From the Birth of the Nation to the Middle of the Twentieth
         Century. New York: Henry Holt & Co., p. 6.
            Julia is an example of the Gothic element in early Amer-
ican fiction.

1957.1   SPENCER, BENJAMIN. The Quest for Nationality. Syracuse:
          Syracuse University Press, p. 31.
              Sarah Wood is one of several authors who sought "to
portray for American girls manners and sentiments and codes consonant
with the national milieu."

1957.2   STIMSON, FREDERICK S. "Spanish Inspiration in the First
          American Adventure Stories." Hispania 40 (March):66-69.
              Brief mention of Wood's use of a Spanish setting in
Julia, though she included no descriptions or local color.

1958.1   LOSHE, LILLIE DEMING. The Early American Novel 1789-1830.
          New York: Frederick Ungar Publishing Co., pp. 52-53.
          Reprint of 1907.1.

1959.1   BROWN, HERBERT ROSS. The Sentimental Novel in America 1789-
          1860. New York: Pageant Books, passim.
          Reprint of 1940.1.

1968.1   CHARVAT, WILLIAM. The Profession of Authorship in America,
          1800-1870: The Papers of William Charvat. Edited by
          Matthew J. Bruccoli. Columbus: Ohio State University
          Press, p. 24.
              Mrs. Wood is a genuine amateur who wrote for her own
amusement "gaudy mixtures of seduction, bastardy, Gothicism, and
morality, most of them set in Europe, the home of sin."

1971.1   BIRDSALL, RICHARD. "Wood, Sally Sayward Barrell Keating."
          In Notable American Women 1607-1950: A Biographical Dic-
          tionary. Edited by Edward T. James, Janet Wilson James, and
          Paul S. Boyer. Vol. 3. Cambridge, Mass.: Harvard Univer-
          sity Press, Belknap Press, pp. 649-50.
              Biography. Brief description of the themes of her
novels. Notes that her purposes were not artistic; she sought through
her publications to do good. Includes bibliography of biographical
sources.

1971.2   PETTER, HENRI. The Early American Novel. Columbus: Ohio
          State University Press, pp. 310-12, 315-16.
              Describes Julia and Amelia in detail and finds fault with
characterization and style in both.

Indexes

Abbreviations

A	Anonymous
AB	Ann Eliza Bleecker
EB	Ebenezer Bradford
EH	Enos Hitchcock
FH	Francis Hopkinson
G	General
GI	Gilbert Imlay
HB	Hugh Henry Brackenridge
Hd'A	Michel-René Hilliard d'Auberteuil
HF	Hannah Webster Foster
HM	Herman Mann
HS	Henry Sherburne
HW	Helena Wells
IM	Isaac Mitchell
JBe	Jeremy Belknap
JBu	James Butler
JD	John Davis
JM	Joseph Morgan
JSM	Judith Sargent Murray
P	Mrs. Patterson
PF	Philip Freneau
PM	Peter Markoe
RT	Royall Tyler
SHR	Susanna Haswell Rowson
SP	Samuel Peters
SR	Samuel Relf
SW	Sarah Wood
TD	Thomas Atwood Digges
WB	William Hill Brown
WW	William Williams

Name Index

Underscored entry numbers indicate fuller treatment of the subject.

173

Kribbs, Jayne K., JD1974.1
Kuliasha, Frances Hoag, HB1969.3
Kunitz, Stanley J., JB1938.1;
 AB1938.1; HF1938.1;
 PM1938.1; SP1938.1;
 SHR1938.1; RT1938.1

L., M.C., JM1905.2
Lathrop, G.P., G1876.1; RT1876.1
L., M.C., JM1905.2
Lathrop, G.P., G1876.1; RT1876.1
Leary, Lewis, AB1971.1;
 HB1942.1, 1965.1, 1971.2,
 1975.5; PF1941.1, 1942.2;
 Hd'A1958.1
Lee, Elizabeth, SHR1921.1
Leisy, Ernest E., G1936.3;
 AB1929.2; HB1929.1, 1936.3;
 WB1936.2; HF1929.2, 1936.2;
 SHR1929.1, 1936.2
Lemay, Leo, TD1969.1
Lennox, Charlotte Ramsay,
 G1940.3
Lewis, Benjamin B., SHR1957.2
Lewis, W.B., HB1973.1, 1975.4
Lewisohn, Ludwig, SHR1937.2
Lischer, Tracy Kinyon, WB1978.3
Littlefield, Walter, WB1894.2
Locke, Jane, HF1855.1
Long, William J., G1917.1;
 SHR1917.1
Loomis, Emerson Robert,
 FH1961.2
Loshe, Lillie Deming, G1907.2,
 1958.1; A1907.1, 1958.1;
 AB1907.1, 1958.1; HB1907.1,
 1958.1; EB1907.1, 1958.1;
 WB1907.1, 1958.1; JBu1907.1,
 1958.1; JD1907.1, 1958.1;
 HF1907.1, 1958.1; Hd'A1907.1,
 1958.2; EH1907.1, 1958.1;
 GI1907.1, 1958.1; HM1907.1,
 1958.1; IM1907.1, 1958.1;
 SHR1907.1, 1958.1; HS1907.1,
 1958.1; RT1907.1, 1958.2;
 HW1907.1, 1958.1; SW1907.1,
 1958.1
Lossing, Benson J., FH1848.1

M., A, RT1791.1
McAlexander, Patricia Jewell,
 G1975.1; A1975.1; HB1975.6;

 WB1975.4; HF1975.1;
 SHR1975.3
McDowell, Tremaine, G1927.1;
 A1927.1, 1929.1; AB1927.1;
 HB1927.1; WB1927.1, 1933.1;
 JBu1927.1; JD1927.1;
 HF1927.1; EH1927.1; GI1927.1;
 HM1927.1; JSM1927.1;
 SHR1927.1; RT1927.1; WW1927.1
Madison, Charles A., SHR1966.3
Marble, Annie, HB1907.2; WB1907.2;
 FH1902.1, 1907.2; 1931.2;
 SHR1907.2; RT1907.2
Marcow, Jane Belknap, JBe1847.2
Marder, Daniel, HB1967.2, 1970.3
Markoe, Peter, biography,
 PM1933.1, 1938.1, 1944.1;
 bibliography, PM1933.1,
 1943.1, 1944.1
Martin, Terence, G1957.1,
 1961.1; AB1961.1; WB1959.1,
 1961.3; HF1961.1; SHR1961.1
Martin, Wendy, HB1969.4, 1971.1,
 1973.4; SHR1972.1, 1974.3
Matsumura, Shoka, WW1970.1
Matthews, Albert, RT1937.2
Mattfield, Mary, HB1967.3,
 1968.2
Maurice, Arthur Bartlett,
 SHR1901.2, 1969.2
Maynadier, Gustavus Howard,
 G1940.3
Mayo, Lawrence Shaw, JBe1926.1,
 1929.2-3
Melville, Herman, G1980.1
Merren, John, A1978.1
Meserole, Harrison, T., G1977.3
Meserve, Walter J., HB1977.2
Metcalfe, John C., HB1914.1;
 RT1914.1
Middlebrook, Samuel, SP1947.1
Mitchell, Isaac, biography,
 IM1933.1
Moltke-Hansen, David, HW1979.1
Montesser, Frederic, HB1975.7
Moore, Jack Bailey, G1967.5;
 A1962.1, 1964.1, 1966.1, 3,
 1967.1, 1976.1; RT1967.1
Morgan, Joseph, biography,
 JM1947.1, 1951.1
Morton, Sarah, A1976.1;
 WB1931.1

Mott, Frank Luther, HF1947.1;
SHR1947.1
Murray, Judith Sargent,
biography, JSM1881.1, 1882.1,
1931.1, 1934.1, 1971.1

Nance, William L., HB1967.4
Nason, Elias, SHR1870.2
Nelson, John H., FH1925.1
Newlin, Claude, HB1929.2,
1932.3, 1937.1, 1968.3
Nydahl, Joel Mellen, G1975.2
Nye, Russel B., SHR1970.3;
RT1970.3

Oberholtzer, Ellis Paxson,
HB1906.1; FH1906.1; PM1906.1;
SHR1906.1; RT1906.1
Orians, G. Harrison, G1937.1
Osborne, William S., WB1970.2;
HF1970.1

Paine, Gregory, G1945.1;
JBe1945.1; HB1945.1;
WB1945.1; SHR1945.1
Paine, Robert Treat, WB1812.1
Paine, Thomas, G1968.1
Parsons, Lynn Hudson, TD1965.1
Palmer, Ormond E., G1952.1
Papishvily, Helen Waite,
HF1956.2
Parker, Patricia L., SHR1976.1-
2, 1981.1
Parma, V. Valta, FH1930.1
Parrington, Vernon Louis,
HB1927.2
Pattee, Fred Lewis, G1935.1;
HB1902.1; WB1935.2; HF1935.2;
FH1935.1; SHR1935.3;
RT1935.3
Paulding, James Kirke, HB1835.1
Pearce, Roy Harvey, G1965.2;
A1965.1; AB1953.1
Pearson, Edmund, IM1928.1
Peladeau, Marius B., RT1972.3
Pendleton, Emily, WB1931.1
Perotin, Claude, HB1976.4
Peters, John S., SP1814.1
Peters, Samuel, biography,
SP1859.1, 1865.1, 1896.1,
1934.1, 1938.1, 1947.1;

bibliography, SP1934.1,
1938.1, 1962.1
Petter, Henri, G1971.2;
JBe1971.2; AB1971.2;
HB1971.3; EB1971.1; WB1971.2;
JBu1971.1; JD1971.1;
TD1971.1; HF1971.2; PF1971.1;
Hd'A1971.1; EH1971.1;
FH1971.1; GI1971.1;
HM1971.1; PM1971.1; JM1971.1;
JSM1971.2; P1971.1; SP1971.1;
SR1971.1; SHR1971.2;
HS1971.1; RT1971.1; HW1971.1;
WW1971.1; SW1971.2
Pitcher, Edward W., G1974.1,
1978.2-3, 1979.2-3, 1980.3-5;
A1977.1, 1978.2-4, 1979.1-2,
1980.1-4, 1981.1-3
Platt, Edmund, IM1905.6
Pochmann, Henry A., WB1957.1
Ponick, Frances M., HW1975.1
Prescott, Frederick C., FH1925.1
Price, L.M., TD1966.2
Prince, Walter F., SP1897.1
Pursell, Caroll W., TD1964.1

Quinn, Arthur Hobson, G1936.4;
A1936. 2; JBe1936.2;
AB1936.1; HB1936.4;
WB1936.3; JBu1936.1;
HF1936.3, 1951.2; EH1936.1;
FH1936.1; GI1936.1;
SHR1936.3; RT1936.3-4;
HW1936.1; SW1936.1

Raddin, George Gates, WB1940.2;
HF1940.2
Rankin, Daniel S., IM1933.1
Redden, Sister Mary M.,
AB1939.1; SW1939.1
Redekop, Ernest, HB1968.4
Reed, Edward B., IM1904.2,
1905.4
Reed, Edward W., IM1905.7
Reilly, Robert J., HB1976.1;
WB1976.1
Reynolds, David Spencer, G1980.6
Richardson, Charles Francis,
SHR1893.1
Richardson, Lyon, JBe1931.1;
HB1931.3; FH1931.3

Swanwick, John, SHR1795.2,
　1796.1
Sweetser, M.F., SHR1889.1

Taft, Kendall B., SHR1947.2
Taft, Mary A., SHR1905.2
Tanselle, G. Thomas, HB1971.4;
　WB1971.3; RT1965.1, 1966.1,
　1967.2, 1974.3
Taub, Andrew, HB1980.3
Taylor, George Robert Stirling,
　GI1911.1, 1969.1
Taylor, Walter Fuller,
　HF1956.3; SHR1936.4, 1956.2
Tebbel, John, WB1972.1;
　SHR1972.2
Thompson, Adele E., HF1903.3;
　SHR1903.2
Tichi, Cecelia, HB1979.2
Tilling, Albert Edward [pseud.
　Stanley Hutton], WW1907.1
Tillinghast, Charles Allen,
　A1974.2; AB1974.1; WB1974.2;
　JDG1974.2; SR1974.1;
　SHR1974.5; RT1974.4
Tomalin, Claire, GI1974.1
Townsend, John Wilson, GI1907.2
Treadway, James Lewis, HB1979.3
Trent, William Peterfield,
　G1903.1; HB1903.1; HF1920.1;
　SHR1903.3, 1912.3; RT1903.1
Trumbull, James Hammond,
　SP1876.1, 1877.2, 1887.1
Tupper, Frederick, RT1928.1,
　1932.4
Turlish, Lewis A., JBe1969.1
Tuttle, JBe1875.1
Tuttleton, James W., IM1972.1
Tyler, Moses Coit, FH1897.1;
　SP1897.1, 1970.1
Tyler, Royall, G1876.1, 1936.2,
　4, 1977.4-5; FH1970.2; biog-
　raphy, RT1880.1, 1928.1,
　1932.4, 1936.4, 1938.1,
　1962.1, 1972.3; bibliography,
　RT1938.1, 1943.1, 1970.2,
　1976.3

Underhill, John, RT1859.1

Vail, Robert W.G., SHR1933.2-3
Van Doren, Carl, G1912.1,
　1917.2; 1940.4; JBe1912.2,
　1940.3; HB1912.3, 1917.2;
　WB1912.1, 1917.1, 1940.3;
　HF1912.3, 1917.1; FH1912.3,
　1940.1; IM1917.1; SHR1912.4,
　1917.2; RT1912.2, 1917.1,
　1940.2
Vinton, John Adams, HM1866.1
Wagenknecht, Edward, G1952.2;
　A1952.2; JBe1952.2; AB1952.1;
　WB1952.1; JD1952.1; HF1952.1;
　Hd'A1952.1; EH1952.1;
　GI1952.1; IM1952.1; SHR1952.1;
　RT1952.1; SW1952.1
Wager, Willis, WB1968.3;
　SHR1968.4; RT1968.2
Walser, Richard, WB1951.2,
　1952.2-3, 1982.2
Ward, William S., G1977.5
Warner, Stephen Douglas,
　RT1972.4
Warren, Robert Penn, HB1973.1
Washington, George, TD1940.1
Watkins, Walter Kendall,
　SHR1919.2
Weber, Alfred, HB1963.1
Wecter, Dixon, FH1940.2
Wegelin, Oscar, G1902.1, 1963.1
Weil, Dorothy Louis, SHR1974.6,
　1976.3
Wells, Helena, biography,
　HW1975.1, 1979.1
Wells, Kate Gannett, HM1895.1
Wenska, Walter P., HF1977.1
Westcott, Thompson, HB1884.1
Wharton, Donald P., A1979.3;
　RT1979.4; WW1979.1
Whipple, Edwin Percy, SHR1876.1,
　1887.2, 1968.5
White, Isabelle, WB1978.4;
　HB1978.2; SHR1978.2
Whittier, John Greenleaf,
　SHR1828.3, 1950.2
Whittle, Amberys R., HB1971.5
Williams, Stanley Thomas,
　G1926.1; JBe1926.2; AB1926.1;
　HB1926.1; WB1926.1;

Title and Subject Index

Underscored titles indicate fuller treatment of the subject.

SHR1905.1, 1964.2, 1970.2, 1971.2

Charlotte's Daughter, reviews, SHR1828.1, 3, 1950.2; criticism, SHR1966.1

"Charlotte Temple: America's First Best Seller," SHR1976.1

"Charlotte Temple by Susanna Rowson," SHR1976.2

"Charlotte Temple in Fact and Fiction," SHR1905.1

"Chevalier and the Charlaton, The," HB1969.4

"Child of Snow," A1966.1-2, 1967.2

"City in the American Novel, The," HB1934.1

"Collections, Topographical, Historical and Biographical," JBe1824.1

Colonial Piscataway in Maryland, TD1962.1

Columbian Magazine, The, A1981.2; JBe1892.1, 1968.1-2

Columbian Magazine and American Literary Nationalism, The, JBe1968.2; AB1968.1; HF1968.1; EH1968.1; FH1968.2; GI1968.1; PM1968.1; SP1968.1; SHR1968.2

Comic Spirit of Seventy-Six, The, FH1976.1

Connecticut Wits, The, Hd'A1943.1; SP1943.1

Constantia: A Study of the Life and Works of Judith Sargent Murray, JSM1931.1

Constantia Neville, reviews, HW1800.1-7, 1801.1-2; criticism, HW1971.1, 1982.1

Constantius and Pulchera, A1907.1, 1936.1-2, 1948.1, 1968.1, 1974.1-2, 1979.3

Coquette, The, review, HF1835.1; introductions, HF1855.1, 1934.1, 1939.1, 1970.1; criticism; HF1901.1, 1904.1, 1907.1, 1912.1-2, 1917.1, 1926.1, 1935.1, 1940.1, 1946.1, 1950.1, 1951.1, 1962.1, 1971.1-2,

1975.1, 1977.1, 1978.1-3, 1979.1, 1982.1

"Coquette and the American Dream of Freedom, The," HF1977.1

"Creation of the American Eve, The," G1975.1; A1975.1; HB1975.6; WB 1975.4; HF1975.1; SHR1975.3

"Critical Biography of Susanna Haswell Rowson," SHR1981.1

Critical Dictionary of English Literature, A, AB1854.1; HB1854.1; WB1854.1; JD1854.1; HF1854.1; PF1854.1; PM1854.1; JSM1854.1; SR1854.1; SHR1854.1; HW1854.1; HW1854.1; SW1854.1

Cultural History of the American Revolution, WB1976.2

Cyclopaedia of American Literature, JBe1855.1, 1975.1; AB1855.1; HB1851.2, 1975.2; FH1855.1, 1975.1; SP1855.1, 1975.1; SHR1855.1, 1975.1; RT1855.1, 1975.1

"Damon and Pythias Among our Early Journalists," RT1896.1

"Daniel Edward Kennedy," WB1966.2

"Deborah Sampson: A Heroine of the Revolution," HM1895.1

Der Amerikanische Essay 1720-1820, FH1968.1

"Development of the Early American Short Story to Washington Irving," G1971.1

didactic fiction, G1907.2

Different Face, A, GI1975.1

"Don Quixote and Modern Chivalry," HB1949.1

"Don Quixote of the Frontier," HB1973.2

Eagle's History of Poughkeepsie, The, IM1905.1

Early American Books and Printing, HB1935.1; WB1935.1; HF1935.3; FH1935.2; SHR1935.4; RT1935.4

"Miscellany. For the Centinel,"
HF1788.2
Miss McRae, Hd'A1907.1,
1952.1; introduction, to
Hd'A1958.1
"Mitchell, Isaac," IM1933.1
"Mitchell's Alonzo and Melissa,"
IM1905.1
"Mitchell's Alonzo and Melissa
a Hug[e] Fraud," IM1905.9
Modern Chivalry, review,
HB1792.1-2, 1808.1; criti-
cism, G1932.2; HB1855.2,
1901.1, 1903.1, 1907.1,
1909.1-2, 1912.1-3, 1917.2,
1922.1, 1926.1, 1927.1-2,
1931.1-2, 1936.1-4, 1937.1,
1944.1, 1945.1, 1948.1-2,
1950.2, 1960.1, 1967.1-4,
1968.2, 1969.2-4, 1970.3,
1971.2-5; 1972.2, 1973.1-2,
4, 1975.5, 1976.2, 4, 1980.3;
introduction to HB1937.1,
1965.1, 1968.3
"Modern Chivalry, The Form,"
HB1967.3, 1968.2
"Modern Chivalry: The
Frontier as Crucible,"
HB1971.5
"Modern Chivalry and 'Young's
Magazine,'" HB1972.1
"Monody, to the Memory of
William Hill Brown," WB1812.1
"Monthly Review of New American
Books," JBe1792.1
"More about the First American
Novel," WB1952.2
"Mothers and Daughters in the
Fiction of the New Republic,"
G1980.2
Mr. Penrose. See The Journal
of William Penrose, Seaman
"Mr. Penrose--America Saisho no
Shosetsu," WW1970.1
"Mrs. Hannah Foster and the Early
American Novel," HF1932.4
"Mrs. Judith Murray,"
JSM1881.1, 1882.1
"Murray, Judith Sargent,"
JSM1934.1, 1971.1

"Names for the American Colonies
in Jeremy Belknap's The
Foresters, JBe1979.1
"Narrative of the Unpardonable
Sin," A1967.1
National Portrait Gallery of
Eminent Americans, FH1862.1
"Native Elements in American
Magazine Short Fiction 1741-
1800," G 1965.1
"Nativism of Royall Tyler,"
RT1932.1
"Neglected American Author, A,"
IM1904.2, 1905.7
"Neglected Early American Short
Story, A," A1966.3
"New England," SHR1944.1
New England Tale, review,
RT1822.1; criticism, RT1955.1
"New Novel," SHR1794.1
"New Wine in Old Bottles,"
G1965.3; HB1965.2; WB1965.1;
HF1965.1; SHR1965.3
New World, New Earth,
HB1979.2
"New York City During the Amer-
ican Revolution," SHR1861.1
New York in Fiction,
SHR1901.2, 1969.2
New York Weekly Magazine,
A1976.1
"North Carolina Sojourn of the
First American Novelist,"
WB1951.2
"Note," A1966.2
"Note on 'Azakia,'" A1977.1
"Note on the Source of 'The
Child of Snow' and 'The Son
of Snow,'" A1978.3
"Notes on Gilbert Imlay,"
GI1924.1
"Notes on Rare Books," TD1941.1
"Novel in America: Notes for a
Survey," G1936.3; HB1936.3;
WB1936.2; SHR1936.2
Novels of Democracy in America,
The, HB1922.1
Novel of Manners in America,
The, IM1972.1
"Novels and Romances,"
RT1798.1, 1802.2

"Obituary Notice of Mrs.
  Rowson," SHR1824.1
"Of Indians and Irishmen,"
  HB1975.3
Oriental Philanthropist, The,
  HS1971.1
Oriental tales, G1980.6
Origins of American Critical
  Thought, RT1959.1
Outline Sketch of American
  Literature, RT1887.1
Outlines of English and American
  Literature, G1917.1;
  SHR1917.1
Oxford Companion to American
  Literature, JBe1956.1;
  AB1956.1; EB1956.1; WB1956.1;
  JBu1956.1; JD1956.1;
  TD1956.1; HF1957.1; EH1956.1;
  FH1956.1; PM1941.1;
  IM1941.1; SP1941.1;
  SHR1956.1; RT1956.1;
  HW1941.1; SW1941.1

"Passive Voice in American Lit-
  erature, The," WB1978.3
Pennsylvania Magazine, The,
  FH1931.3
Personal Memoirs and
  Recollections, SHR1852.1
Peter Markoe (1752?-1792),
  PM1944.1
Peter Porcupine in America,
  SHR1939.2
"Peters, Samuel Andrew,"
  SP1934.1
"Peters, Samuel, D.D.,"
  SP1864.1
Philadelphia, G1903.1
Philadelphia Magazine, The,
  HB1892.1
Philadelphia Magazines and
  Their Contributors, JBe1892.1
Philenia, The Life and Works of
  Sarah Wentworth Morton,
  WB1931.1
Philip Freneau, PF1967.1
Picaresque Element in Western
  Literature, The, HB1975.7
Poems of Philip Freneau, The,
  HB1902.1

"point de vue théorique des
  romanciers dans les préfaces
  des premiers romans
  américains, Le," G1977.2
"Polishing God's Altar, The
  Emergence of Religious Fiction in America," G1980.6
Popular Book, G1950.1; AB1950.1;
  WB1950.1; HF1950.1;
  SHR1950.1; RT1950.1
Power of Sympathy, The,
  review, WB1789.2; introduction to, WB1894.2, 1961.1,
  1969.1, 1970.2; criticism,
  G1936.4, 1952.2; WB1907.1,
  1932.2, 1933.2, 1935.1-2,
  1937.1, 1944.2, 1945.1,
  1951.1, 1952.1-2, 1954.1,
  1960.1, 1968.1-2, 1971.1-2,
  1973.1, 1974.2, 1975.1, 4,
  1976.2, 1978.1-4; HF1917.1
"Power of Sympathy Recon-
  sidered," WB1975.1
"Powers of Genius," RT1804.2
"Precosité Crosses the
  Atlantic," WB1944.2
"Pretty Story, A," FH1791.1,
  1862.1, 1897.1, 1906.1,
  1907.1, 1909.1, 1912.2-3,
  1926.1, 1929.1, 1931.1,
  1932.2, 1936.1, 1961.2,
  1968.1, 1971.1, 1976.1
"Profile: Susanna Rowson, Early
  American Novelist," SHR1974.3
Profession of Authorship in
  America, SHR1968.1; SW1968.1
Prose and Poetry of the
  Revolution, FH1925.1
Prose of Royall Tyler,
  RT1972.3
"Pulled Out of the Bay:
  American Fiction in the
  Eighteenth Century," G1974.2;
  A1974.1; WB 1974.1;
  SHR1974.4; RT1974.2; WW1974.1
"Puritan Preacher's Contribution
  to Fiction," G1948.1

Quest for Nationality, The,
  WB1957.2; EH1957.2; PM1957.1;
  JSM1957.1; SHR1957.3;
  SW1957.1

Wit and Humor of Colonial
    Days, HB1912.2, 1970.2;
    FH1912.2, 1970.1
Women in Eighteenth-Century
    America, WB1935.1; HF1935.1;
    SHR1935.1; RT1935.1
Women of the American Revolu-
    tion, A1850.1; GI1850.1;
    HM1969.1
Women's Fiction, WB1978.1;
    HF1978.1; SHR1978.1
"Woman's Place in Early American
    Fiction," HF1903.3; SHR1903.2

"Wood, Sally Sayward Barrell
    Keating," SW1971.1
"World Introduced: The Writing
    of Helena Wells," HW1979.1
World of Washington Irving,
    HB1944.1; WB1944.1; HF1944.1;
    RT1944.1

Yankee in London, review,
    RT1810.1
"Yonora: An American Indian
    Tale," A1965
Young's Magazine, HB1972.1